THE FAMILY
KITCHEN GARDEN

TIMBER
PRESS

THE FAMILY
KITCHEN GARDEN

Karen Liebreich, Jutta Wagner & Annette Wendland

Karen: to my parents, Kitty and Freddy, who taught me to pick, to my children, Sam and Hannah, who eat their vegetables, and above all to Jeremy who cooks what I grow.

Jutta: to my family, especially my grandparents, Katharina and Karl Merz.

Annette: a heartfelt thank you to my sister, Barbara, and to my parents for their continued support and ever-ready assistance. Thanks also to my close friends for their lasting enthusiasm.

The Family Kitchen Garden
Copyright © Frances Lincoln 2009
Text copyright © Karen Liebreich, Jutta Wagner and Annette Wendland 2009
Photographs copyright © Annette Wendland 2009
Line drawings copyright © Jutta Wagner 2009

Published in 2009 by Timber Press, Inc.

The Haseltine Building
133 S.W. Second Avenue, Suite 450
Portland, Oregon 97204-3527
www.timberpress.com

2 The Quadrant
135 Salusbury Road
London NW6 6RJ
www.timberpress.co.uk

ISBN-13: 978-1-60469-050-7

Printed in China

A catalog record for this book is available from the Library of Congress and the British Library.

3 5 7 9 8 6 4 2

CONTENTS

FOREWORD

Anyone who has fallen in love with Frances Hodgson Burnett's *The Secret Garden*, or Mr. McGregor's kitchen garden in Beatrix Potter's *The Tale of Peter Rabbit*, will also be inspired by the power of the forgotten English walled garden in this book. The opportunity for urban children everywhere to witness and partake in the pleasures of planting, nurturing, tending, and harvesting food for the table cannot be underestimated.

Three women from London, endowed with remarkable good sense and thrift, have created a small miracle within the old walls of Chiswick House, in central London. With the help of school children from all over the city, they have renovated this centuries-old garden, brought it back to life, and in the process, have invested in the lives of these kids.

At the heart of this story is every child's desire to engage with the real world through authentic work and good old-fashioned sweat and dirty fingernails. As Americans, so many of us have strayed from the pleasure of honest labor, drawn to the siren songs of technology, the ease of industrial food, and the continuous strain of doing more. We have forgotten the perfume of freshly dug earth, the outrageous biology of a compost pile, the pleasures of creating a garden oasis, and sharing it with other creatures on this earth. This book shows us how to reengage with this world.

In essence, this garden world is the same in San Francisco, New York, and Akron as it is in London. All the vegetables and other plants the authors describe are as delectable in North America as they are in Kent. If you live in an especially warm, cold, wet, or dry part of the continent, you may need to make small adjustments to the authors' seasonal calendars, which are based on a climate that is similar to that of the Middle Atlantic or Pacific Northwest. Beyond that, you can take the authors' hard-won experiences and suggestions to the bank.

The Family Kitchen Garden reminds us that children are great workers and capable of amazing tasks when we let them. This un-fussy and informative book, with a distinctly British view of the world, provides us with a kid's-eye view of a great garden project. The common-sense advice and step-by-step instructions will help anyone interested in digging in. So get out your secateurs (pruning shears), hook up your water butts (rainwater barrels), slip into your Wellies (rubber boots), and get started!

Arden Bucklin and Rachel Pringle,
San Francisco Green Schoolyard Alliance

INTRODUCTION

> 'God Almighty first planted a garden, and indeed it is the purest of human pleasures. It is the greatest refreshment to the spirits of man.'
> Francis Bacon, 'Of Gardens', *Essays*, 1627

Five years ago one of us climbed over a wall and discovered a secret garden, overgrown and neglected for decades. Three centuries earlier, it had been laid out as a garden for pleasure and productivity. Now it was a jungle of bindweed and bramble, lying not far from one of the busiest main roads linking central London to its principal airport, a long-forgotten corner of the grounds at Chiswick House. We began to restore it, bringing in hundreds of local schoolchildren to work and learn and garden and eat. Over the past four years we have worked with literally thousands of people – children and adults – to create a working kitchen garden. None of us was paid, and all was done on a shoestring, but done well nevertheless. This book is the fruit of that experience.

The Family Kitchen Garden is for anyone with an interest in gardening, food, beauty and eating well. Although aimed at families and those wishing to garden with children, this is not a book that makes concessions by creating little 'kiddy projects'. Children are integrally included, for in our experience children can do pretty well everything grown-ups can do – just not for as long, and a bit more messily. If you include the children in the growing, they will find it far more interesting both to work and to eat the results. It is the canniest way we know of encouraging them to eat healthy food. We believe that a garden is for everyone and for pleasure – the pleasure of working in it and the pleasure of harvesting from it, whether the results be edible or pleasing to the senses. Flowers would have been grown in traditional kitchen gardens, and form an integral part of a productive garden, whether for cutting, companion planting and biodiversity, or even simply for the aesthetic pleasure they provide. By presenting a selection of vegetables, fruit, flowers and herbs that would suit a family, in terms of both ease of growing and suitability for family meals, we hope to encourage adults and children to have a go.

'When I found out I was digging I was so happy.'
Luke, aged eight

But while beginners will find clear instruction, we also hope that more experienced gardeners might discover new information and inspiration.

In a time of stress (and what time is not stressful?), surrounded as we are by increased urbanization, fears and realities about global warming, pollution, economic or personal worries, the little oasis we can create for ourselves in our gardens or outdoor spaces is increasingly important. By showing people how to garden – at the Chiswick House Kitchen Garden and in this book – our aim is to enable as many adults and children as possible to experience such pleasures.

You can start small with kitchen gardening – just dig up a little corner, or get a few containers, sow some seeds and look forward to harvesting several pounds of produce. Even if your kitchen garden consists only of a few pots and troughs with tomatoes, runner beans, rainbow chard, herbs and lettuces, the result will be your achievement and one that children can equally enjoy. Whether it is the joy of getting muddy, or the satisfaction of accomplishing a task, there is something very cheering for children about gardening. Older children can often talk to you better while working, and younger ones enjoy burning off energy positively out of doors.

Start small, but you might find kitchen gardening grows on you and thoughts of self-sufficiency begin to creep into your dreams. The things you grow will not be perfectly uniform, like the ones you find at the supermarket; you will probably have to pick off the odd slug. But the vegetables will taste stronger and better; the flowers will be fresher; the herbs more tangy; and the fruit more healthy – because you and your children will have grown it yourselves.

We garden organically as a matter of course. For us it was simply a matter of common sense that we would be reluctant to use any kind of poison where children and pets play, and on plants that we wanted to eat afterwards. Whether the vegetables grown in soils that have been tended organically for a while are in fact more nutritious, vitamin-rich and healthy than conventionally grown vegetables is a moot point, but if the produce grows without chemicals, why use them? Trying to create a balanced environment in your garden and encouraging beneficial wildlife

is an integral part of good gardening. So you will not find any instructions on chemical spraying here. If you are growing your own food, you might as well do it organically; for your daily pesticide ration, you could continue topping up at the local supermarket.

Organic gardening requires a holistic approach (though we apologize for employing a term over-used by New Age therapists). The overall aim is simply to prevent pests and diseases and to grow healthy plants.

Organic gardening means you:
- do not use chemical substances in your garden
- use pest barriers instead of pesticides
- encourage a wide range of beneficial wildlife to live in your garden
- use compost and organic fertilizer to improve your soil

'I really enjoyed picking the beans, and I keaped on and on picking the big beans.'
Khalid, aged seven

- remove weeds by hand instead of using herbicides
- improve plant health through companion planting.

If you follow these principles, your plants should be healthy, and healthy plants are more resistant to the attacks of pests and diseases that target weaker plants.

All the plants in this book can be grown without a greenhouse, although quite a few will need to be started off on the windowsill. A little extra protection, such as a cold frame or a few little cloches, would be useful, but we have assumed little in the way of additional equipment.

One of the old-timers down at the common used to say, 'It's got two chances: it'll either grow or it won't', and that was pretty good advice. Read on – we hope you find inspiration – and then go and just do it. Seeds and young plants are pretty cheap: experiment, plant stuff, water it, keep an eye on it, then with any luck you'll be able to eat it or pick it and admire it. Life is too short to worry about all the techniques too much;

> *'If well managed, nothing is more beautiful than the kitchen garden.'*
> William Cobbett, *The English Gardener*, 1829

chances are it will flourish anyhow. Then come back to this book and maybe get some tips about how it could be done a bit better next time. But most of all, enjoy your little bit of growing space.

*plant
grow
see
touch
smell
pick
eat
enjoy*

Cucumber plants with pot marigold companion planting.

THE
BASICS

GARDENING WITH CHILDREN

There is a school of thought that says that one cannot garden while one's children are young, or while they wish to play in the garden, but in the case of kitchen gardening, although we accept that it can sometimes be frustrating we do not agree that it cannot be done. Digging, sowing, planting, watering, harvesting – all these are surprisingly fascinating activities for children if approached in a suitably amiable way.

In the kitchen garden that we run we usually garden with children – including often at least one or two of our own, who range from toddler to teenager – and with whole school classes. We have about 1,000 children per year, so our experience is not based only on a particular type of child. Our main tip for gardening with children is to let them do pretty well everything (except pruning in the case of the younger ones) themselves – obviously with your guidance – and involve them completely; otherwise they get bored very quickly. Well, wouldn't you, watching someone else gardening?

The most essential piece of equipment you will need is **a relaxed attitude.** Things are going to take longer and be less perfect or planted less straight than you would ideally like. Go with the flow – if a child becomes distracted by a worm, stop to wonder at it and discuss.

Short sessions

Try to be child-oriented, rather than task-oriented. Quit while you are ahead. On the other hand, children should finish what they started, so decide on manageable jobs. There is a balance to be drawn between finishing the task and not running off halfway, and stopping while they are still keen. You will need to factor your child's attention span into that equation. Come to terms with the fact that you are just not going to get those two hours of concentrated gardening done with them.

Grow more

Grow enough seedlings to have some in reserve to supplement the inevitable casualties. For instance, grow enough flowers so that they can help pick them, even though the stalks will probably be too short and the petals macerated by eager and over-firm little fingers. Accept that there will be a high casualty rate (of plants, not children). Sow enough seedlings so that children can drop, squeeze or stand on a few without you having a nervous breakdown.

Encouragement

Children may not plant seedlings in a perfect straight line. Either accept that this does not matter or sneak out later when they cannot see you and straighten the line up a bit. If a seedling was planted to death by an eager young gardener, either explain it kindly, or – if you feel the gardener is too young or too emotionally attached to their work to accept the explanation – discreetly replace it after they have gone to bed.

Digging up carrots among the nasturtiums (left); an armful of summer squash, cucumber and onion (right).

Safety

- Always insist that equipment is handled carefully.
- Forks (pitchforks to Americans) should be either stuck in the ground or laid with points facing downwards. Always lay rakes points downward, and spades (shovels) with blade downwards. If you are working with a couple of children, keep them spaced out – they are like magnets and are irresistibly drawn too close together, which can result in non-deliberate companion-bashing. All equipment must be kept below hip height. No flailing forks or rakes.
- No running in the garden with equipment; no throwing anything.
- Keep any pruning equipment well away from children. If they are picking flowers and you think they are old enough and sensible enough, use small children's scissors (with blunt points) over which you keep a careful eye.
- Wash hands properly.
- All of the above is good practice for grown-up gardeners too!

Seeds

The easiest seeds to sow with small children are the larger ones. Peas, beans, spinach and onion/garlic sets are perfect. The other main criterion is that seeds should be cheap and plentiful. If you are sowing a packet with only five seeds, you will be reluctant to lose any; a packet containing several hundred is another proposition and makes for a far more relaxed supervisor.

Growing and eating your harvest

If you can avoid passing on any preconceptions about the vegetables that children might like to eat, and leave them to make their own decisions about eating the crops they have helped to grow, you may be surprised at the breadth of their adventurousness.

Give them the work of picking and let them help washing and preparing it, so that they see that they grew it themselves.

If left unprejudiced by comments such as 'You won't like this, it's a vegetable', children will eat most things with an open mind. You may scoff and think your children are different, but after years of weekly school sessions we know what we are talking about. We have had children staring dubiously at a tray of vegetables they have grown and picked, and

by the end of the picnic they are literally fighting to eat rocket leaves, broccoli florets or nasturtium flowers, with teachers and parents watching open-mouthed as they ask for 'more please'. So next time you despairingly put some vegetables on your child's plate, just think about whether your language or body language is expressing your doubt that they will even have a go or whether you are giving the food a real chance.

We have a rule at the garden – and at home – that you do not have to like something, but you have to try it, and you have to try it with an open mind. (The same could apply to gardening in general.) Everything in this book has been grown and enjoyed on that basis.

Harvesting is satisfying, whatever your age.

PLANNING YOUR CROP

One of the best things about gardening is planning your crop. It is mid-winter. The rain is sheeting down outside, the skies are grey and grim. Settle down with a pile of catalogues or an Internet connection, and a cup of hot chocolate (or a glass of whisky), and make plans for all the great things you can grow next year. Discuss it with your family – what do they want to plant and eat? Seed mail order catalogues are generally well illustrated, and children could spend a pleasant rainy-day session cutting out and pasting images of future crops on to a rough plan of the garden, familiarizing themselves with the plants. If each person in the family, old and young, has chosen a couple of plants they particularly wish to grow, they already have a vested interest in the result.

Choice of plants

After working out all the fruit, herbs, vegetables and flowers that you would like to grow and eat, check your list against the following criteria.

Ease of growing and yield for effort

If you are a gardening virgin, for your first attempts choose plants marked 'easy' in the A–Z of plants that begins on page 114.

Think about 'yield for effort': how much work you have to put in to get a result. There are plants that do not need much effort but provide a bumper crop – beans, courgettes (zucchini) and pumpkins, for example. Then there are others that require a bit more work: tomatoes are a perfect example – you will have to build a support for them and keep pinching them out. Then there is stuff that is cheap and local and available in most supermarkets, such as celery: rather than waste space and effort on them, prioritize something more worthwhile. The lists beginning on page 211 will help you with the decision-making process, and the cultivation details can be found in the A–Z of plants beginning on page 114.

Take into account how much time realistically you can spend gardening on a regular basis, especially with children helping. Your kitchen garden is supposed to be a pleasure garden, not an extra source of stress in your life. If you are going to have only half an hour a week, consider growing fruit bushes and trees. If

> 'A garden is never so good as it will be next year.'
> Thomas Cooper

you think you have time for twenty minutes every evening, then you have a wider choice. If you have a few window boxes that will receive daily attention, and a larger garden for weekends only, then put the attention-seekers close by and the tougher stuff further away.

Which varieties?

The variety (or cultivar) can make all the difference. Each plant may exist in several different forms, selected by breeders over the years and given a unique variety name to distinguish their specific characteristics. Carrots, for instance, can be long and thin, short and round, orange or purple, early season or late. We have grown some vegetables and declared we would never bother again, only to be recommended a different variety that has forced us to reconsider.

- **'AGM' varieties** The Royal Horticultural Society carries out trials where hundreds of plants are grown and tested for consistency, pest resistance, ease of growing and so forth. The best receive an Award of Garden Merit (AGM); this is a good indication of a worthwhile plant, and is noted in seed catalogues.
- **Disease-resistant varieties** These should reduce problems with pest control. New varieties are introduced every year as research progresses, so keep an eye out for these – for example, tomatoes resistant to blight.
- **Harvesting times** Plants are sometimes marked 'early', 'maincrop' and 'late', and you should pay attention. Choosing the right varieties means you can pick certain crops over a long period of time. Using the right kind at the right time is also important. For instance, if you sow late beetroot too early, it will probably bolt.
- **Heritage varieties** These are ancient varieties stocked by specialist suppliers but no longer grown commercially. Some have unusual tastes,

shapes or names. 'Nun's Bellybutton' beans, 'Drunken Woman' lettuce … Some heritage varieties, however, can be prone to diseases and in some cases it becomes sadly clear why they are no longer widely grown.

- **Your own taste and experience** This is the most important. Keep a garden diary where you note what you grew each season. You may think you will remember, but you won't. If you sowed leeks that became rusty immediately, or a tomato that was wonderful, note it. In this way your garden will gradually evolve to supply your own preferences. Your children can participate in this, helping to create a family scrapbook that provides a useful source of information, as well as memories for later.
- **Holiday (vacation) season** If you know that you regularly go away on holiday at a certain time of the year, plan your crops accordingly. It should be possible to avoid the maincrop being ready just when you are away. For more on timing, see the monthly calendar on pages 214–19.

How much to grow?

A seemingly obvious question, but the temptation is strong to plant an entire row, or to finish the seed packet, resulting in a wasteful glut. Bear in mind that the experience of growing your own should be pleasurable, not stressful; even the great gardener Christopher Lloyd once complained, 'I don't like being hounded by my vegetables.' We planted a bed of kale one year and loved it, but by the time we had had kale soup every night for three weeks

Short round carrots (the snappily named 'Paris Market 4 Baron') and long thin ones ('Sugarsnax').

running, we had had enough and needed a decade's kale break.

First position the plants that will be in the same spot for a long time, like fruit bushes and trees, perennial herbs, or perennial vegetables such as asparagus or artichokes. Decide how many you need and find the right places, preferably around the edges of your garden, leaving a dedicated space for other vegetables.

In order to decide how much to grow, consider whether you want to freeze surplus, and whether you have the time or inclination to do any other preserving. At one end of the scale is growing a few salad leaves; at the other lies self-sufficiency. For more information on yields see page 213.

Bear in mind that these numbers are just guidelines. You could start with these recommendations in your first gardening season and then make your own adjustments in following years.

If you are pressed for space, consider your options carefully. One artichoke looks stunning, but you could probably grow enough chard for the whole family in the same spot.

Take into account how long plants take to mature. Again, if you are short of space you should perhaps grow many crops with a short growing period, instead of sprouting broccoli that will sit there for almost the whole year. On the other hand, if you love winter vegetables you could squeeze in some, even in a tiny garden … On a square 1.2 x 1.2m/1.3 x 1.3yd you could grow two Brussels sprouts, one kale 'Cavolo Nero' (black kale) and one sprouting broccoli – which would give you sprouts for Christmas dinner and greens into spring.

Successional sowing, intercropping and catch crops

Some vegetables mature very fast (6–8 weeks) and, especially in smaller gardens, this should be exploited.

- **Successional sowing** Some fast-growing plants should be sown every few weeks – little and often – to ensure an even supply for most of the year. There is no point having, for instance, eighty lettuces one week and nothing for the next few months. For a continual supply, sow lettuce, rocket, radishes, spinach, spring onions and French beans every 2–4 weeks throughout the growing season.

- **Intercropping** This means sowing a quick-growing crop in between plants that need a long time to reach maturity. For example: Brussels sprouts need a great deal of space – 60cm/2ft between plants. But when just planted as seedlings, there will be empty space around them, and you can use this to grow lettuce or spinach. By the time the sprouts need the space, you will have eaten the lettuces or spinach.

- **Catch crops** The same plants can also be grown in any space where one crop has been cleared, and before the next long-standing one is planted. So you seize ('catch') the opportunity to grow one more crop.

How to plant?

Ideally rows within beds should run north to south to benefit from the sunshine. Plant tall crops on the north side of other crops to minimize shade.

For vegetable beds use companion planting and crop rotation. Both techniques minimize attacks by pests and diseases and improve the health of the vegetables.

Crop rotation

If plants are grown on the same spot year after year, soil pests and diseases that attack particular plants can build up seriously. This applies not just to the same plant but to plants within the same family that share the same diseases and often also use the same

level of nutrients. Proper crop rotation is therefore an important element of effective organic gardening. If you are interspersing your productive plants in general flower beds, then a formal crop rotation is hard to achieve, but you should still try to move the vegetables around within the beds.

For rotation purposes, plants are divided into groups with similar needs or from similar families. Ideally, divide your plot into four equally sized quarters and move the groups from one quarter to the next each year.

Over four years, in each quarter of your plot grow one group of plants, each year moving the group on to the next quarter.

FAST-GROWING CROPS	
Chard for baby leaves	Radishes
Leaf lettuces	Rocket (arugula)
Oriental leaves (salad greens)	Spinach
Pak choi (bok choy)	Spring onions (scallions)

GROUP 1
Brassicas and tomatoes

Brassicas and tomatoes are heavy feeders. Plant these together because the tomatoes' distinctive scent helps keep brassica pests at bay.

Lime beds in winter, prepare with good compost or well-rotted manure.

Large cabbages are happy about extra nitrogen-rich fertilizer as top-dressing; tomatoes require additional tomato fertilizer in summer. Only the smaller brassicas, such as radishes or rocket (arugula), are fine without extra food.

Lettuces and spinach can be grown as catch crops.

Broccoli
Brussels sprouts
Cabbages
Kohl rabi
Lettuces – after early brassicas
Oriental leaves (salad greens)
Pak choi (bok choy)
Radishes
Spinach
Tomatoes

GROUP 2
Root vegetables

Most of these plants do not like freshly manured ground, so grow them the year after the well-fed brassica group. Only if gardening on poor soil, add some well-rotted compost before planting or sowing.

The exceptions are celeriac and leeks which enjoy additional fertilizer.

Beetroot (beets)
Carrots
Celeriac
Chard
Garlic
Leeks
Lettuces
Onions
Parsnips

GROUP 4
Legumes, annual herbs and flowers

These plants are content with leftovers from the hungry Group 3 feeders. Only if your soil is poor, add compost. Peas and beans collect nitrogen and store it in their roots, and this will be available for the brassicas that follow.

There is only one hitch: legumes need the same growing conditions and therefore are good grouped together, they are not good neighbours, so plant annual herbs or flowers between beds containing peas and beans.

Broad beans (fava beans)
French beans (string beans)
Lettuce
Runner beans (flat pole beans)
Peas

GROUP 3
Potatoes and the cucumber family

These plants are heavy feeders again but – as opposed to the brassicas – they prefer balanced food.

Four weeks before planting work in half-rotted compost or well-rotted manure. If any plants look needy in summer, feed them with tomato food or liquid seaweed.

The plants will appreciate rows of annual herbs or flowers planted in between, to attract pollinating insects.

Courgettes (zucchini)
Cucumbers
Peppers and chilli peppers
Potatoes
Pumpkins
Spinach
Sweet corn (corn)

Companion planting

Companion planting means growing certain plants together for a variety of beneficial reasons.

- To attract insects to pollinate your crops. Early-flowering nectar plants such as rosemary attract bumblebees that pollinate broad beans, currants and gooseberries. Honeybees love herbs such as hyssop.
- To attract insects whose larvae will eat aphids and other pests. Hoverflies love orange flowers such as calendula, nasturtium and French marigolds. Plants in the parsley family attract lacewings.
- To benefit other plants. Combining specific plants makes each of them grow better, although this method is still controversial and there is little scientific evidence. Some plants also inhibit one another's growth, and some should not be grown together because they share diseases.
- To deter pests. Mixed planting can help to confuse insects and mask certain smells; for instance, throwing carrot fly off the scent by putting strong onions nearby.

Sometimes the information on offer about companion planting is contradictory. We compared several existing lists with our own experiences, but suggest you do your own experiments too. One thing is certain: companion planting may not only prove useful, but it is also more attractive than any kind of monoculture.

For further details, see suggestions in the A–Z of plants.

The poached egg plant (*Limnanthes douglasii*) (above), which attracts useful insects, and cabbages and celeriac (below) make good neighbours; French marigolds are always useful.

CLIMATE AND POSITION

When choosing plants to grow, you will have to take some account of the conditions you can offer them: shade, slopes, shelter, frost pockets, prevailing winds. There can be surprisingly significant differences between the microclimates of gardens even within the same area. For instance, if your garden is partially shaded you will not have much success with sun-lovers such as tomatoes or pumpkins. If it never drops below –5°C/23°F where you live, then you can garden and harvest throughout the year. In colder areas everything pretty much stops from November onwards.

Two of the most crucial dates in your calendar are those of the first and last expected frosts. You need to know these in order to orientate yourself within the gardening year. Another problem, particular to much of the UK, is the combination of mild winters and late last frosts, because it means that plants are tempted to start flowering early, only to be knocked back.

The short answer to both is: from early spring onwards always keep some horticultural fleece (or cover cloth, such as 'Reemay') close to hand to protect susceptible plants – or choose different crops.

Any walls in your garden provide one big advantage: they heat up during the day and slowly release their warmth during the night. Traditional kitchen gardens were always surrounded by brick walls about 2m/7ft high and these were used for growing fruit espaliers. Small gardens enclosed by walls can be up to several degrees warmer at night, but note that each wall and building has a dry zone along its base that requires extra watering.

> *'I consider every plant hardy until I have killed it myself.'*
> Sir Peter Smithers

You may have to adapt your crop choice according to the conditions, but there are always cases where a plant flourishes where it is not 'supposed' to be – or the other way round. This is what makes gardening so unpredictable and interesting. And occasionally frustrating.

Early blossom is essential for bees, and bees are essential for blossom.

Sensitivity of plants to cold temperatures

Type of plant	Temperatures	Examples
Hardy plants	Survive frost down to –10°C/14°F and cope even if it stays around –5°C/23°F for weeks.	Fruit bushes, strawberries, Brussels sprouts, kale, chives.
Half-hardy plants	Survive an occasional light frost, down to –5°C/23°F.	Sprouting broccoli, artichokes, chard, pot marigolds, nigella.
Tender plants	Need temperatures of at least +5°C/41°F. Grow on the windowsill until it is warm enough.	Tomatoes, peppers, beans, French marigolds, zinnias, basil.

PREPARING THE PLOT

Tools

Garden supply stores encourage you to buy a whole shedload of tools, but in fact a bare minimum will do. Container gardeners will need nothing more than a trowel and a watering can, others a bit more. We recommend that you treat yourself to few but good-quality tools.

The most important is a good fork (or pitchfork), preferably of stainless steel and with the right length of handle for your height. A tough trowel with a comfortable handle is also essential; there is something very dispiriting about a poor trowel. Secateurs (pruning shears) are the one tool where it pays most to invest in quality. It is helpful to buy smaller tools in bright colours, so that they are easy to find. Get a watering can with a good rose for seedlings, and invest in some water butts or barrels in which to collect rain and grey water.

Your spade should be made of stainless steel, not too heavy and the right height, with a tread at the top of the blade so that you can use your boot and weight. A rake is necessary to prepare a smooth seed bed; a hoe for weeding. A garden line – two sticks and a length of string – helps you to make straight rows and edges. A wooden plank does the same thing, and is also practical to work from when you do not want to compact the soil.

In small gardens you can make do with a trug or large bucket, but in larger ones a wheelbarrow is handy. Two-wheeled versions are easier to

A well-stocked shed would contain most of these tools, but a trowel and fork are the bare essentials.

manoeuvre, but not good for very narrow paths. Maintaining the recommended tyre pressure makes everything easier, as does always loading two-thirds of the weight towards the front to keep the weight off the handles.

Tools for children

- Get some small gloves – and the patience to make sure the right number of fingers go in the right holes.
- Brightly coloured plastic is not necessary; rather get good-quality scaled-down versions of adult tools which work well and make children feel like serious gardeners.
- Grown-up trowels are fine. Only for erratic toddlers use plastic trowels rather than metal.
- Wellies with warm socks for winter.

Starting a new plot

First note any plants that you want to keep. Also take a closer look at the weeds before you rip them out, because they offer important clues about your soil.

The second reason for looking carefully is to make sure that you get rid of them the right way.

If you are faced with a jungle, borrow a strimmer (weed trimmer), scythe or loppers and cut everything down to ground level. At least then you can see the bigger picture.

The next step is to dig over the ground and remove all weeds, especially roots. Old-timers say, 'How do you eat an elephant? A little bit at a time.' So, faced with an impenetrable jungle, concentrate on a small area. It is better to do this thoroughly and plant it up, and just keep the rest of your plot roughly under control and non-seeding for the first season than rush

Indicator plants

Name of weed	Conditions indicated
Horsetail	Wet soil, heavy clay
Creeping buttercup, couch grass	Compacted soil
Cleaver, thistles, nettles, chickweed	Fertile, nitrogen-rich soil
Clovers, vetches	Low nitrogen content
Dock, heartsease, moss	Acidic soil
Sow thistle, wild mustard	Alkaline soil

> *'I've had enough of gardening ... I'm just about ready to throw in the trowel.'*
> Author unknown

onwards and work on a large area of ill-prepared soil, or clear and clear for weeks on end and not sow anything in the first season. Working this way will encourage you to take the next bite.

Using a rotavator (rototiller) is an option, but only if your plot is free of perennial weeds. Otherwise it just multiplies the problem because from every tiny chopped-up bit of root a new plant will grow. We are sorry to say that for clearing the ground there is nothing better than hand clearance: digging through it with a fork, metre by metre, and picking out the weeds. Non-organic gardeners would zap it with weedkiller and start with a fresh slate. But smug, masochistic organic gardeners will regard weed clearance as a work-out in the fresh air.

For more on weeds, see page 38.

If the ground is not too hard, children will enjoy removing weeds, especially clearly defined and challenging ones, such as bramble. It can also make weeding more fun to turn it into a game – for instance, the weed with the longest root wins. After a short time they will have had enough, but then they can dig a large hole to the centre of the earth, or collect worms, while you continue to do the actual weeding.

A proud young gardener wheels home the harvest.

SOIL

The automatic reaction when reaching a section on soil is to turn off one's brain and turn over the page – this was our initial reaction too. But soil quality is absolutely key to good crops, so stay with us here.

Before you get going with your first crop, assess your soil and improve it if necessary – soil is one of the few things in your garden that you can directly influence. One of the main principles of organic gardening is to improve your soil constantly, because a well-fed plant is a healthy plant.

To make the best of your soil, and know how to improve matters, check two things first: texture and pH level.

Soil texture

Soil texture is determined by the size of the soil particles: the largest are in sand, the next in silt and the smallest in clay. Soils are usually a mix of these, but one often dominates. When the three types are in equal proportions, you have loam.

Take a small sample of moist soil and rub it between your fingers; children can have fun with this one too. How does it feel?

*   Forms a ball without crumbling, feels smooth, sticky and not gritty: clay.
*   Forms a ball without crumbling, but feels rough: clay loam.
*   Forms a ball, but falls apart quickly: loamy sand.
*   Does not roll into a ball and feels gritty: sand.

As a generalization it is trickier to grow root vegetables in heavy soils, whereas brassicas are unhappy on sandy soils. You could just accept this and grow only a certain range of plants – or you could improve your soil. Read on …

pH level

You can measure the pH level of your soil very easily by buying a cheap little tester kit at the garden centre, costing a few pounds. The weeds growing on your plot may already have provided a hint (see Indicator plants, page 23). The pH of your soil is its level of acidity and alkalinity, determined

How to recognize your type of soil	Consequences for your garden
Sandy soil Easy to work Not many earthworms. Tends to be acid	Never waterlogged, but water drains away quickly. Nutrients wash out quickly. Heats up quickly in spring, but loses warmth quickly in cold nights, so plants are more prone to late frosts.
Silt Easy to work with when reasonably moist. In dry weather hard to dig.	Usually water-retentive and fertile. Compacts very easily, so try not to step on it too much – work from a plank.
Loam Easy to work. Good soil structure. Good amount of earthworms.	Ideal mix of good water retention with good drainage and a good nutrient-holding capacity.
Clay Digging is very hard work. Few earthworms. Unworkable for days after rain.	Tends to be compacted and waterlogged. Stores water and nutrients well. Warms up very slowly in spring, but water in the soil stores warmth, which helps at night. Can be difficult for plant roots to penetrate, especially root crops.
Chalk Shallow soils. Often contains white lumps of chalk or flint. Not much organic matter. Alkaline.	Free draining. Nutrients are quickly washed out. Needs lots of organic matter.
Humus-rich loam Dark colour. Rich smell of earth. Easy to work. Lots of earthworms.	Warms up quickly in spring. Nutrient-rich. Water-retentive. The ideal to which we aspire.

< extremely alkaline				neutral					extremely acidic >	
9.5	9	8.5	8	7.5	7	6.5	6	5.5	5	4.5
				vegetables and herbs						
						fruit				
				majority of all plants grow in this range						

on a scale by the amount of calcium in it, with 1 as the strongest acid and 14 as the strongest alkali; 7 is therefore neutral.

You need to know about your soil's pH because nutrients will not be available to your plants if it is not right for them. Your soil may well contain plenty of nutrients, but if at the same time it is too acid or too alkaline, these nutrients will be useless to your plants – however much fertilizer you add.

If your soil is too acidic, lime will raise the pH. If the soil is too alkaline, sulphur chips will reduce the pH, although very slowly.

Even when your pH is fine, an application of lime every four years or so is recommended. Any soil that is intensively worked – such as your productive beds – will become more and more acidic over the years. This is even more so in free-draining soils, where calcium will also be washed out easily. Earthworms, which are the most important creatures in your soil,

do not like acid conditions. (For how to apply lime, see page 45.)

How to improve your soil

Whatever your soil, it will always be beneficial to work in organic matter.

What is organic matter? It consists basically of remains of dead plants, manures and other animal vestiges. Soil creatures break organic matter down and the end product is called humus. Humus particles are dark coloured and have a special structure which enables them to store nutrients and water. As the humus develops, microbes secrete sticky matter that holds the particles together, creating soil crumbs. Between these crumbs is air, and thus humus also improves the aeration of the soil. This is beneficial for any kind of soil. If you increase humus levels, sandy soil will retain water and nutrients better, while the other extreme, loam, is also improved by the aeration.

Healthy soil makes a productive garden.

EARTHWORMS

'It may be doubted whether there are many other animals which have played so important a part in the history of the world, as have these lowly organized creatures.'
Charles Darwin, *The Formation of Vegetable Mould through the Action of Worms,* 1881

Organic matter also makes earthworms happy, and happy earthworms mean happy plants, as worms drag organic matter down into the soil, eat it and produce nutritious casts. Their tunnels drain and air the soil.

Children generally enjoy worms, and can be encouraged to count them; the more worms there are, the better your soil. You may need to intervene to save worms and other mini-beasts from too enthusiastic an interaction with younger children.

If the soil in your garden is poor, compacted or waterlogged, dig in organic matter regularly until the situation has improved. After this point less digging will be necessary, and simply mulching regularly with organic matter will be equally beneficial.

Organic matter – what can I use?

- **Garden compost and manure, half- or completely rotted**
  These soil improvers also produce a fertilizing effect (see page 42).
- **Mushroom compost**
  Fertilizes and raises pH (see page 24).
- **Leaf mould**
  Low fertility, but improves soil structure.
- **Composted bark, fine grade**
  Low fertility, but improves soil structure; ideal for improving clay and silt.

DIGGING AND PREPARING BEDS

> *'It was really nice to be in the mud.'*
> Natalie, aged eight

> *'Why do you like digging so much?'*
> Molly, aged eight

Love it or hate it, digging is the main way to add organic matter, remove weeds and open up compacted soil. Children generally love digging, and can enjoy the activity from toddlerhood, although at this age their efforts are unlikely to be very productive. Older children can dig usefully for a while and then enjoy themselves creating holes and barrowing compost around.

Digging the easy way

- Spread a layer of organic matter on the section to be dug and then just turn it in.
- Dig down to one spit deep. A spit (nothing to do with saliva) is the depth of one spade.
- Work methodically, starting at one end and working backwards, so that you do not stand on the earth you have just dug. Children weigh less, but even so it is better if they do not walk on the area just dug.
- As you are working, remove any perennial weed roots you come across.
- If you are digging in autumn, try to finish by the end of the year, as later in winter the soil may be too wet.

The only time you might really need to **double dig** is if your garden has been driven over by diggers and has been really flattened. Then you will need to go down further and break up a soil pan (a layer of compacted earth that will retain water) to undo the damage.

DO NOT DIG IF:
- The soil sticks to your boots and you leave footprints behind that retain water – the soil is still too wet and you will just compact it by walking on it.
- The top layer of soil is frozen – digging the frozen layer under will chill the whole bed, which will then take much longer to warm up in spring. Instead, start digging when the soil has warmed up in spring.

Every now and then you hear reports about the fabulous **'no-dig'** method. As long as your soil is compacted or waterlogged and lacks organic matter, you should dig. When your soil has achieved a better structure and balance, there is indeed no real need for frequent digging: you would only disturb the microcosm that has developed under the soil surface. You could continue to add organic matter just by mulching.

Preparing beds

- Remove all weeds thoroughly.
- Incorporate soil-improving materials and/or fertilizer (see page 42).
- Use a rake to even out the bed – if the bed is bumpy, watering will be uneven and seeds can be washed away. And frankly, it just looks better if it is all neat and even. Children generally enjoy raking as much as digging but are unlikely to produce a very even bed without help.

PROPAGATION

Sowing

Sowing is great fun. However old you are, however often you have done it before, there is still a little prickle of excitement at the thought that these little spots of dried matter can turn into plants. Seed germination is a fascinating process to watch, and not only for children.

With a few packets of seeds you could theoretically fill a whole garden. But try not to get too carried away: you do not have to finish off the packet. Otherwise you will end up like us one year with 200 Brussels sprout seedlings, theoretically requiring 150 sq. m/180 sq. yd and producing over 100kg/225lb of sprouts. Most seeds can be stored for a few years, so you are not obliged to use them all up at once. For seed storage times, see individual plants in the A–Z of plants.

Remember that very small children will have difficulties with very tiny seeds, so choose larger

> *'I find it hard to believe that you make a lot of your plants from tiny little seeds.'*
> Francesca, aged nine

seeds for the youngest. But by the age of seven or eight, children will often be better with small seeds such as lettuce than adults. Encourage them to work carefully and meticulously, spacing the seeds out evenly, and point out that when the seeds germinate the accuracy of their work will be revealed.

Sowing under glass

Sowing under glass is necessary for some tender plants to ensure the season is long enough for them to produce fruit.

Some require temperatures of around 20°C/68°F for germination and are best grown on a warm windowsill; others do not need particularly warm temperatures but just appreciate some protection from frost. These can also be sown in a cold frame; for details, see individual entries in the A–Z of plants.

Containers

You can use all kinds of trays and pots, recycled or purpose-bought, as long as they have drainage holes in the bottom. Square pots are more space-saving for a windowsill.

Modules are seed trays divided into little chambers so that each plant has enough space in its individual pot. Peat-free Jiffy 7s come as flat coir pellets that are rehydrated for twenty minutes in a saucer of water, whereupon they turn into little pots. The advantage of all these is that the seedling that grows in each pot will not need pricking out (see page 30): it can grow on until ready to be planted out.

Sowing compost

Buy special sowing compost; or you can mix multi-purpose compost with one-third horticultural sand. Try to ensure that your seed compost is freshly bought from the garden centre; old bags can contain fungi.

MINERALS

- **Vermiculite** is a natural mineral that retains water and air, and also insulates against fluctuations in temperature. Some seeds need light to germinate, so you should not cover them with soil, but vermiculite prevents them drying out, while still being light enough.
- **Perlite** is a volcanic mineral that is used to increase air in potting compost, but does not hold water or nutrients.

How to sow

Fill each container with moist soil. Tap it on a hard surface a few times and firm the soil down lightly. Make sure the surface is even, and that there is enough room left in the container to water the soil without the water overflowing – possibly carrying the seeds with it. This is especially important if a child will be watering the seeds (and watering is a favourite task).

Try to sow the seeds thinly, and well spaced. Cover thinly with a layer of compost, usually as thick as the seeds themselves are. Some plants require light to germinate: cover these with vermiculite (for details, see individual entries in the A–Z of plants). Water the

seeds carefully with a watering can with a fine rose. Always water seeds and seedlings with tap water; water from a water butt (or barrel) might encourage fungal infection. Label your seeds: ideally note the plant, variety and date of sowing.

Seeds that love warm moist climates will appreciate a propagator lid, or simply a piece of glass on top of the tray or a clear plastic bag held in place with an elastic band. Cover trays with some layers of newspaper but check every day, and as soon as they start to germinate, take the paper off and put them on a light windowsill. Keep the seeds moist.

Sowing outside

You do not necessarily need a windowsill to start your crops: most plants can also be sown directly outside. The exact date of sowing will depend on their hardiness. For some of them, especially root crops, there is no other way of sowing, since they hate to be moved and should be sown *in situ* (for details, see the A–Z).

Start sowing outside only when the soil is dry and warm enough in spring; the 'muddy-boot-rule' applies – if the soil sticks to your boots, wait. Theoretically the soil should be at least 10°C/50°F,

and the precise measurers among you will be out there with your soil thermometers, while the rest of us are dithering. Usually it is better to wait a bit rather than start too early, in which case the seeds just rot away in cold weather and you end up wasting them. You can, however, warm up the bed by covering it with horticultural fleece (or cover cloth), starting a couple of weeks before you want to sow.

Sowing in drills

If you have heavy soil that compacts quickly, work from a plank. After raking the bed, make a drill about 1–2.5cm/½–1in depth with a trowel, getting a straight line by using the edge of the plank, a string

When sowing seeds directly into the soil, don't sow too densely.

or a bamboo cane. Remove stones and break up clods along the drill; try to get an even depth, as otherwise your seedlings will germinate irregularly. The larger the seed, the deeper it should be planted. If the drill is dry, water it before sowing. Sprinkle the seeds thinly into the drill, cover with fine soil and firm it down a bit. If you sow sparsely and regularly, you will have less work thinning afterwards. Children can do all this brilliantly; pour a small quantity of seed into their hand or a small tub, to cut the losses if they spill it, and to encourage careful work. The last job is to water again, using a watering can with a rose. Try to encourage children to create water like a gentle drizzle, rather than like a river torrent. Keep the soil moist until the seedlings emerge.

For specific information on depths, distances, pests and seasons, see individual entries in the A–Z of plants.

Broadcasting

This is the term for sowing not in rows, but by scattering seeds all over an area. It might be done with salad leaves or root crops, or with flowers that you wish to grow as a drift. The advantage of planting in rows is that you can recognize your seedlings (the weeds are not in rows) and it is easier to hoe and weed between them.

Station sowing

Some seeds germinate erratically, parsnips being a good example. In such cases you can sow three seeds every 15cm/6in. When the seedlings come up, you remove the two weakest, leaving a row of single plants.

Pricking out and thinning

Pricking out means lifting seedlings from crowded conditions in their seed tray or pot and giving them more room to grow. This can be done as soon as the little plants are large enough to handle; this is usually when they have the first pair of true leaves (in general, the first leaves that look like the adult plant, not the baby leaves). Before you start, water well. Do not wait too long, as otherwise the plants' growth may be stunted and the seedlings will become susceptible to damping off (see page 51).

Children can do this very well, as long as you have sown more than you really need, since there might be a few casualties. They may need help separating out plants' roots if the seedlings are very crowded.

> *'The seeds were so tiny, and then I sneezed.'*
> Sam, aged sixteen

You can prick the seedlings on into modules – one plant per little pot – or into small pots of 6–9cm/2½–3½in width. Fill the pots as described for sowing on page 29. Using a little dibber (or an old pencil or fork), lift the seedlings carefully out of the seed tray. Always hold the little plants by their leaves, never by the stem; if you break a leaf it might live, but if you break the stem … Make a hole with your dibber and sink the plant into it, slightly deeper in the compost than it was before – the seed leaves should almost rest on the compost. The little stem up to the seed leaves can make roots, so you can use this ability to grow sturdier little plants. Push the soil carefully around your little plant with the dibber. Water well with a fine rose. And do not forget the label …

Keep the seedlings out of full sunshine for a few days until they have recovered from this operation; then you can grow them on under cooler conditions. After two weeks they will enjoy a dose of liquid seaweed fertilizer (see page 45).

Seedlings sown directly into a bed require only thinning out. If you have the time, thin them in two stages, reaching the final distance on the second thinning. You may be able to use the thinnings, either to eat or, if they are strong enough, to transplant elsewhere. Children with small fingers are useful for thinning, although beware of them standing back to admire their work and trampling on another row… Afterwards, firm the soil gently back around the stems of the remaining plants.

COLLECTING SEEDS

This is a satisfying thing to do. It hits the right buttons of recycling, getting something for nothing, having more lovely flowers next year and having extra to give to friends.

Note that seeds from F1 hybrids will not come true, so there is no point in collecting those. Most other plants will be cross-pollinated by insects or wind, whereby pollen is transferred between different flowers of the same kind of plant. This is nature's way of increasing genetic diversity, but also means that you might not get exactly the same result again. Don't let this stop you collecting seeds, though, especially from flowers; just be prepared for some surprises. Some vegetables, however, are self-fertile and will produce the same plants in the following year: beans, peas, peppers and tomatoes.

Seed collecting starts around August and runs throughout autumn. Allow the seeds to ripen – otherwise they will not germinate – but be careful not to leave it too long, or else they may start spreading themselves around. Many flowers, beans and peas produce dry capsules or pods; these are only ready when dry and brown. Keep a close eye on plants from which you want to collect seeds.

- Collect seeds on a dry day, preferably in the afternoon. It is more fun for children if they have a little pot or tub in which to collect their own seeds. Take a little time to point out to them which is the seed and which is just the distribution mechanism, or the remains of the old petals.
- After collecting, spread them out for about a week in a dry room. Any moisture that may remain should evaporate.
- Separate the chaff from the seeds. Vegetables such as tomatoes, cucumbers and squashes carry their seeds inside moist fruits. Wait until the fruit is slightly over-ripe. Scoop the seeds out into a container, and rub or sieve them to separate the flesh from the seeds. Dry on a plate, and then on layers of kitchen towel.

Store all cleaned and dried seeds in the dark in paper envelopes or bags, labelled and dated. A shoebox in a cool room is ideal.

> *'I like pricking out the crowded seedlings.'*
> Teenage gardener with an ASBO

Division, offsets and cuttings

Also referred to as 'vegetative propagation'. These are the only ways to get more of a plant with exactly the same genetic material. Some varieties can only be propagated by cuttings or division because their seeds do not come true.

Division

By this method fibrous-rooted plants such as perennial herbs can be multiplied and also rejuvenated. Dig up the plant or take it out of the pot and slice the root ball into portions that are no bigger than a fist. Plant each one anew outside or pot them up.

Offsets

Offsets are shoots with roots, small plantlets, which can be taken from the outside of a well-established plant, such as an artichoke. Dig them up, trying to retain as many roots on each plantlet as possible. Make sure you leave at least three shoots on the original plant.

Softwood cuttings

Typical examples of plants that are suitable are lavender, sage, rosemary and verbena. If they are long enough, you could use the little bits that you pruned off when giving your plant a summer trim. The perfect time for this is spring and summer.

- Use a shoot without a flower, about 5–8cm/2–3in long.
- Cut below the node, and remove any leaves growing at this node.
- Put three cuttings into a small pot with seed compost and cover with a cloche or a plastic bag. Check and air regularly to avoid mildew.
- The cuttings usually make roots in 3–6 weeks and can then be uncovered.

Hardwood cuttings

These are used for propagating fruit bushes such as currants and vines. They are usually taken in winter while the shrubs are dormant. For a full description, see blackcurrants (page 171).

Pinching out

Once your seedlings or cuttings are growing on, it is a good idea to pinch them out. Pinching out makes plants bushier and more compact. It feels unnatural at first to be removing hard-won growth, but it encourages the plant to create more side shoots, and

Cut with a sharp knife or scissors just below the node (the point where the leaves join the stem). Place cuttings around the edge of the pot.

therefore more flowers and fruits. Use your thumb and forefinger and pinch out each growing tip of a plant. You may feel nervous about letting small children do this, so perhaps this is better kept as an adult task. Different plants require this at different stages; for details, see individual plants in the A–Z of plants.

'I made a hole. I pot in the cabbages. I had fun.'
Oliver, aged five

PLANTING OUT

'We planted out beans and butternut squash and other things. It was awesome.'
Anna, aged eight

Hardening off

Hardening off means acclimatizing plants that have been growing under warm conditions inside to cooler temperatures outside. You need gradually to prepare such plants by giving them longer and longer periods out of doors. Either place seedlings in a cold frame, a few weeks before you actually want to plant them out. Open the windows of the frame for longer and longer periods on warm days and get them used to fresh air. Or, if you have no cold frame, carry the plants to a sheltered spot outside and take them back into the house in the evening, gradually leaving them outside for longer and longer. The whole process should take 2–3 weeks.

Planting into beds

The big day has come and your seedlings or other container-grown plants are large enough to be planted out. When you are planting out, avoid days with extremes – it should not be very hot, very windy or very cold because the operation is stressful enough for them anyway.

Before you start, water the plants. The bed should be prepared (see page 27). With a trowel, dig a hole that is large enough to take the rootball easily; none of the rootball must be proud of the earth after planting. Put one hand over the top of the pot with a finger gently on either side of the plant's stem to hold it, turn it upside down and lift the pot off. Children can do this too, although take care that the top of the plant is not being damaged while they focus on extracting the roots from the pot. Once the plant is in the soil, firm the soil gently around it. Younger children may need an adult on standby while they do the whole operation.

After planting, water well – even if you are working

These pea seedlings were sown on the windowsill; it is now warm enough for them to go out into the soil, after being hardened off.

Veg and herbs in containers: not just tasty but pretty as well.

in a light drizzle. Watering ensures that the soil encloses the roots perfectly and this makes settling in easier for the plant.

POTTING SOILS AND COMPOST MIXES

The number of brands and types of commercial potting soils (called compost mixes in the UK) is astonishing. Various mixes can contain wetting agents, fertilizers, vermiculite, and worm casings, to name a small number of additives. As a general rule, most commercial mixes contain sphagnum peat moss, sand, and perlite and have been sterilized. We try to avoid using peat in the UK because ninety-four percent of all British peat bogs have been destroyed in the last fifty years. Even though peat is much more available and sustainable in North America due to the hundreds of millions acres of wild peatlands in Canada, many North Americans still prefer to avoid mixes that come from wild-harvested peat. Mixes with more decomposed bark or other organic matter such as coconut fibre are excellent substitutes for peat-based mixes.

We do not recommend using soils with synthetic fertilizers. If you plan to keep an organic garden, you should also seek out those commercial mixes that are certified organic. It is possible to reuse commercial potting soils, provided that the remnants of plant roots, fungus, weeds and insects are removed from the mixture through heating before new planting can take place.

Planting in containers

You can use any container, as long as it has enough holes in the bottom for decent drainage.

Lots of vegetables, herbs, fruit and flowers can be successfully grown in containers. The main criterion is that they are watered properly, because plants in pots dry out fast in summer. For details, see the A–Z of plants.

For vegetables, use:
- shallow containers of 8–15cm/3–6in deep: lettuces, rocket (arugula), radishes
- mid-depth containers of 20–50cm/8–20in: beetroot (beets), kohl rabi, French beans (string beans), chard
- large pots containing at least 10 litres/2 gallons (12 US quarts) of soil: tomatoes, peppers, chilli peppers, potatoes.

Growbags are popular, but we are sceptical: see page 155.

CROP PROTECTION

Protection from cold and frost

Cloches

If you cannot wait to get going in the spring, you can cover a bed with a cloche, warm the soil up for about two weeks and plant little lettuces or sow your first carrots. You can also use cloches to protect susceptible crops after they have just been planted out, or during a cold spell. They can be moved as needed. Cloches come in several shapes:

- Those that look like a mini polytunnel, usually made of plastic sheeting over metal hoops: these can be used to cover a row of plants.
- Beautiful dome-shaped 'Victorian' glass cloches (very expensive!) or cheaper plastic variations, working downwards to cut-off water bottles, that can be used to cover single plants.

Cold frames

A cold frame is a more substantial, stationary shelter that protects seedlings against cold, damp and wind. It provides a useful halfway house between an indoor windowsill and the outside garden, and can be used for hardening off.

Horticultural fleece

Horticultural fleece (available in the U.S. under the name 'Reemay') is a godsend and has become an essential piece of equipment. It can be bought in smaller sheets or larger rolls, and acts as a blanket that protects plants but lets moisture through. Fleece can be used in several ways:

- If a late frost is threatened, throw a sheet over sensitive plants.
- Use a sheet of fleece to warm up the soil for a few days prior to sowing or planting.
- Make a little cloche from it by draping it over susceptible seedlings. If it sits directly on the plants, be careful to provide enough air and remove it on warm days so that fungi and slugs do not enjoy the warm conditions underneath.
- Use it to protect plants from pests.

Protection from pests

There are two barrier materials that provide protection against insects, such as carrot fly and flea beetle: horticultural fleece and mesh. Crops can be watered through both.

Better for keeping insects off your plants for longer, although slightly more expensive, is fine mesh, usually available as 'Enviromesh'. It comes in different mesh sizes; the finer one works for smaller insects.

Cloches extend the growing season (left). Nets keep the birds off strawberries (right), while a bed of straw keeps the fruit clean.

WATERING

How often?

This depends on the type of plant and the weather. Plants should not be subjected to extremes of dryness and should be watered before they wilt. Don't forget the drying effect of wind.

- Seed beds and freshly planted seedlings should be watered thoroughly every day in dry periods; once seedlings are established they can cope with less water.
- Flowers and vegetables in containers dry out quicker than those planted directly into soil, so water them every day in dry spells.
- With established vegetable plants, stick your finger a few centimetres into the soil. It might look dry on the surface, but if it is damp below the first layer, you could wait another day.
- Established trees, shrubs and woody herbs like lavender need the least water.

The most important thing is to maintain regularity; irregular watering causes crops to split. Well-watered, plump fruits and vegetables simply taste better.

How?

- The best time for watering is early morning or early evening. Too late on a sunny morning and the leaves of the plants might scorch, as water droplets act like magnifying glasses; too late in the evening and the plants remain moist overnight, making them susceptible to slugs and fungal diseases.
- Make sure you provide enough water; moistening the surface of the soil alone is useless. Often recommended: counting to ten while holding the watering can or the hose over the roots of each plant.
- Try to water around the plants; do not spray cold water directly on to them, especially if they come from warmer climates (tomatoes, cucumbers, peppers). When watering with a hose, a lance will make this task easier.
- The aim is to moisten the soil down to 10–15cm/4–6in deep to encourage plants to grow deep healthy roots. In a bigger garden this can become

quite a task, but if you water properly, you will not have to do it every day.

- For very small seedlings, turn the holey part of the rose upwards so that they are not flattened.
- Sprinklers are wasteful – one hour of sprinkling uses as much water as a family of four in a whole day and on very hot days much of the water evaporates anyhow.
- Children are very fond of watering. This can be a bit of a liability, as they are likely to get themselves soaking wet, while small seedlings can be drowned. Wherever possible, encourage them to use a watering can, while you use the hose.

Make the most of it

- Collect rainwater, install as many water butts (or barrels) as possible and divert water from your drainpipes into them.
- Plant in slight depressions in order to retain water around the plant, especially on slopes.
- Place a bottomless plastic bottle next to thirsty plants like runner beans or courgettes (zucchini), burying it with the neck of the bottle pointing downwards; then when you fill the bottle with water it can soak right down close to the roots.
- Companion planting and intercropping are also useful for conserving water: if the soil is shaded, less water is lost.
- After watering thoroughly, apply a mulch of 5–8cm/2–3in after planting to delay evaporation. Mulching (see page 46) also helps to incorporate organic matter into your soil, which will make it more water-absorbent in the long term.
- Run out of mulching material? At least hoe away the weeds that compete with your plants for water.

But can you water too much? Yes. The effect is not as obvious as with plants that are grown too dry, and initially they will grow away happily as long as the soil does not become waterlogged. But the roots may be superficial, the plants' tissue too soft and sappy, making the plant susceptible to disease, and the fruit less tasty.

WEEDS

Depressing as it is to devote a section to this rather tedious subject, it is important. Some people even enjoy weeding as a way of getting close to their plants, and the effect of removing competitors and creating a tidy bed can be therapeutic for plant and gardener. Children, however, generally only enjoy weeding for a short period.

Why bother to weed at all? Isn't a weed just a plant in the wrong place? Weeds are in direct competition with your plants for food and water; some weeds can literally smother seedlings, and many weeds host pests and diseases.

Regular and frequent weeding is the secret. Rather than having a six-monthly blitz, try doing ten minutes a day. Just remember the doom-laden but accurate saying 'one year's seeding is seven years' weeding'. So if you notice some weeds that are about to seed, prioritize those.

The conventional solution for dealing with an overgrown plot is to use weedkiller, usually glyphosate. The organic way is hand clearance or covering beds with membrane or some other material so that weeds have no access to light. The problem with covering weeds is that to be effective, it has to be done for at least two years, which is rarely practical. Hand clearance means hoeing, digging and forking out weeds. Even after a bed is cleared, be prepared for weed seeds to germinate again a few weeks later, and for perennials to re-appear. Stay alert.

There are two main types of weed, and they have to be dealt with in different ways. The most important thing to understand about weeds is the difference between annuals and perennials.

If you can prevent an annual weed from flowering and setting seed, you will have won, even if some of the original plant remains; whereas a perennial will be there for ever unless you definitively kill or remove every bit of root.

Annuals

- The plant itself lasts only one year.
- Annuals can be hoed off, preferably in hot weather. Hoeing in wet weather will just transplant them.
- Annuals can be composted (see page 40) if not in seed.

These are some of the worst offenders.

- **Chickweed** Easy to remove, but be quick: otherwise it can smother your seedlings.
- **Cleavers or goosegrass** Sticky fun for children but not for gardeners. It scrambles over your plants, eventually smothering them completely. It comes out quite easily but flowers discreetly, so before you know it is has seeded everywhere.

- **Groundsel** Loves heavy soils, and self-seeds happily with little parachutes like dandelions, so make sure they never get that far.
- **Hairy bittercress** A small but very effective plant: after flowering it produces little seed capsules that explode at the slightest touch, spreading very rapidly and producing several generations per year. Be quick and hoe them off, preferably before any little white flowers appear.

> '*Advice on dandelions: if you can't beat them, eat them.*'
> Dr James Duke

Perennials

- These have to be dug up or killed in some other slow and painful way. Slow and painful for the gardener, that is.
- They must be discarded or burned, or stored in plastic bags or a bucket of water for a few months until they have rotted down, after which they can be composted.

Perennials subdivide into groups, depending on their different root structures:

Perennials with tap roots

- **Dandelion** The leaves form a rosette close to the ground; the flowers look pretty and children love the seed heads, but if you let them play dandelion clock, remember that each seed they blow off can make a plant with a nasty tap root that can grow even through tarmac.

- **Horsetail** The traditional advice is not to buy a house with a garden that contains horsetail. One of the most ancient plants, horsetail has deep roots and spreads by spores. It is rarely eliminated, but you can annoy it by pulling it up and hoeing it off. Maybe a non-organic friend could apply weedkiller when you are not looking ...

- **Creeping thistle** It has attractive purple flowers and can reach a height of 1m/39in. The roots are truly annoying: the plant produces a long tap root, from which lateral roots branch off and spread everywhere. Dig it up as soon as you see it.

Perennials with runners or rhizomes

These also have to be dug up, as every small piece of root can make a new plant. Sift through the soil with a digging fork. Of the following, the first two have runners above ground, and the rest have roots or rhizomes below ground.

- **Creeping buttercup** Pretty but a real nuisance: remove the runners while they are small. Once established they are very hard to remove and spread quickly.

- **Brambles** Brambles spread rapidly, both above and below ground. While the roots are spreading unseen, any strand of bramble that touches the ground soon grows roots and creates a new plant.
- **Bindweed** Bindweed roots can go down 5m/16ft. The chemical method of removal is to provide bindweed with a stick to grow up and then apply glyphosate to the leaves. If

you are a purist organic gardener, however, you are going to do a lot of digging, and eventually the plant will be weakened. Meanwhile enjoy the large white trumpet-shaped flowers of the large bindweed or the little pink flowers of the lesser.
- **Couch grass** Looks like rough tufty grass and spreads underground by rhizomes. Solution: dig it up, and make sure you follow each stringy bit and remove it completely. The only positive aspect is that the roots are white and stand out against the dark soil.

- **Ground elder** One of the nastiest and hardest to deal with of weeds – make sure you dig up every bit of the roots regularly. Work methodically and thoroughly, although it

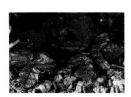

can be tricky to untangle from the roots of other plants.
- **Japanese knotweed** One of the less glorious achievements of the Victorians was to bring in this incredibly invasive plant. The solution is to dig up each bit of the root. As it is a notifiable weed, you are not allowed just to throw it away: you must burn it *in situ* or take it to a special waste site.
- **Stinging nettle** Likes good, humus-rich soil, and spreads through rhizomes and seeds. Nettles are valuable plants for wildlife, make a wonderful soup and are also useful for making an excellent liquid manure, so you could keep some plants in a corner of your garden.

COMPOST

> *'My favourite bit was putting the grass mixed with mud and pink worms in the wheelbarrow with a long fork.'*
> Sam, aged six

Throughout the gardening year you will create a large amount of waste plant material, and you can use this to produce your own compost, a homemade and free fertilizer and soil improver. Compost typically contains a balanced mix of nitrogen, phosphorus, potassium (see page 43) and other nutrients that, when you incorporate the compost into your soil, will benefit your plants.

When made the right way, compost is not smelly and does not attract vermin. The result is a crumbly material that smells similar to woodland soil.

Site and container

Choose somewhere for your compost heap that you do not have to look at, but where you have good access. The right space also depends on the climate in which you are gardening: in cool and wet climates choose a sunny place, in dry areas a partially shaded spot under a tree is ideal.

You can put compost in a container or you can simply pile it up. Containers are tidier and save space. Place your compost containers directly on the ground, so that worms and microbes can enter from below. Look for containers that you can open at the front, instead of having to dismantle the whole thing. Homemade containers from palettes are brutish but effective, and there is a whole range of stylish but impractical models on offer. Plastic compost bins with lids, often supplied cheaply or free by your local council, are very common and handy for small gardens. If possible, get two; then when you have filled one up, you can leave it while you fill up the second. Three are even better …

Pay some attention to layering what you put in. It also helps if you tip the bin over every few months, mix everything thoroughly and then put it back in.

YOU CAN USE:

Soft, 'green' materials, nitrogen-rich and moist:
- Remnants of vegetables, annuals and perennials – disease-free; chop thicker stalks or shred them.
- Fruit peelings – chop, mix with dry compost and cover to keep away flies.
- Weeds – without seed pods or roots.
- Grass clippings – mix with other materials; never create a single thick layer. Do not use if treated with weedkiller.
- Ground coffee and tea bags.
- Horse and cattle manure – store for a while first, as if fresh it can get too hot and kill worms and friendly bacteria.

'Brown', woody materials, carbon-rich and rather dry:
- Prunings and hedge trimmings – rot very slowly; better shredded.
- Leaves – most rot very slowly and are best mixed with green materials or composted separately (see right).
- Pet bedding – straw and sawdust. Mix with green material; good for aeration.
- Wood ash – very rich in potassium and calcium; do not add too much at once.
- Paper and cardboard (non-glossy and no colour print) – low-nutrient content, but good for absorbing moisture in a too-wet heap, torn up, crumpled or shredded.
- Egg shells – calcium-rich; will rot very slowly, so crush them.

How to do it

The main principle is very simple: you try to maintain an even consistency – not too wet and not too dry. It might be necessary to water it in summer, and to keep it covered, for instance with cardboard, to retain moisture in summer and prevent it from getting too cold and wet in winter.

Nitrogen-rich materials increase the temperature in the heap and the speed of decomposition, but if there are too many thick layers of soggy material your compost can become wet and slimy. If you have put in lots of moist kitchen waste, add some newspaper or shredded bank statements. There must always be enough air in the heap.

Carbon-rich materials produce the desired crumbly soil structure but if there is too much carbon-rich material it will rot too slowly. If your compost heap looks too dry for a happy worm, add something wetter like grass clippings.

Organic activators might be useful when you start your very first heap, but once you have a heap going you can use a few well-rotted layers from an old heap to activate the new.

Just try and mix soft with woody, moist with dry, rough with fine. If you fear it has gone wrong and no compost is emerging, tip it out and have a mix. But in general, just add a variety of material and leave it to get on with the process.

> 'My whole life had been spent waiting for an epiphany, a manifestation of God's presence, the kind of transcendent, magical experience that lets you see your place in the big picture. And that is what I had with my first compost heap.'
> Bette Midler

> 'Behold this compost! behold it well!'
> Walt Whitman

Mixing compost

Mixing your heaps speeds up the whole process: instead of waiting for a year or two, you could be using it after 6–9 months. Some gardeners insulate their compost (for instance with cardboard or plastic sheeting) in order to raise the temperature in the heap and get even quicker results. However, this means that not much air can get to the compost, so it is even more important to turn it several times. But if you do so, your compost will be ready for use that much quicker.

So your decision is: to mix or not to mix? In other words, do you just want to compost your garden waste without too much hassle, or do you want to spend more time and produce more compost, more quickly?

Leaf mould

Leaf mould is compost made only from dead leaves. If you have several trees in your garden it is definitely worth making it. It is low in nutrient levels but unbeatable as a soil conditioner or mulch, because it provides a very stable form of humus and has the enormous advantage of being weed free.

Build a frame with chicken wire, and pile the leaves in it. Depending on the type of leaves, it will take up to 18–24 months until the leaf mould is ready. Some leaves such as oak, chestnut, plane and evergreen leaves decay very slowly. To speed up decomposition, spread out the raked-up leaves and run a hover mower over them, collection box attached. The addition of a bit of grass will make it rot even better. The leaves should be damp in order to rot well. Check once in a while to see that it is not too wet or too dry.

In small gardens put leaves into a plastic bin liner (garbage bag) with 1 litre/1½ pints (2 US pints) of water. Make some holes in the bag with a fork and leave in a corner until rotted, turning occasionally.

FERTILIZING AND IMPROVING THE SOIL

A rich, healthy soil is the basis of successful gardening, especially successful organic gardening. The more you understand about what your plants need, the more you can help them to flourish and be productive.

Why should we feed our plants?

Every plant needs a specific amount of nutrients. If it cannot find these, it will be weakened and prone to pests and diseases. In a natural habitat plants take nutrients from the soil, grow, die down in winter and rot; and the rotting organic material provides nutrients and humus for next year's plants. Only plants that are happy with the specific conditions of a habitat grow there; if the conditions change for some reason, they vanish and other plants that prefer the new conditions will replace them.

In your garden, however, this natural process cannot take place because you are removing a quantity of organic matter to eat or to fill your vases. You want to grow a whole range of fruit and vegetables, not just the few that might grow naturally in your soil. And if this were not enough, cultivated varieties are more demanding than the original wild-growing plants. So for all these reasons you should help out.

Which products are organic?

Chemical-based fertilizers are widely available and you can achieve quick effects with them because the plants absorb the nutrient solution immediately. The downside is that it is very easy to over-apply them and plants that have been fed too much fertilizer are sappy with watery tissue that will be more prone to pests and diseases. To make matters worse, chemical fertilizers contain salts that will build up over the years in your soil; worms and many micro-organisms dislike these salts and vanish, and thus the whole process of developing a humus-rich soil is disturbed.

The main objective of fertilizing in organic gardening is to apply products of natural origin to achieve soil that is rich in humus, micro-organisms and earthworms (see page 26). The advantage is a

COMMON TERMS
Balanced fertilizer – contains approximately equal amounts of nitrogen, phosphorus and potassium.
Base dressing – fertilizer that you either rake into the ground before planting or mix into the soil when planting larger plants such as shrubs and trees.
Top dressing – fertilizer that is spread on top of the soil around established crops.
Foliar feed – this is dissolved in water and sprayed on leaves, which are able to absorb nutrients. A good emergency measure: works very quickly, but is usually more expensive than other fertilizers.
Soil conditioner – products that improve the texture of the soil.

more balanced and natural feeding and nurturing of plants and soil. The main objective is to maintain the soil in this condition through regular applications of organic matter. You can have one or two quick-acting fertilizers for emergencies to hand and that is it.

Bulk-spread fertilizers

These are the ones you add by the shovelful or barrowload. They are applied once a year, usually in late winter or early spring, and under normal conditions they are effective for most of the year.

Garden compost

When we refer to compost, we mean your own homemade material (see page 40). This is the best and most cost-effective fertilizer for your garden. It contains a very stable form of humus that will be beneficial for your soil. Do not confuse this with seed compost bought in sacks from the garden centre. Compost is used in two forms:

Well-rotted

Raked or forked in, from spring onwards. Good compost is usually well balanced with a relatively high content of phosphorus and potassium. The amounts you will need to maintain a reasonably good garden soil are surprisingly small – a 10 litre/2 gallons

THE MAJOR NUTRIENTS YOUR PLANTS NEED

Nitrogen (N)
- Encourages leaf growth, so much appreciated by leafy vegetables.
- The more humus-rich your soil is, the more nitrogen is available for your plants.
- Deficiency is shown by pale or yellow leaves; plants are small and inferior.
- Too much nitrogen leads to many dark green leaves but few flowers and fruits.

Phosphorus (P)
- Needed for the development of flowers, fruit and new roots; especially loved by root vegetables.
- Helps improve soil structure.
- Deficiency is shown by a purplish tinge to leaves. This happens rarely, as there is usually enough phosphorus in most soils, apart from very acidic ones.

Potassium, aka potash (K)
- Boosts disease resistance, and is needed for the development of sugar and starch in plants, so important for all fruiting crops.
- Usually there is enough potassium in garden soils, but micro-organisms must work on it to make it available. So the more active your soil is, the more potassium there will be for your plants. Sandy and/or acid soils are most likely to show a deficiency.
- Deficiency is shown by a lack of flowers and poor-quality fruit; plants look limp and leaf edges may be brown.

Calcium (Ca)
- Important element for a healthy soil.
- Deficiency leads to poor root growth and acid soil. If soil is too acid, potassium cannot be absorbed.

Magnesium (Mg)
- Deficiency is shown by yellow leaves; typically only the veins remain darker green. Fruit trees may develop brown blotches along the veins.
- Loams and clays are usually well supplied with magnesium, but sandy soils can be deficient.

(12 US quart) bucket per 3 sq. m/3½ sq. yd for hungry feeders on poor soil and the same bucket full for 10 sq. m/12 sq. yd for sparse feeders on good soil.

Half-rotted

You might still find larger pieces floating around in this compost, but there should no longer be any green material that could attract slugs. You can use half-rotted compost for two purposes:
- As a nurturing mulching material. The earth creatures dig it in themselves, although at a slow pace. Apply a layer about 5cm/2in deep.
- To improve soil structure. Dig it in to a bed several weeks before you intend to sow or plant into it. Spread a layer a few centimetres deep on the bed before digging in. Apply regularly for a few seasons, until your soil structure has improved.

If you have just started gardening or your own compost heap is not supplying enough, what else is available?

Mushroom compost

Organic mushroom growers often sell off their spent compost, advertising it in the classifieds in gardening magazines. The mushrooms are grown in a manure-based substrate, which is usually sterilized, so weed free. The compost is alkaline, so it is perfect if your soil tends to be acid. It is not cheap, but it provides a great kick-start if you have just taken over a patch with poor soil. Apply as garden compost.

Farmyard manure

In theory, you should use only manures and products from organic farms; otherwise farmyard manure is likely to contain residues of animal medicines, including antibiotics. Official organic gardening guidelines, however, permit non-organic farm manure after a six-month rotting period.

Manure – usually horse, but also cow or pig – should never be used fresh, since it can burn the roots of young plants. Manure also usually contains high quantities of bedding straw or sawdust. If you dig these in too soon, the soil will use up nitrogen in rotting them down, so you will produce exactly the opposite of what you are trying to achieve: namely, a nitrogen deficit.

Pile the manure next to your compost heap. Make sure it is moist, and then cover it with a tarpaulin or plastic sheet. This prevents the rain from washing out the nutrients and starts the rotting process. Leave it for about six months, until it is completely rotted.

Adding manure to your compost heap is a good way of producing more compost (see page 40).

Poultry manure can be five times as rich as the average stable manure and is always best added directly to your compost heap.

You can buy ready-for-use organic farm compost in bags at garden centres.

As a mulch, apply a layer about 5cm/2in deep, using only well-rotted material.

Sprinkle-spread fertilizers

Unlike bulk-spread fertilizers, these are sprinkled on in handfuls rather than dug in in bulk. While their application does not directly affect soil texture (unlike bulk-spread fertilizers), they affect the soil condition by facilitating increased beneficial microbial activity.

Products from animal residue

These are waste products from the meat industry that rot slowly and are therefore effective for several months. Like composts, they supply plants over a continuous period, starting about six weeks after application for the very fine-ground ones. Coarser, more granular products need longer to become effective, so are perfect for plants that are in the soil for a longer time but not very useful for quick plants like radishes or lettuce.

According to the authorities it is safe to use these, since they should have been pressure-cooked and all pathogens destroyed. This is supposed to prevent transmission of any diseases, but they still recommend wearing gloves and perhaps a face mask.

- **Blood, fish and bone** (5:5:6.5)
  Balanced, general fertilizer for leaf, fruit and root growth; releases nutrients slowly. Use if there is not enough compost available.
- **Hoof and horn** (13:0:0)
  Slow-release source of nitrogen, especially for leaf crops like brassicas.
- **Bone meal** (4:15:0)
  Phosphorus rich, and therefore good for root growth. Sprinkle in the hole when planting fruit trees and shrubs. In poor or sandy soil can be beneficial for root crops and other plants with bulbs and tubers (dahlias, tulips).

Non-animal fertilizers and soil conditioners

- **Ash from untreated wood**
  Good source of potash. Gooseberries, currants and all plants from the onion family respond well. Very alkaline and washed out quickly, so use only in small amounts: not more than 300g/11oz per sq. m per year.
- **Seaweed meal**
  Fertilizer and soil conditioner in one product. Contains many minor nutrients and alginic acid, which helps to bind sands and separate clays. Apply three months before planting.

LIQUID PLANT MANURE

These are easy to make, cost nothing and are quite effective. The main disadvantage is that they are very pungent. If you are prepared to put up with this, try making one of these:

- Comfrey manure: high in potash and trace minerals, for potash-loving plants like tomatoes, all berries and all plants of the onion family.
- Borage manure: high in nitrogen.
- Nettle manure: high in nitrogen, increases resistance to diseases, repels insects.

The principle is the same for all: collect 1kg/2¼lb of plant leaves (comfrey, borage, nettle) and put them into a woven bag or net. Steep in a 10 litre/2 gallon (12 US quart) bucket of water. Cover with a lid and wait for two weeks. Use diluted, one part manure to ten parts water.

Borage: use the little blue flowers in your Pimm's, and then use the rest of the plant to make nutritious liquid plant manure. Drink one and apply the other to your plants.

- **Lime**
  Not a fertililizer in itself, but helps to make nutrients available. Raises pH level and improves soil structure. Always use granulated lime, which does not scorch plants (for more on pH, see page 24). If the pH of your soil is lower than 6.0, apply 200g/7oz per sq. m per year each winter until you have reached the desired pH. Other soils need regular liming only every 3–4 years, because soil acidifies over the years. For these, apply 150g/5½oz per sq.m per year in winter.
- **Rock dust**
  A by-product of quarrying; contains many trace elements. Good for sandy soils, improves water retention and boosts soil fertility.

Fertlizers for quicker results

Your garden could be happy all season living off its spring treatment. But a few hungry plants may get stressed or peckish halfway through the year. So it is useful to be able to read the signs and have a few emergency solutions to hand. None of these fertilizers should be used after August on any plant that will overwinter, as plants that put on extra tender new growth just before winter risk damage in the first frost.

- **Organic chicken pellets** (5:3:3)
  Good source of nitrogen, can be used as top dressing for hungry plants or as base dressing in poor soil if compost is lacking. Nutrients are released at medium speed (a few weeks, depending on weather).
- **Liquid organic tomato food** (3:3:6)
  Available in garden centres; good for all plants that like extra potassium in summer, i.e. any flowering and fruiting plants.
- **Liquid seaweed extract**
  Very rich in minor nutrients, can be used as quick acting foliar spray. Good for emergencies, but relatively expensive.

QUANTITIES?

Maybe there are some gardeners with scales in their sheds, but for the rest of us here are some guidelines for 1 sq. m:

100g/3½oz = 1 small yoghurt pot full
25g/1oz = 1 heaped tablespoon

MULCHING

*'The best was having a go with the wheelbarrow
and digging the compost.'*
Louis, aged six

In nature the soil is never bare. Plants that die down provide natural mulch and eventually become compost that feeds the soil. Following this example in your garden brings huge benefits:
* moisture retention
* weed suppression
* improvement of soil structure
* reduced risk of compaction and erosion
* regulation of soil temperature by retaining warmth in autumn and protecting from frost later
* and last but not least, fertilizing.

What can you use?
There are organic and non-organic mulches.

Organic mulches have the major advantage of feeding your soil while they rot down. The following are suitable as organic mulches:

With fertilizing effect (see also page 42):
* Half-rotted garden compost – without any residual green material, as otherwise it attracts slugs.
* Manure – only well rotted, as otherwise weeds are spread with the mulch.
* Organic mushroom compost – alkaline, therefore good for vegetable beds, less so for fruit.

Without much fertilizing effect, but still beneficial for the soil:
* Leaf mould (see page 41).
* Shreddings, made from prunings – compost a few months before using.
* Chipped bark – good for weed suppression. Apply nitrogen-rich fertilizer such as hoof and horn before mulching with it, because it takes nitrogen from the soil while rotting down.
* Straw – good short-term mulch for plants such as strawberries.

Non-organic mulches, mainly used for weed suppression:
* Black plastic sheeting.
* Cardboard or newspaper (at least 8–10 sheets thick).
* Matting from synthetics or coir.

These materials suppress weeds reliably and retain moisture, but have no beneficial effects on the soil. They have one big advantage, however, in that they keep for several years. The downside is that they are rather ugly. To make the area look more appealing you can cover them with other materials such as chipped bark or shreddings.

How and when?
* Wait until the soil has warmed up. If you mulch too early, you lock in the cold beneath the mulch. The best moment is usually late winter or early spring, when the soil is still moist from the winter rains.
* Mulch only after removing all weeds including roots.
* Do not pile mulch against the stems of plants: leave around 5cm/2in free of mulch, as otherwise the stems can rot. Also be careful not to cover the crowns of perennial plants once they start to grow in spring.
* 5–10cm/2–4in depth is ideal.

Children are generally enthusiastic wheelbarrow drivers, and enjoy filling barrows, and particularly tipping out the contents and raking muck around, so they should be able to participate, although not for too long.

PEST CONTROL

> *'I found it a bit disgusting picking up the bugs, but I liked drawing them.'*
> Paula, aged nine

Pest control in organic gardens is different from the more conventional method – the first aim here is prevention. To do this:
- Choose pest-resistant varieties.
- Rotate your crops, thereby reducing the build-up of soil-borne diseases.
- Use companion planting – pests spread slower than under a monoculture.
- Grow healthy, well-fed plants.
- Encourage beneficial predators.

The more diverse the planting in your garden and the more beneficial wildlife it has, the better. Within a couple of years there should be a natural balance, and pests and diseases should be reduced to a minimum.

In an organic garden, children need not keep away during spraying, but on the contrary can learn about wildlife, encouraging ladybirds (ladybugs) and worms or stamping on slugs.

Attracting allies

By attracting beneficial wildlife you will not only be helping yourself in terms of pest control but also doing a good thing for the protection of these animals in general. Once you cut down on chemicals, they will gradually come back to your garden.

If you have the space, plant some shrubs or even a hedge near your kitchen garden. This will provide shelter and food for wildlife. Even in small gardens you can help out by planting some evergreen climbers on a fence or wall. Especially beneficial are native plants such as honeysuckle, elder or ivy.

Also remember wildlife in winter. Tidying your vegetable beds is important to prevent the build-up of pests, but leave some leaves and logs in corners of your garden for wildlife.

Encourage allies such as ladybirds (ladybugs), hoverflies and lacewings with flowers such as cosmos, parsley and poached egg plant (*Limnanthes douglasii*). Centipedes predate on slugs and their eggs.

Hedgehogs and frogs are great slug-eaters. Insect-loving birds such as robins, wrens, tits and song thrushes eat huge quantities of aphids, caterpillars, snails and other pests. Earwigs are a problem with some plants, namely dahlia flowers and calabrese (broccoli), but otherwise useful.

Pests
Aphids

Aphids distort and weaken plants, and also spread viruses while sucking. They come in different forms – greenfly, blackfly and mealy cabbage aphid; sometimes they are yellowish, and they may or may not have wings. They propagate at an alarming rate.

Prevention:
- Well-fed (but not over-fed) plants are less susceptible to aphids than weak ones.
- Rub the aphids off with your fingers or pick off infested leaves and shoots as soon as you spot them.
- Encourage aphid predators such as ladybirds and their larvae, hoverflies, lacewings and earwigs to live in your garden. Be patient for a few weeks to let these allies build up their strength.
- Nasturtiums are more attractive to blackfly than any other plant, so you can use them as a trap.

How to get rid of them if they are overwhelming your plants:
- Wash them off with a powerful jet of water from the hose.
- For a simple and effective homemade pesticide, add one or two drops of washing-up liquid to several gallons of water – the fatty acids in this solution break down the insects' casings. Make sure the solution is very dilute. In extreme cases use pyrethrum.

> *'If it moves fast, it's a predator – let it continue to predate. If it moves slowly, it will eat plants – remove it!'*
> Old gardeners' wisdom, with one exception: earthworms

> *'On every stem, on every leaf, and both sides of it, and at the root of everything that grew, was a professional specialist in the shape of a grub, caterpillar, aphis, or other expert, whose business it was to devour that particular part.'*
> Oliver Wendell Holmes

Cutworms and leatherjackets

Both pests cause the most depressing damage in gardening: overnight they can completely slice through the roots of small plants. Cutworms also attack potatoes and other root crops.

To reduce the damage:
- If a plant has been affected, search in the soil around the plant for the pest and kill it.
- Protect young plants with collars made of plastic tubes stuck into the soil a few centimetres/1–1½in deep or grow plants from seed under fine mesh to prevent adults laying their eggs near by.
- Heavy rain or heavy watering kills larvae.

Leaf miners

If you find a pale squiggly pattern on leaves, hold it up to the light and you may see a little maggot literally within the leaves: the larva of a leaf miner. Susceptible plants are celeriac (celery root), chard, beetroot (beets) and many flowers of the daisy family.
- Pick off affected leaves at the first sight and squash the larva.

Leaf miner larvae affect not only the look of the plant but its health too.

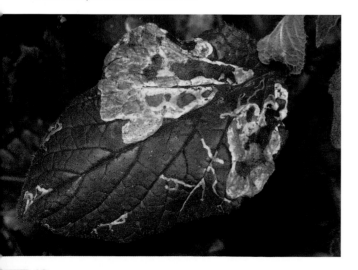

Millipedes

You can distinguish millipedes from centipedes because the millipedes have two pairs of legs on most of their body segments. They move slowly, unlike centipedes, who prey on them. Millipedes love peas and beans, and can also attack roots and other tubers. Dig gently around the damaged plants and try to find and remove the millipedes.

Rabbits

If rabbits are a problem in your area, the only way to keep them out of your patch is to erect a rabbit-proof fence. Surround your vegetable patch with a fence of chicken wire with 2.5cm/1in mesh size. The fence should be about 1.2m/4ft high, with 30cm/1ft dug in under soil level, angled outwards.

Slugs and snails

When it comes to slugs, even the gentlest gardener can become amazingly aggressive. The only mitigating factor is that on the compost heap they can help to break down organic matter.

Prevent them:
- Keep your beds clear of rotting leaves, which attract slugs.
- Keep the garden tidy – slugs love to hide under pots, trays and pieces of wood.
- Encourage other animals that eat them.

Build barriers:
- Slugs and snails don't like to crawl over bumpy, spiky surfaces such as gravel or shredded twiggy material.
- Copper rings and tapes seem to work, giving the snails little electric shocks. But they are only handy for single plants or plants in pots and containers, and they are expensive.
- Recycle coffee grounds by spreading them as a barrier around plants. The big café chains often offer them for free.

Catch them:
- With beer traps – they like lager best – but emptying out the traps is revolting.
- By hand. Go out into the garden on a damp evening with a torch, or get up early and hunt them out. Message boards are full of discussions about what to do next, but the quickest is a stamp. We have also heard of 'flying snails', but that is most unneighbourly.

Along with slugs, snails are every gardener's favourite enemy.

Kill them with:
- Nematodes – there is a product available that consists of nematodes harmful to snails, though not slugs. Dilute and then water your garden with it. Most effective in gardens with boundary walls.
- Slug pellets. Organic gardeners do not use conventional slug pellets because they can harm birds, hedgehogs and even pets. The latest generation of slug pellets, however, is made from ferric phosphate, which is not harmful to any creature other than slugs.

The most effective way is probably a mix of several methods.

Squirrels
Grey squirrels can be a real nuisance in the garden. They dig up freshly planted tulip and crocus bulbs and nibble fresh plant shoots. The only way to keep them off is to use netting or chicken wire with 1cm/½in mesh size. For pots planted up with bulbs you can use a 2cm/1in layer of grit. It is some consolation to know that if you can defend your bulbs the first year, they will not dig them up the following year – they are lazy and only take the freshly planted ones in easy-to-dig soil.

Deer
Suburban deer can be a terrible nuisance in North America, and sometimes the only solution will be a tall fence and netting around the vegetable plot. The best deterrent to deer is a family dog, but failing this, various pepper sprays and commercial products can be tried. Even coyote urine is sold as a deer repellent!

Wireworms
While digging you might come across little worms 2cm/1in long with a slightly orange, stripy skin. Wireworms can eat into beets, carrots and potatoes; sometimes they also eat seeds. They are the larvae of click beetles, whose favourite habitat is grass, so typically problems with wireworms occur after digging up a grassy patch for vegetables or if growing near a lawn. If you want to check if there are any present in your soil, bury some pieces of potato, mark the site and look again after a week.

If you have wireworm:
- Dig the ground over and leave it for birds to pick at the worms, if possible several times.
- Grow something other than root vegetables and potatoes in this bed, and hoe frequently during the season to enable birds to do their work.
- If you have no choice but to grow root vegetables in this bed, harvest the crops before September,

The most common offenders, their predators and how to attract them

Pest	Eaten by	Support for allies
Larvae and eggs of insects, and caterpillars	Birds	Hedges, bird boxes and bird baths. Provide bird food in winter.
Aphids	Larvae of lacewings and hoverflies, and ladybirds (ladybugs)	Plant flowers of plants of the parsley family (dill, fennel), and poached egg plant (Limnanthes douglasii) for hoverflies. Make insect hotels (see page 101).
Slug and snail eggs	Beetles	Mulch beds, as beetles live in mulch.
Slugs and insects	Frogs and toads	Hiding places under log piles, stones and leaves. Create ponds.
Slugs, beetles, maggots and woodlice	Hedgehogs	Hiding places under log piles and leaves. Don't use conventional slug pellets.
Moths and midges	Bats	Install bat boxes.
Slugs, insects and woodlice	Blindworms and lizards	Hiding places in stone walls, around ponds, and under log piles and leaves.

because after that the problem will get really bad.

- Some people plant 'sacrifice potatoes' in the first season to catch as many wireworms as possible, and then continue with their normal crop rotation.

It is probably no consolation to know that after 4–5 years of cultivation they should be eradicated.

Pigeons

Pigeons are particularly annoying, eating brassicas, chard, peas, lettuces … unless they are fleeced or netted. Or made into a pie (the pigeons, not the brassicas; or perhaps both together). Net, net, net.

Biological controls

This means the introduction of pest predators. Some are exotic, and often they are meant for use in a greenhouse, but you can also buy lacewings and ladybirds for your garden, usually by mail order.

We are sceptical about the exotic ones; good examples of the use of biological controls that went wrong include the cane toad in Australia, and more recently and closer to home, harlequin ladybirds. Having arrived in Britain as recently as 2004, harlequins are galloping northwards and can no longer be stopped, to the detriment of our native species. Biological controls are offered in gardening magazines and via websites; read the details carefully before ordering.

Diseases

Plant diseases can appear as fungi, bacteria and viruses.

By preference, **fungi** attack plants that are already weakened, often because of a lack of water and/ or food. Weakened plants have softer tissue, which makes it easier for the disease to enter. Fungi are spread by spores that can be transmitted in dry conditions by wind or in damp weather by rain splash. Some fungi, such as that which causes clubroot in brassicas, can remain viable in the soil for many years; others overwinter in plant remains that were affected the

Many a ladybird (ladybug) larva has been exterminated by ignorant gardeners: treasure these 'baby ladybirds'.

season before. So your main objective should be to prevent the spread of fungi by good garden hygiene and by not planting seedlings too close together, so ensuring enough ventilation between plants.

Bacteria can enter a plant only through wounds, caused by pests or pruning. Examples of bacteria are cankers and fire blight on fruit trees. There is not much you can do except cut back affected branches until you reach healthy tissue.

Act quickly as soon as you spot fungal or bacterial diseases. Often it is sufficient to pick off affected leaves in the first stages, and then try to improve the growing conditions of the plant. Remember to put the rubbish in the dustbin, not on the compost heap.

The following diseases affect a whole range of plants. Others relevant only to certain plants are described in the A–Z of plants.

Powdery mildew on a courgette (zucchini) leaf.

Damping off

This could be one of the first diseases you come across, since it affects seedlings. The little stems of the seedlings keel over and the plants die. Damping off is a fungal disease that spreads quickly and happens when conditions are too damp, or when seedlings are sown too close together or pricked out too late. Lettuces, tomatoes, antirrhinums, salvias and zinnias are very susceptible.

Conventional gardeners use chemicals to prevent and treat it, but in organic gardening the main thing is to work as hygienically as possible and avoid the causes.

- Only use mains water for watering seedlings; do not overwater.
- Wash trays and pots that were affected with the disease properly before re-using.
- Make sure you sow seeds thinly.

Downy mildew

This is a fungal disease that attacks many plants, often young ones. Yellow patches show on the leaf surface, mould on the underside. This happens especially in damp conditions. The fungus survives in the soil and in plant debris.

Powdery mildew

This fungus shows as a powdery white coat on leaves. It can attack almost all plants, especially if the days are warm and dry but the nights are cold. If plants are too dry in general they are also susceptible.

Grey mould

Leaves or fruit are covered with fungal grey mould. It can be prevented by growing healthy plants and good general hygiene. Remove all dead plant parts. Do not plant too densely, so as to ensure good air circulation between plants.

Rust

If you find little pustules in shades of yellow and red on plant leaves, they have caught rust. The onion family and mint are particularly susceptible. The treatment for all these is more or less the same:

- Avoid overcrowded conditions.
- Cut off affected leaves at the very first sign; do not compost.
- Improve conditions – feed and top up mulch if necessary.
- Water in the morning so that the leaves can dry off before a cold or humid night.

Viruses

A wide range of plants can carry viruses without showing any signs, but for a few plants viruses are particularly harmful. Since viruses are spread by sap-sucking insects, such as aphids, be especially watchful for these and fight them if necessary.

MONTH
BY
MONTH

Note: North American readers in zones 6 and below will want to consider adding a delay of one month to recommendations.

JANUARY

winter

January is usually the coldest month of the year, at best crisp and bright, but perhaps dour and slushy. A time to help birds and other wildlife to make it through the winter, to wonder whether it will ever be summer again, and to try to remember why you live in this country. But wrap up and get out; the children have got cabin fever and could do with some fresh air. Get outdoors even if the days are short, and try to finish winter pruning and digging.

SOW NOW

Windowsill
Sweet peas

PLANT NOW

In frost-free areas
Rhubarb
Bare-rooted fruit trees and bushes
Sweet peas sown in autumn – pot on, keep pinching out and keep on a light windowsill or in a cold frame

DO NOW

Brassicas Keep beds tidy, pull off any damaged leaves, and ensure soil surface is free of debris and provides no shelter for lurking pests and diseases.
Fruit trees Check that stakes are firm, and ties and guards not too tight. As you inspect the bare branches, try to remember how beautiful the blossom will be and how tasty the fruit.
Apples and pears Prune now. Twiggy prunings can be kept to use as pea sticks later on, and thicker logs can be piled up to create shelter for wildlife.
Blackcurrants and gooseberries Prune now. Thorny

Sow sweet pea seeds in root trainers on the windowsill.

gooseberry prunings can be used to keep cats off seed beds.

Weed and add compost Make sure beds are free of perennial weeds and distribute a layer of compost 5cm/2in deep over beds where necessary.

Test soil If your soil is too acidic (below pH6), sprinkling lime at a time when nothing much is growing will raise the pH and benefit fertility (see page 24).

Check storage Apples, pears, dahlia tubers, potatoes. Remove any that are damaged or rotting before they infect their neighbours. Eat the last pumpkins and squashes.

Potatoes Visit your nearest potato day to find a wider range of varieties. Set purchased potatoes out to chit (sprout).

Order seed catalogues and select your crops for this season.

Birdfeeders Keep well filled: this is a tough season for birds.

HARVEST NOW

Brussels sprouts
Winter cabbages
Kale
Leeks
Parsnips
Welsh onions

In mild areas or under cloches
Chard
Oriental leaves (salad greens)
Spinach
Bay
Parsley
Rosemary
Sage
Thyme
Winter savory

'Instead of watching TV it is good to spend time to do gardening.'
Malika, aged eight

If the temperatures in your area remain above −5°C/23° F in winter, you can still find plenty to harvest in January.

EAT NOW

Parsnip crisps

Homemade vegetable crisps. A healthy take on a children's favourite. We do not recommend getting your kids to make these because of the hot fat, but they will love eating them.

When seasoning the crisps, try out different herbs and spices such as paprika, chilli powder or crushed herbs such as thyme. Also try making fresh sweet potato or beetroot (beet) crisps in the same way. Just make sure they are dried off properly before cooking, as otherwise the oil will spit.

Serves 4
6 large parsnips
450ml/15fl oz sunflower oil
    (2 cups)
salt

Peel the parsnips and slice very thinly across the root. It is best to use a knife rather than a mandolin, as long as the slices are very thin. Lay the parsnips on paper towel to absorb any excess liquid.

Heat the sunflower oil in a medium-sized saucepan until it is very hot. You can tell if it is hot enough if a piece of bread goes golden brown immediately when dropped in. Add the parsnip slices, about 10–12 at a time. Beware: they may spit. Be careful to keep children and clumsy adults at bay at this stage.

Watch very carefully and remove the parsnips with a slotted spoon after about 20–30 seconds when they turn pale golden brown. Place the crisps on paper towel to absorb the excess oil. Taste them: they should be very crisp. When all the crisps are done, place in a bowl and add a pinch or two of salt. Any other seasoning could be added at this stage. Give them a good shake and for the best taste serve immediately.

'We have found that if the children dig effectively enough they don't usually get severe frostbite.'
Chiswick House
Kitchen Garden mailshot

FEBRUARY

late winter

As soon as the soil has warmed up a little – usually by the end of the month – the mulching season has arrived. The soil should be thoroughly damp by now and the mulch will help to retain the moisture. Clearing out your compost heap – get the children barrowing and spreading compost – will create some room for the new season's debris. And by the end of the month, spring is finally beginning to arrive.

Forced rhubarb, grown under a dark pot, will be ready earlier and taste more tender than unforced.

SOW NOW

Windowsill
Summer cabbages
Lettuce
Onions
Antirrhinums
Sweet peas

Cold frame/cloche
Broad (fava) beans
Early peas – in guttering or pots
Spinach

PLANT NOW

Early potatoes – at the end of the month, under fleece (or cover cloth)
Mints – pot up and take into the house or a cold frame
Fruit trees and fruit bushes – last chance
Rhubarb, after division

DO NOW

Potatoes If you put them out to chit (sprout) last month, check that they are the right way up. Sometimes when they are dormant it is hard to tell.

Apples, pears and gooseberries Last chance to prune before they start to leaf up.

Autumn raspberries Cut down the old canes to the ground and tidy the bed.

Rhubarb Mulch with compost, and cover with a pot or bucket to keep out the light and force more delicate-tasting stalks.

Strawberries Cover some plants with cloches for earlier crops.

Blueberries Feed with ericaceous fertilizer, or pot on with ericaceous compost.

Dahlias Start dahlia tubers: either buy new ones of special varieties, or bring last year's out of winter storage to a sunny cold frame or a cool windowsill and start watering them.

Sweet peas Pinch out tips to create bushy, compact plants, rather than one-strand tall thin ones.

Weed thoroughly and spread compost as mulch under trees and between plants.

Seed beds If your seed beds are all ready and prepared, and you have cloches and fleece, you can cover them to start warming up the soil.

HARVEST NOW

Early sprouting broccoli
Late Brussels sprouts
Kale
Leeks
Parsnips
Welsh onions
Rhubarb, forced

In mild areas or under cloches
Chard
Oriental leaves (salad greens)
Spinach
Bay
Parsley
Rosemary
Thyme
Winter savory

Kale 'Red Russian'.

Kale 'Cavolo Nero' or 'Black Tuscan'.

EAT NOW

Side dish of quick-fried chard or pak choi (bok choy)

This is a quick way to create a tasty side dish that can be used with many of your favourite vegetables. Try making your own combinations. Just remember to add the vegetables needing a longer cooking time first.

Serves 4

2 garlic cloves, sliced
2 tablespoons olive oil
4 large pak choi (bok choy) or 4 handfuls of chard
1 teaspoon soy sauce
1 teaspoon walnut or sesame oil (optional)

In a pan, fry the sliced garlic in the olive oil for 2–3 minutes, making sure you do not burn it. For chard, wash and separate the stems from the top leaves and crudely chop the stems. For pak choi, small plants can be cooked whole; with larger ones either cook the leaves separately or cut in half lengthwise.

Add the stems to the garlic. Fry at a high heat for 3–4 minutes, stirring occasionally. Add the remaining chopped leaves, the walnut or sesame oil (if you wish) and continue to cook for 2–3 minutes, stirring occasionally. Add the soy sauce and finish cooking for a further 30 seconds and serve.

Cook pak choi in the same way.

Side dish of kale with Portobello mushrooms

This is a variation on the above recipe. For greater visual effect, use different types of kale.

Serves 4

2 garlic cloves
2 tablespoons olive oil
150g/5½oz kale, roughly chopped (about 4–4½ cups)
4 Portobello mushrooms, sliced, or 12 shitake mushrooms, whole
1 tablespoon soy sauce
2 tablespoons roasted pine nuts

In a pan sweat the garlic in the olive oil and then add the Portobello mushrooms or shitake mushrooms and the kale. Add the soy sauce to taste and cook for 5–10 minutes. Serve with the roasted pine nuts sprinkled over the vegetables.

'Everybody complains about the weather, but nobody does anything about it.'
Charles Dudley Warner

CREATE NOW

Willow wigwam weaving

Willow is a wonderfully flexible, natural material. A wigwam for sweet peas or other climbing plants is a satisfying and fairly simple structure to build, and although not suitable for the very young, slightly older children can work on their own wigwam, with some help on finishing and manoeuvring the withies.

For a basic structure you will need:
8 sturdy willow rods for the frame (see below)
17–21 thin flexible willow rods (withies), 2m/6ft long
  (different lengths are available)
pot 45cm/18in in diameter
compost
string
scissors

You can buy a variety of willows. Green willow, for example, is freshly cut and although it does not need soaking and is very flexible it will take root if planted in the garden. Brown is good for wigwams,

as the withies have been steamed and will not grow; they will, however, need to be soaked before use. Ideally, source pre-soaked willow from a specialist supplier; otherwise check with the supplier about exact soaking times.

Fill the flower pot with compost. This pot will be used to hold your rods firm while you build your wigwam, and will not be needed afterwards.

Select eight sturdy rods and distribute them evenly in the compost around the edge of the pot. Make sure the natural curve of the willow bulges outwards, making it easier for you to gather the rods in the centre and fasten them together with a piece of string.

Now start weaving, always being careful with children to ensure that the ends of the withies are not going to poke anyone. Select two, preferably of equal length, of the more flexible willow withies and start weaving them in front of and behind the uprights in a crisscross pattern, with the withy that comes from the back of the upright always ending up below the other one (so that the two withies end up intertwined in one another as well as woven around the uprights). Once you come to an end, leave about 2cm/1in of withy – you can trim this later. Choose

Weave alternately over and under, and trim off anything sticking out at the end.

another two withies and lay them overlapping by 5cm/2in over the end of the previous ones and repeat the exercise at least twice more. This is now your base band.

For the next band, remove the string and tie it tightly further up the rods. Repeat the weaving process three times in the centre part of your now developing wigwam. Step back from the structure from time to time to make sure that you are weaving evenly. The time to make any adjustments is while the wigwam is taking on shape and structure.

Before starting the third and final band wrap one of the withies around the top several times before tying a knot to hold it together. Now start the final band, using two rows.

You can make the bands thicker by weaving another row; you can also connect the bands by weaving upwards diagonally.

Once you have finished, remove the structure from the pot and trim off any loose ends. Place the finished structure in position and plant sweet peas or other climbers around it.

MARCH

early spring

The big sowing month – make space on your windowsills . . . Also the perfect month for planting herbs and perennial cutting flowers.

Planting and sowing outside in March depend on the weather. If you sow too early, seeds will either rot in the moisture or fail to germinate in the cold, and you will have to do it all again. Seed sowing is a fun thing to do for children of all ages.

Remember that each seed will be a seedling that will need even more room on the windowsill . . .

SOW NOW

Windowsill
Celeriac (celery root)
Peppers and chilli peppers
Sweetcorn (corn)
Tomatoes
Basil
Chives
Coriander (cilantro)
Marjoram
Parsley
Thyme
Antirrhinum
Aster
Sunflowers
Zinnia

Cold frame/cloche
Brussels sprouts
Cabbage for summer
Chard
Kohl rabi
Leeks
Lettuces

Oriental leaves (salad greens)
Peas – in guttering
Rocket (arugula)
Alpine strawberries
Cosmos

Outside
Broad (fava) beans
Beetroot (beet), early varieties
Carrots
Onions
Parsnips
Peas (depending on the weather)
Radishes
Spring onions (scallions)
Spinach
Dill
Calendula
Nigella

PLANT NOW

Garlic (if not planted last winter)
Onion sets
Early potatoes
Shallots – in colder areas
Herbs such as chives, mint and thyme, after division
Herbs such as lavender, lemon balm, marjoram, mint, rosemary, sage, bought in
Vines, container grown
Dahlias – pot up
Sweet peas

DO NOW

Asparagus Mulch with compost. Order new plants and prepare beds. These need to be very well done – deep and thorough – so leave enough time, because once the crowns arrive you will need to plant them as quickly as possible.
Spring cabbages Feed with chicken manure pellets.
Rhubarb Uncover forced rhubarb and let it grow naturally from now on. You can still pick it, as long as you do not take too many leaves from each plant.
Weeding This is when weeds can begin to get a hold. Keep on top of them now if you can.

HARVEST NOW

Sprouting broccoli
Last Brussels sprouts
Kale
Leeks
Welsh onions
Rhubarb

In mild areas or under cloches
Chard
Winter lettuce
Spinach
Bay
Parsley
Rosemary

'Bad seed is a robbery of the worst kind: for your pocket-book not only suffers by it, but your preparations are lost and a season passes away unimproved.'
George Washington

Purple sprouting broccoli: one of the few vegetables in this 'hungry gap' before the next season's crops kick in.

'Every year, back comes Spring, with nasty little birds yapping their fool heads off and the ground all mucked up with plants.'
Dorothy Parker

EAT NOW

Rhubarb cake with vanilla cream and meringue

Rhubarb is the first fruit of the season and many an over-enthusiastic gardener may wonder what to do with so much of it. Rhubarb, peeled, chopped into 5cm/2in long pieces, can easily be frozen for use later in the year, making this recipe a year-round pleasure. This recipe also works well with gooseberries, as they too have the tangy taste that goes so well with the sweetness of the meringue. Even the very young can help rolling out pastry, and if there is any pastry left over they could make a separate little tart.

Serves 4

1 packet of good-quality sweet shortcrust pastry (12oz sweetened pastry dough)
750g/1½lb rhubarb
250ml/8fl oz single cream (1 cup light cream)
2 egg yolks
1 tablespoon cornflour (cornstarch)
100g/3½oz sugar (½ cup)
½ vanilla pod (vanilla bean)
2 egg whites
100g/3½oz icing sugar (¾–1 cup confectioner's sugar)

Preheat the oven to 180°C/350°F/GM4.

Roll out the pastry to 0.5cm/¼in thickness. Line a buttered round baking tin, 25cm/9in in diameter, with the pastry. Blind bake the pastry for 20 minutes in the middle rack of your oven until golden brown.

While the pre-baked pastry is cooling, prepare the rhubarb. If necessary, peel it and cut into 5cm/2in long pieces. Then in a pot, with a little water – just enough to cover the base – cook down the rhubarb to a compote consistency.

In a pan add the single cream, egg yolks, cornflour and sugar, and the scraped-out seeds of the vanilla pod. Over a low heat whisk the ingredients together until they are thick and creamy. Remove from the heat and add the cooked rhubarb.

Using a clean dry bowl and hand mixer, whisk the egg whites and icing sugar until you get stiff white peaks.

Fill the pastry form with the fruit and vanilla mixture. Then top up with spoonfuls of the meringue and return to the preheated oven at 180°C for a few minutes, until the meringue peaks turn a light caramel colour. Remove from the oven and let it cool before serving.

CREATE NOW

Easter egg decorations using garden herbs and vegetables

Eggs have always symbolized Easter, so why not try this herbal variation on the traditional theme? Use it to make hard-boiled eggs to eat or hollow eggs to hang as decoration. The very young will find this too fiddly, but slightly older children enjoy being creative with the patterns, as long as you can help them towards the end.

You will need:

white eggs
pair of skin-coloured tights (pantyhose)
selection of herbs such as parsley and sage, with
    leaves large enough to give a good outline (smaller
    leaves such as thyme may not show up)
handful of brown onion skins
1 litre/1½ UK pints water (4 cups)
white wine vinegar
corkscrew, egg pricker or metal skewer
matches
string, for hanging
slotted spoon
scissors

For hard boiled eggs

Make sure you prick the rounded end of the eggs with an egg pricker to avoid cracking when boiling.

Cut a piece of the tights approximately 10cm/4in long, large enough to make a knot at each end and to hold the egg snugly. Make a knot at one end, put your egg carefully inside and add a variety of herbs in between the egg and the tights. The herbs must be pressed tightly against the surface of the eggs in order to create a pattern on the egg. Carefully tie the other end of the tights, making sure that the herbs stay in place against the outside of the egg. It may be easier to tie with string.

In a saucepan add the onion skins, and white wine vinegar. Bring to the boil and let simmer for a few minutes so that the water absorbs the colour from the onion skins.

Now, using a slotted spoon, gently place the eggs into the gently boiling water with the onion skins. Make sure the egg is completely immersed so that it will become evenly coloured.

Cook until hard boiled. Timings will vary depending on what eggs you are using – chicken eggs 8–10 minutes, duck eggs 15–18 minutes. Once cooked, remove the eggs and run them under cold water. Discard the tights and herbs and let the eggs dry.

For hollow eggs

Carefully make two holes, one at each end of the egg, using a corkscrew or metal skewer. Make the hole at the bottom of the egg slightly larger so that a match can be slotted in lengthways. Now empty the egg, blowing though the top of the hole and collecting the contents into a bowl (use to make omelette). Secure your egg and herb decoration in a piece of tights, as above.

Instead of boiling the egg in the vegetable dye you can just immerse the egg into a previously prepared mixture (either hot or cold) and let it sit for 15–20 minutes, depending how dark you want the colour to be. Remove the eggs and dry them.

To hang each hollow egg, cut off the tip of a match and tie a piece of string around the middle of the remaining match. Pass the match lengthwise through the larger hole at the rounded end of the egg. Jiggle the egg about very gently to move the match crosswise, so that you can hang your decorated egg up by the string.

Eggs and daffodils, symbols of spring.

APRIL

spring

Probably the busiest month of the gardening year. Seedlings are waiting to be pricked out, new plants have arrived in the shops and there is still lots to sow. Put on the wellies and get the whole family outside. Everything is bursting forth; fruit trees and the first flowers are already in blossom.

Radish seedlings.

SOW NOW

Windowsill
French (string) beans
Runner (flat pole) beans
Courgettes (zucchini) and marrows
Cucumbers
Oriental leaves (salad greens)
Pumpkins
Squashes
Sweetcorn (corn)
Tomatoes
Basil
Coriander (cilantro)
French marigolds
Nasturtiums
Zinnias

Outside
Beetroot (beet)
Broad (fava) beans
Brussels sprouts, late varieties
Autumn cabbages

Calabrese (broccoli)
Carrots
Chard
Early kale
Kohl rabi
Leeks
Lettuces
Peas
Radishes
Rocket (arugula)
Spinach
Spring onions (scallions)
Chives
Dill
Lemon balm
Welsh onions
Asters
Calendula
Cosmos
Nigella
Sunflowers
Sweet Williams

> *'I always used to think gardening was boring. It was really great.'*
> Sam, aged seven

PLANT NOW

Artichokes
Asparagus
Broad (fava) beans sown earlier in pots
Summer cabbages
Kohl rabi
Lettuce
Onions, from seed
Oriental leaves (salad greens)
Second early potatoes – early in the month
Maincrop potatoes – later in the month
Tomatoes – pot up when 8cm/3in tall; keep indoors
Marjoram
Thyme
Antirrhinums
Asters
Sweet peas

Young lettuces, ready to be planted out
in the big wide world.

DO NOW

Peas Support.
Herbs Divide chives, thyme, lemon balm and any other fibrous-rooted herbs to make more.
Sage Trim to create a compact low bush.
Blackberries Keep canes under control and tie them in as they grow for easy picking later.
Forced rhubarb Pick the last harvest, and then feed with general fertilizer and turn your attention to the unforced.
Figs Prune and start feeding with chicken manure pellets.
Strawberries Place straw under the fruit around each plant and net before the birds help themselves.
Vine Keep under control by pruning out unnecessary growth – anything that grows two leaves beyond a developing bunch.
Weed.

HARVEST NOW

First asparagus
Sprouting broccoli
Leeks
Welsh onions
Rhubarb
Sage
Winter savory

In mild areas or under cloches
Winter lettuces
Spinach
Spring onions (scallions)
Bay
Parsley
Rosemary

> *'I hope the peas are getting on well.'*
> Caitlin, aged eight

EAT NOW

Asparagus, broad (fava) bean and crabmeat salad

Savour your first homegrown batch of asparagus. Once you have a constant supply from your garden, it is nice to dress it up a bit. Delicious as a side dish or a starter, this salad uses broad beans and lettuces from the garden too. For an alternative, use the warm salad, without the lettuce, over freshly cooked linguini.

Serves 4

400g/14oz green asparagus spears (about 14–18 spears)
salt and pepper
400g/14oz broad bean pods (about 1 cup shelled fava beans)
1 teaspoon Dijon mustard
juice of ½ lemon
4 tablespoons olive oil (¼ cup)
12 cherry tomatoes, quartered
10g/⅓oz dill, chopped (about 3–4 tbsp)
10g/⅓oz chervil leaves, chopped (about 3–4 tbsp)
300g/11oz white prepared crabmeat (1¼–1½ cups)
1 head of lettuce, cos or semi-cos is best

Cut the woody ends off the asparagus and gently simmer in salted water for 5–10 minutes until tender. Using a slotted spoon, lift and drain them, and then set aside. (At this stage you could just serve the asparagus as a side dish or a starter with a knob of butter and a squeeze of lemon juice, adding salt and pepper to taste.)

Prepare the broad beans by shelling the pods and cooking the beans in salt water for 5–10 minutes until tender. If they are young enough you do not need to remove the white shell enclosing the bean.

In a bowl make the dressing by mixing salt, mustard and lemon juice together before adding the olive oil and finishing off with freshly ground pepper.

In a salad bowl place the warm broad beans, quartered cherry tomatoes, chopped dill and chervil leaves. Then add the crabmeat and two-thirds of the salad dressing. Mix gently.

To serve, place the washed and dried lettuce leaves in individual plates or a wide large bowl, making a bed for the salad. Dribble half the remaining dressing over the leaves. Top the lettuce with the salad mix and then drape the asparagus spears over it. Finish by dribbling the rest of the dressing over the asparagus spears and salad.

CREATE NOW

Plant labels

Spring is a busy time in the garden, when gardeners are full of enthusiasm and gusto. Unfortunately the weather can be tricky, but this project can be done inside and will keep you and your children focused on your future harvest.

You will need:

wooden clothes pegs/dolly pegs
miniature terracotta flower pots
paint, waterproof for outdoors
paintbrushes
hay, to fill the flower pots
bamboo or wooden sticks approximately 60cm/2ft high

Make a list of vegetables, flowers and herbs that require labels. Divide the list between those that are in pots and those that will be planted outdoors. For the potted plants, use the clothes and dolly pegs. For large planters or for outdoor plants, use the miniature terracotta pots. Make sure children are wearing old clothes or big aprons.

For outdoor plant labels, prime your pots before you paint them with waterproof paint. Priming, although not a necessity, will keep the pots looking better longer. After the first coat of colour has dried, choose a fine paintbrush and paint the letters of the plant name on the pot. Thinning the paint can help to make this easier. You may want to mark out the first few labels in pencil to get the size and spacing of the letters right and practise doing the lettering on a piece of paper first.

Once the pots are dry, stuff the bellies with enough hay for a snug fit. Then turn them upside down and balance on a bamboo stick in a flower or vegetable bed. As well as functioning as a plant label, these hay-filled pots will encourage welcome predators such as lacewings and earwigs.

For the clothes pegs, the paint does not need to be waterproof. To avoid too much mess, clip several clothes and dolly pegs around a pot and then paint them. Remember to paint the lettering vertically so that you can read the plant labels when on the pots.

Plant labels and insect hotel.

> 'If you have a garden and a library, you have everything you need.'
> Cicero

MAY

late spring

This is one of the most beautiful months, with gardens nearing fullness but still fresh and bursting with energy. But in many regions mid-May can be a risky time, when it seems like early summer but a last frost could sneak up on unsuspecting gardeners and blossom and wreak havoc. Once this danger has passed, tender plants can be sown or planted out without cover. But if your evenings are still cool, tender plants will appreciate a cloche or a fleece cover.

> *'The month of May was come, when every lusty heart beginneth to blossom, and to bring forth fruit.'*
> Thomas Malory, *Le Morte d'Arthur*, 1485

Red and white radishes: 'Hailstone' and 'Sparkler'.

SOW NOW

Windowsill/cold frame, before the last frosts are over

French and runner (string and flat pole) beans
Courgettes (zucchini) and marrows
Cucumbers
Pumpkins
Squashes
Sweetcorn (corn)
Coriander (cilantro)
Nasturtiums

Outside

Broad (fava) beans
French and runner (string and flat pole) beans (after danger of frost)

Beetroot (beets)
Sprouting broccoli
Calabrese (broccoli)
Winter cabbage
Carrots
Chard
Late kale
Kohl rabi
Late leeks
Lettuce
Peas
Radishes
Rocket (arugula)
Spinach
Dill
Summer savory
Calendula
Cosmos
Nigella
Sweet Williams

PLANT NOW

Brussels sprouts
Cabbages
Kohl rabi
Lettuces
Sunflowers

Only after danger of last frosts

French and runner
  (string and flat pole)
  beans
Celeriac (celery root)
Courgettes (zucchini)
  and marrows
Cucumber
Peppers and chilli
  peppers

Pumpkins
Tomatoes
Squashes
Basil
Asters
Dahlias
French marigolds
Zinnias

Courgette flower: a great delicacy, but if you pick it you won't get the courgette.

DO NOW

Broad (fava) beans Pinch out tips once the pods have formed.
Potatoes Earth them up.
Tomatoes Pinch off side shoots and take off any subsidiary growth that may waste the plant's energy.
Blackberries Tie in new canes.
Plums Set pheromone traps for plum moths.
Soft fruit Start to net.
Vines Anything that grows two leaves beyond a developing bunch – remove.
Annual flowers Thin out directly sown seedlings to the recommended distances.
Sweet peas Keep tying them in as they grow.
Weed and water Continue to weed and water in dry spells.

HARVEST NOW

Asparagus
First broad (fava) beans, sown last autumn
Spring cabbages
Early carrots
Lettuces
Oriental leaves (salad greens)
First peas
Radishes
Spring onions (scallions)
All herbs
Rhubarb

Oriental salads: not just very easy to grow but also very attractive.

Opposite: garlic chives also produce pretty and edible (though strong-tasting) flowers.

EAT NOW

Risotto with fresh peas

This is a satisfying and easy dish to make. You could substitute roasted butternut squash for the peas.

Serves 4

1 medium-sized onion
1 garlic clove
1 tablespoon olive oil
320g/11oz Arborio rice (1¾ cups)
juice of ½ lemon (or 150ml/5fl oz dry white wine)
1 litre/1½ UK pints organic chicken stock (4 cups)
300g/11oz peas, fresh or frozen (2 cups)
4 tablespoons Parmesan cheese, grated (¼ cup)
1 teaspoon butter
salt and freshly ground pepper

Finely dice the onion and garlic. Then in a large saucepan add the olive oil and sweat the onion and garlic over a medium heat until soft. Add the rice (it does not need soaking or washing) and stir until it is coated with oil; then add the lemon juice (or wine) and stir until the liquid has evaporated. Add one ladleful of the stock and turn the heat down a bit. While continuing to stir, add the stock ladle by ladle once each ladleful has been absorbed by the rice. The rice will take approximately 18 minutes to cook. Add the peas to the rice after about 12 minutes and then continue cooking until the rice is tender. You may need more or less of the chicken stock, depending on your stirring and the heat.

Before serving, add the Parmesan cheese and butter, and give it a good stir. This will add flavour and give your dish a lovely gloss. Season with ground pepper and salt to taste.

CREATE NOW

Drying herbs

Drying your garden herbs preserves them for later use, and you can make them into gifts for friends and family. You can make teas from them, prepare single varieties or mixtures for cooking, or even use them to freshen your linen cupboard or indulge in a scented bath.

When choosing which herbs to dry, try rosemary, thyme, mint, bay and lavender. Generally soft herbs such as basil, parsley and chives contain a high percentage of moisture and so are prone to mould; these are best used fresh or frozen.

You can use a dehydrator or a microwave, but air drying is the most cost effective and straightforward method.

You will need:

Good pair of scissors or secateurs (pruning shears)
  and children's scissors for the younger helpers
twine
paper bag

For the best flavour, cut your herbs mid-morning and before they flower. Remove any damaged leaves or stems. To avoid any hidden insects, give your herbs a shake.

Gather the herbs in a bunch at the stems. Do not make the bunches too big, as you want air to circulate freely. Gently tie some twine around the stems to hold them in place without bruising. Make sure you leave enough length on the twine to hang the bunches up later. Cover the leaves with a paper bag, not least to keep away any dust, secure at the top and hang your herbs in a dry and airy space for about two weeks.

Check that all herbs are dry and remove any mouldy leaves or stems. Store the dried leaves in an airtight container or experiment with herb mixtures.

To make teas

Use 1 teaspoon of dried herb per cup. Stew the herbs for a few minutes and then remove before drinking.

Try chocolate mint for the aroma without the calories, lemon balm for a healthy start to the morning or sage when suffering from a throat infection.

To make pre-mixed herbs for the kitchen

Variation on *herbes de Provence* for cooking: crush and mix 3 parts thyme, 2 parts each rosemary and marjoram and 1 part bay leaf and a few lavender flowers. Keep in an airtight jar.

Spicy mixture: crush and mix 2 parts dried lemon thyme, 2 parts rosemary and 1 part dried crushed chilli pepper (dried in the same manner as herbs). Keep in an airtight jar.

For your linen cupboard

Fill muslin squares with dried lavender flowers and fragrant dried rose petals.

JUNE

early summer

Berry month. Now comes the reward for planting in the depths of winter, and digging and mulching and weeding and feeding and seeding … Let children just pick and eat from the bush.

French lavender cuttings.

SOW NOW

French and runner (string and flat pole) beans
Late beetroot (beets)
Sprouting broccoli
Calabrese (broccoli)
Maincrop carrots
Last courgettes (zucchini) and marrows
Last cucumbers
Late kale
Kohl rabi
Late leeks

Lettuces
Late peas
Last pumpkins and squashes
Radishes
Rocket (arugula)
Coriander (cilantro)
Dill
Nasturtiums
Summer savory
Calendula, nigella and other rapid growers – last chance

PLANT NOW

Sprouting broccoli
Late Brussels sprouts
Autumn and winter cabbages
Celeriac (celery root)
Courgettes (zucchini) and marrows
Kale
Kohl rabi

Leeks
Lettuces
Peppers and chilli peppers
Pumpkins
Squashes
Sweetcorn (corn)
Last tomatoes
Calendula

Peas forming within the pod.

Let my beloved come into his garden, and eat his pleasant fruits.
Song of Solomon 4:16

DO NOW

Carrots Net with Enviromesh to prevent carrot fly from laying its eggs.

Potatoes Keep earthing up and checking that no tubers are near the light.

Tomatoes Keep tying them in and pinching them off.

Herbs Take cuttings.

Soft fruit Net and mulch to keep the birds off and the moisture in.

Gooseberries Shorten side shoots and look out for gooseberry sawfly – these little caterpillars will strip the leaves off your bushes given half a chance.

Figs Prune off any extra-long shoots.

Raspberries Hoe off suckers that pop out of the row or crowd the existing canes.

Strawberries Peg down runners (not more than three per plant) and lay straw under fruits.

Vines Keep under control by removing surplus growth.

All fruit Water thoroughly once a week in dry spells. Check if the bushes are still well mulched; if not, top up mulch to retain moisture.

Annual flowers Thin out directly sown ones.

Sweet peas Keep tying in the new shoots.

HARVEST NOW

Artichokes
Asparagus
Broad (fava) beans
Early beetroot (beets)
Summer cabbages
Early carrots
Early garlic
First kohl rabi
Lettuces
Onions
Oriental leaves (salad greens)
First peas
Early potatoes
Radishes
Rocket (arugula)
Shallots
Spinach
All herbs
Gooseberries
Raspberries
Rhubarb
Strawberries
Calendula
Cosmos
Nigella
Sweet peas
Sweet Williams (sown in previous year)

EAT NOW

Fruit ice pops for kids and granitas with a kick for adults

Making these is a healthy, fun and easy way for all the family to enjoy homegrown fruit over a long period. Explore different flavours and combinations using your favourite fruits.

Granita is similar to a fruit sorbet. The difference is that granita usually contains less sugar, and no egg white. It therefore has an edgier texture than sorbet but is easier to make.

Serves 4
5 tablespoons sugar (⅓ cup)
200ml/7fl oz water (scant cup)
5 tablespoons lemon juice (⅓ cup)
400g/14oz raspberries (about 3–4 cups)

or
600g/21oz red plums
125g/4½oz sugar (⅔ cup)
160ml/5fl oz apple juice (⅔ cup)

1 shot vodka or Crème de Cassis (optional)
fresh fruit and mint leaves, to serve

Before you start, there are two things to remember. First, the amount of sugar needed depends on your taste and the sweetness of the fruit. A rough guide is up to one-third sugar and at least two-thirds fruit. So tasting while cooking is essential.

Second, if you plan to have your ice lollies and granitas in the freezer for more than a couple of weeks, it is best to cook the fruit first so that the colour is preserved.

For raspberries, mix the sugar, water and lemon juice in a pan. Simmer on a medium heat for a few minutes, stirring until the sugar has dissolved. Let it reduce until it has a syrupy consistency, and then set aside to cool. Mix the raspberries in a food processor until smooth. Sieve the raspberries through a medium mesh, as not everyone likes 'bits'. Now add a little syrup at a time to your fruit pulp, until you have found the right sweetness for your taste.

If you are using plums, pit them and cut into quarters. Cook the plums with the sugar and apple juice for at least 5 minutes until they are soft. Remove from the heat and mix with a hand blender until smooth.

Fill ice pop forms with the fruit mixture and place in the freezer. Alternatively pour the mixture into a container and stir in a shot of alcohol for a kick. Crème de cassis or vodka goes very well with raspberries. After approximately 1–2 hours, when ice crystals are starting to form, remove the granita. Break up the ice crystals with a fork and stir before placing back in the freezer. Repeat this every 1–2 hours another three times or until the granita is smooth.

Place the granita in the refrigerator 30 minutes before serving. Garnish with fresh fruit or a few mint leaves.

CREATE NOW

Fruit leathers

The words 'sticky' and 'yummy' come to mind when trying to describe fruit leathers. They are fun for kids to eat and an excellent healthy and portable fruit snack. For best results, use berries, plums or peaches. Experiment, using your own fruit surpluses. Try also the red plum mixture used to make the ice pops and granita (page 85). You need a bit of patience to let the leathers dry, but once they have, you can just rip off a piece whenever you feel peckish.

Makes one sheet of leather

500g/18oz strawberries (about 4½–5 cups)
2–3 tablespoons sugar
9 tablespoons water
or
4 peaches
9 tablespoons water
75ml/5 tablespoons maple syrup

Preheat the oven to 70°C/160°F/GM¼.

Whichever fruit you use, make sure it is fresh and unblemished. Fruit with stones needs to be pitted. Remove the stalk from soft fruits such as strawberries. Peel and cut the fruit into rough pieces.

In a saucepan put the fruit, water and sugar or maple syrup and cook for 5 minutes. Using a hand blender or food processor, mix until very smooth. Line a square or rectangular baking tray, approximately 30 x 30cm/12 x 12in, with greaseproof paper or baking parchment. Pour the mixture on to the tray in a thin layer, 0.5cm/¼in deep.

Dehydrate in the oven for 5–6 hours. Check your leathers after a few hours as ovens vary: the mixture should not become too dry. Leathers should feel sticky, but firm and not wet.

Once finished and cooled, cover with a piece of cling film and flip over. Remove the greaseproof paper and cover with a second piece of cling film. Now you can roll them up and store in the fridge for up to 2 months.

JULY

summer

Usually the hottest month – water butts (rain barrels) come into their own now. The garden should be in the fullness of its glory … All the hard work you put in earlier in the year should be repaid by masses of flowers and food. Children on holiday can help you pick.

Striking deep pink antirrhinum.

SOW NOW

French (string) beans – last chance
Spring cabbage
Kohl rabi
Lettuces
Oriental leaves (salad greens)

Pak choi (bok choy)
Late peas
Radishes and mooli (daikon)
Rocket (arugula)
Spring onions (scallions)

PLANT NOW

Sprouting broccoli
Winter cabbages
Last kale

Kohl rabi
Late leeks
Lettuces

'Our England is a garden, and such gardens are not made
By singing: "Oh, how beautiful!" and sitting in the shade …'
Rudyard Kipling, 'The Glory of the Garden'

DO NOW

Potatoes and tomatoes Watch out for blight; remove and discard affected leaves.

Tomatoes Pinch out the top after five trusses.

Herbs Take cuttings.

Apples If you want larger fruits, thin overcrowded clusters to one hand apart. Leave only two fruits per cluster.

Gooseberries Check for mildew and sawfly.

Cherries Prune sour cherries after fruiting.

Strawberries Feed plants after harvest with potash-rich fertilizer; peg down more runners.

Vines Keep under control by removing surplus growth and any leaves shading bunches.

Cutting bed This will be at its peak now: enjoy (see Flower arranging, page 92).

HARVEST NOW

Artichokes
Broad (fava) beans
Beetroot (beets)
Summer cabbages
Calabrese (broccoli)
Carrots
Chard
Courgettes (zucchini)
Garlic
Kohl rabi
Lettuces
Onions
Spinach

Spring onions (scallions)
Peas
Potatoes
Radishes
Rocket (arugula)
Shallots
All herbs
Currants
Blueberries
Cherries
Gooseberries
Raspberries
All flowers

Freshly harvested radishes.

EAT NOW

Summer berry layers

A delicious dessert that is easy to create but makes a big impression. Maybe too fiddly for the littlest to help prepare, but they can help picking the berries and make a wonderful mess eating it.

Serves 4

400g/14oz good-quality puff pastry (see below)
4–6 tablespoons icing (confectioner's) sugar, plus some for sprinkling
600–800g/1¼–1¾lb mixed berries: strawberries, blueberries, red currants, blackberries
300ml/½ UK pint whipping cream (1¼ cups)
1 teaspoon vanilla sugar
200g/7oz mascarpone cheese (about 1 cup)
4 tablespoons plain yoghurt (¼ cup)
4 teaspoons strawberry jam

Try to buy a good-quality puff pastry that comes already rolled out, which will save you some time.

Pre-heat the oven to 220°C/425°F/GM7.

Cut the pastry into portion-sized triangles and place on a tray lined with baking paper.

Using a fine sieve, sprinkle some icing sugar over the top; this will give them a nice gloss and a crunchy finish. Bake the pastry triangles in the oven for 10–15 minutes until they have risen and are golden brown.

Let them cool slightly and cut them horizontally, being careful not break them, giving you a top and bottom, in between which the filling will go.

Carefully wash and dry the fruit. Cut strawberries in half, lengthwise; other berries can be left whole.

Whip the cream in a bowl until it makes soft peaks. In another bowl add the vanilla sugar, icing sugar and mascarpone, and mix until you have a smooth consistency. Fold in the whipped cream.

For each puff pastry triangle, place the bottom on a plate, and spread over it some jam and then a thin layer of fruit. Place the halved strawberries on the edge and smaller fruits on the inside. Then top with a spoonful of the cream mixture and cover with the top of the triangle. Sprinkle some sieved icing sugar over the top and add a few fruits to hint at the variety inside.

CREATE NOW

Flower arranging

Picking a bouquet of flowers from your garden for yourself or someone else brings much joy and quiet satisfaction, and a more personal touch than a florist-bought bunch.

Perhaps you would never consider a flower-arranging course, but wouldn't you like your flowers to look a bit less as if they have been just plonked in the vase? Read on.

You will need:

sharp secateurs (pruning shears) or scissors (children's scissors for your young helpers)
a bucket with water (if you plan to cut many flowers and take your time)
a garden full of blooms and interesting vegetables
vases or containers

Picking

The best time to pick flowers is either early morning or early evening. Avoid midday, as your flowers will wilt quicker. Place each cut flower in the bucket of water while you cut more. The easiest way to do this with children is to make sure that you have grown enough flowers to be able to sacrifice a few; and give them their own bucket in which to collect their blooms. You will probably want to keep an eye on the cutting so that not too much damage is done to the plant.

Flowers used in an arrangement might be at different stages in their life – in bud, in bloom or even seed head. And do not forget to consider vegetables in terms of visual appeal too. An artichoke head, for instance, makes quite an impact; curly kale can look great too. See also Combinations, below.

Preparing

Once you have all your blooms, prepare them by stripping any leaves off the stems that may touch the water. Cut stems at an angle – the steeper the cut, the more water they will be able to absorb. Woody stems need a bit more help, so insert a 2–3cm/1in deep vertical cut in the base.

Containers

The main rule is to remember that the wider the opening of your vase or container, the more flowers you will need, but rules are there to be broken ...

Besides vases, look for interesting containers to use, from colourful tins to wooden vessels – be as creative as you like. If the container is not watertight, place a glass inside it to hold your flowers.

Make sure your vases are clean, as any residue will shorten the life of your blooms.

Combinations

When deciding which flowers to put together, look at colour, shape and texture, and remember to include vegetables or even weeds with architectural ambitions, such as horsetail. Also consider the container itself. A bouquet is great, but in the right container just a couple of stems may be sufficient. You could use the opportunity to discuss colour, shape and textures with your children.

- **Colour** The safest option is to stick to one colour range, resulting in an understated and elegant look. For a more vibrant and lively combination, match up complementary colours, such as yellow and purple, red and green or blue and orange. Such combinations create the strongest contrasts. If you use a variety of different colours, try to stay in the same tonal range or add just one different tone as a highlight.
- **Shape** Think about combining different shapes for interest – round dahlia heads, for example, with long slim snapdragon stems.
- **Balance** Start by placing larger blooms in the centre, and then add different shapes for interest, finishing with some fillers such as nigella, flowering asparagus or kale leaves.

Aftercare

For the longest-lasting blooms, replace the water daily. Avoid placing your flowers in direct sunlight, and do not place them next to a fruit bowl, as the flowers wilt more quickly.

Don't restrict yourself to using only flowers for your arrangements: pink dahlias, curly kale leaves, green chilli peppers, pale green amaranth and cape gooseberries.

AUGUST

late summer

Pick and enjoy. Or, if you are off on holiday, think about planning better for harvesting times for next year. If you have to go away, get a neighbour to pick and enjoy on your behalf: at least that will keep some crops productive, and in return perhaps they will do some watering for you.

Start on the year's second round of seed sowing for winter vegetables and begin collecting your own seeds.

French marigold 'Simba'.

SOW NOW

Spring cabbages
Late carrots
Kohl rabi
Lettuces for autumn and winter
Oriental leaves (salad greens)
Pak choi (bok choy)
Winter radishes and mooli (daikon)
Rocket (arugula)
Spinach
Spring onions (scallions)
Parsley

PLANT NOW

Kohl rabi
Lettuces
New strawberries

'Gardening requires lots of water – most of it in the form of perspiration.'
Lou Erickson

DO NOW

Beans Pick broad, French and runner (fava, string and flat pole) beans at least every second day; otherwise they will stop producing new ones.

Cabbages Check the undersides of leaves for little rows of caterpillar eggs.

Tomatoes Continue to feed. Look out for blight; remove and destroy any affected leaves.

Herbs Cut back herbs that have flowered, such as lavender. You can still make cuttings from rosemary and bay.

Apples and pears Summer prune, removing water shoots. Prop up heavily laden branches if necessary with stakes.

Plums Watch out for brown rot; remove affected fruit and bin or burn. Prune after picking.

Raspberries Cut out old canes and start tying in new ones.

Strawberries Pot up runners.

Vines Keep under control by pruning excess growth.

Cutting garden Keep picking and feeding flowers to keep your garden colourful as long as possible.

Keep watering.

HARVEST NOW

Broad (fava) beans
French and runner
 (string and flat pole)
 beans
Beetroot (beets)

Summer cabbages
Calabrese (broccoli)
Carrots
Chard
Courgettes (zucchini)

and marrows
Cucumbers
Garlic
Kohl rabi
Lettuces
Onions
Peas
Peppers and chilli peppers
Potatoes (second earlies)
Radishes
Rocket (arugula)

Spring onions (scallions)
Summer squashes
Sweetcorn (corn)
Tomatoes
All herbs
First apples
Blackberries
Red and white currants
Plums
Raspberries
All flowers

EAT NOW

Oriental summer rolls

This dish is great for getting the kids involved, as there is lots of rolling and filling.

Serves 4
200g/7oz vermicelli rice noodles (about 4 cups)
8 large rice paper wraps (see below)
1 avocado, sliced
1 red pepper, deseeded and sliced
2 spring onions (scallions)
1 carrot
1 bunch of fresh mint
1 bunch of fresh coriander (cilantro)
16 king prawns (jumbo shrimp), cooked and peeled
 (or two cooked chicken breasts, sliced)

For the dipping sauce:
1 tablespoon soy sauce
1 tablespoon fish sauce
1 tablespoon rice vinegar
1 red chilli pepper
½ cucumber

Each wrap can be varied slightly by using a different combination of fillings. Rice paper wraps are available in some supermarkets or in Thai food stores. There are usually two sizes available: go for the larger size, approximately 22cm/8½in in diameter, as they are easier to handle. You can make the rolls in advance, wrap them individually in cling film and keep in the fridge for up to a day.

Prepare the rice noodles by pre-cooking them and then putting them under running cold water so that they stop cooking and cool off. Prepare the rice paper wraps by soaking them in cold water.

Slice the vegetables into 8–10cm/3-4in sticks. Add

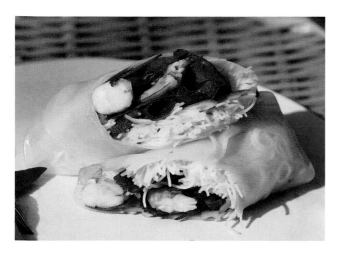

one or two mint leaves and a bit of coriander.

For the dipping sauce, mix the soy sauce, fish sauce and rice vinegar, topping it off with a few bits of red chilli and cucumber very finely diced.

Get everyone to make their own wraps. First gently take out a soaked rice paper wrap and place it flat on your plate. (Be careful not to tear the wraps if you have more than one soaking at a time.) In the middle place a thumb-sized row of cold rice noodles, leaving a space of about 5cm/2in at the edge of the wrap on each side. Add 1–2 king prawns (or slices of chicken), a few slices of avocado, some spring onion, red pepper and mint. To wrap, fold each side into the centre, fold the bottom over the filling and then roll the wrap. If you find that your roll does not close, do not worry: it will stick if you leave it a few minutes.

CREATE NOW

Garden herbs for oils and vinegars

Another great way to extend the aroma of your garden herbs is to use them to flavour oils and vinegar. If kept in a cool dry place they will keep for 3–6 months. Use them freely to enhance the flavour of your everyday dishes and salads.

As well as herbs, consider using edible flowers and fruit – there are endless combinations you can make. Most combinations follow a general recipe.

Pick herbs in their prime (see the A–Z of plants), gently wash them and pat them dry. Make sure they are totally dry before immersing them, especially in oil, or else they will grow mould.

Place them in a clean, dry jar and cover with vinegar or oil. Close the lid tightly and let the mixture sit for 2–3 weeks, giving it a daily shake.

Use either a coffee filter or a muslin cloth to filter the oil or vinegar into its final container. You may want to re-use the original bottle in which the oil or vinegar came. Alternatively, enjoy hunting around for beautiful shaped bottles to add extra flair.

Do not be tempted to add fresh ingredients to your filtered oils or vinegars. The liquid may cloud and your ingredients will discolour.

One more tip: if you are using olive oil, choose one whose scent will not overpower your herbs.

Here are some tried and tested favourites.

Basil vinegar

500ml/17fl oz white wine vinegar (scant 2¼ cups)
7 sprigs of basil
Use for summer salads; especially good with tomatoes.

Raspberry vinegar

1 litre/1½ UK pints cider vinegar or white wine vinegar (4 cups)
300g/11oz raspberries (about 2–3 cups)
Lovely colour and wide range of uses in salads all year round.

Strawberry vinegar

1 litre/1½ UK pints cider vinegar (4 cups)
300g/11oz strawberries, stalks removed and cut in half (about 2½–3 cups)
6 basil leaves
Soft sweet smell.

Thyme and chilli pepper oil

500ml/17fl oz olive oil (scant 2¼ cups)
4 large sprigs of thyme
1–3 chilli peppers, depending on type and strength
Use to spice up grilled chicken or roasted vegetables.

SEPTEMBER

early autumn

End of summer, back to school . . . While the garden continues preparing stores for the winter larder, there is still a chance to sow seeds for autumn and winter crops. Most of these plants mature very quickly. If you live in an area with mild winters, you should be able to pick them for a few months, especially if you can provide some late protection.

SOW NOW

Lettuces
Oriental leaves (salad greens)
Rocket (arugula)
Spinach
Spring onions (scallions)

PLANT NOW

Spring cabbages
Garlic
Lettuces
New strawberries

DO NOW

Tomatoes Pinch out growing tips and side shoots; as long as the weather holds you should still be able to pick.
Basil Cover these tender plants with cloches at night.
Plums Remove any brown rotted fruit.
Strawberries Plant new ones, remove straw and tidy up old ones.
Vines Keep under control by pruning out excess growth and any leaves shading bunches.
Fruit trees End of month: start to fix greasebands around trunks.

Dill flowers (left); handfuls of plums (below).

HARVEST NOW

Broad (fava) beans	Peas
French and runner (string and flat pole) beans	Peppers and chilli peppers
Beetroot (beets)	Maincrop potatoes
Autumn cabbages	Radishes and mooli
Calabrese (broccoli)	Rocket (arugula)
Carrots	Summer squashes
Chard	Sweetcorn (corn)
Courgettes (zucchini) and marrows	Tomatoes
Cucumbers	All herbs
Kohl rabi	Apples
Lettuce	Blackberries
Onions	Grapes
Oriental leaves (salad greens)	Hazelnuts
Pak choi (bok choy)	Pears
	Plums
	Autumn raspberries
	All flowers

Summer squash amongst chard leaves.

EAT NOW

Homemade ketchup

There are two versions, the second of which is closer to a barbecue sauce, but since it is very more-ish we could not leave it out. The cooking method is the same for both.

Makes a medium-sized jam jar full.

Version 1

1 red onion
2 garlic cloves
500g/18oz tomatoes
1 carrot
1 celery stalk
1 handful of basil
1 thumb-sized piece of ginger
½ handful of parsley
1 teaspoon salt
1 teaspoon soy sauce
½ teaspoon allspice
4 tablespoons brown sugar (¼ cup)
5 tablespoons vinegar (⅓ cup)
freshly ground pepper

Version 2

½ red onion
2 garlic cloves
500g/18oz tomatoes
1 carrot
1 red pepper
1 chilli pepper (see below)
1 handful of basil
1 thumb-sized piece of ginger
1 teaspoon salt
1 teaspoon allspice
5 tablespoons sugar (⅓ cup)
2 tablespoons balsamic vinegar
2 tablespoons rice wine vinegar
freshly ground pepper

For version two, choose a moderately hot chilli pepper – if you grow your own chillies you will know which ones are hot and which are mild – as a very hot one will overpower the rest of the ingredients.

Sweat the chopped onion and garlic in oil and add the washed and roughly chopped tomatoes. Dice the carrots and celery or, for version 2, chilli pepper and add them to the pan, followed by the basil, ginger and, for version 1, parsley, then the salt, soy sauce and all spice.

Cover and cook at a medium to low heat for about 30 minutes until all the ingredients are tender. Purée the sauce in a mixer or with a hand-held blender and strain through a sieve. This takes a bit of patience but is worth it for the extra smoothness. Return the mixture to the stove, adding the sugar and vinegar, and reduce it, stirring from time to time, until a heavy flowing liquid consistency is achieved. Adjust the seasoning and put the ketchup in sterilized jars. Keep in a dark cold place and use within 3 months.

CREATE NOW

Build a ladybird (ladybug) and lacewing nesting house

Ladybirds and lacewings are very welcome visitors to the garden, as they feast on unwanted aphids. So it is worth encouraging them by offering them a comfortable place such as this to overwinter. Children are always happy to find a ladybird; perhaps it is something to do with its colouring. Make sure the contents are tightly packed.

You will need:
hack saw with fine blade
10–15 bamboo stems
2m/about 7ft garden wire
2 x 15cm/6in lengths of wood, 10–15cm/4–6in wide
hammer
4 nails
wood glue
string, for hanging the house

Saw the bamboo into 15cm/6in pieces. Lay them out in a row and wind wire around each end. You should have something resembling a railway track in front of you. If you just wrap wire around the whole bundle of bamboo, the canes will simply fall out. Roll the bamboo tightly together and secure with a piece of wire.

To make the roof, take the two pieces of wood and, using a hammer, nail them together at right angles, one end on top of the other. To secure the roof to the bamboo nesting home, first glue the bamboo to the roof with wood glue. Then secure by winding a piece of wire around the nest and roof three times, ending with a little hook.

Attach string to the hook and hang up the house, at a slight downward angle so that the tubes do not get waterlogged.

OCTOBER

autumn

October is Harvest Festival, with special school assemblies and pumpkin carving. Everything is hanging on, ready – unless there is an Indian summer – to tip over into the greyness of winter. As the nights begin to draw in, the plants lap up the last rays of sun. It is the beginning of the tidying-up season. Golden pumpkins and squashes must be harvested for winter nourishment. But planting bulbs, onions and garlic offers the promise of the next season.

SOW NOW

Broad (fava) beans
Peas in areas with mild winters
Sweet peas

PLANT NOW

Spring cabbages
Garlic
Onion sets in areas with mild winters
Herbs – pot up and take into the kitchen

DO NOW

Asparagus Cut down ferns and mulch.
Apples Go to an apple-tasting day to choose new varieties ready to plant in the winter.
Dahlias Lift tubers after the first frost has browned the leaves.
Organic matter Start to dig in organic matter.

> *'Season of mists
> and mellow fruitfulness …'*
> John Keats, 'Ode to Autumn', 1820

A last burst of orange from dahlias and pumpkins before everything shuts down into winter monochrome.

> 'Season of lists and callow hopefulness ...'
> Katharine S. White, 'Onward and Upward in the Garden', 1958

HARVEST NOW

Before the first frost

Last French (string) beans
Beetroot (beets)
Carrots
Kohl rabi
Last peas
Pumpkins
Last tomatoes
Winter squashes
Nasturtiums
Summer savory
Autumn raspberries
Flowers

Oriental leaves (salad greens)
Spring onions (scallions)
Pak choi (bok choy)
Winter radishes and mooli
Rocket (arugula)
Spinach
Bay
Chives
Mint
Parsley
Rosemary
Sage
Thyme
Welsh onions
Winter savory
Apples
Hazelnuts
Pears

When you need them

First Brussels sprouts
Autumn cabbages
Celeriac (celery root)
Chard
Leeks

Red cabbage (above); beetroot varieties (below) including 'Burpees Golden', which can also be eaten raw, and 'Bull's Blood'.

EAT NOW

Tagliatelle with butternut squash, porcini and sage

Butternut squash has a wonderful flavour that is brought out well by roasting. Instead of tagliatelle, you could serve the squash mixture over grilled chicken.

Serves 4

1kg/2¼lb butternut squash, peeled
salt and freshly ground pepper
2 small dried red chilli peppers, crumbled, or 2 pinches of chilli flakes (red pepper flakes)
2 tablespoons olive oil
30g/1oz dried Porcini mushrooms
1 red onion
2 garlic cloves
25g/1oz fresh sage leaves (about 1 cup)
1 tablespoon butter
1 glass of dry white wine (½ cup)
200ml/7fl oz double cream (scant cup heavy cream)
500g/18oz tagliatelle (fettuccine) or homemade egg noodles

Preheat the oven to 185°C/350°F/GM4.

Cut your butternut squash in half lengthwise and then de-seed it, before cutting the flesh into 1cm/½in cubes. Place the cubes on a baking tray and season with salt, chilli and a drizzle of olive oil. Bake in the oven for approximately 30 minutes or until tender, turning the cubes halfway through.

Place the dried mushrooms in a bowl and just cover with boiling water. Rehydrate for 20 minutes or as per instructions on the packet. Once they are ready for use, drain them, retaining the infused liquid.

In the meantime finely dice the onion and garlic and roughly chop the sage. Sweat these in a little olive oil in a large pan. Add the drained mushrooms and the butter. Stir and let cook for a good minute; then add the white wine and reduce it by a third. Add the cream and a couple of spoonfuls of the mushroom liquid, being careful not to include any sediment that may remain. Reduce it further and then add the pieces of butternut squash. Season with salt and freshly ground pepper to taste.

Bring a pan of water to the boil and cook the tagliatelle (or homemade egg noodles) until al dente. Serve with the butternut squash mixture over it.

> 'The discovery of a new dish confers more happiness on humanity than the discovery of a new star.'
> Jean Anthelme Brillat-Savarin, *The Physiology of Taste*, 1825

NOVEMBER

late autumn

A time to batten down the hatches before the winter frosts and gales; a last chance to harvest what is tender and to tidy up a bit. Also a time to review what worked – and what did not.

SOW NOW

In mild areas
Broad (fava) beans
Peas

PLANT NOW

Garlic – last chance this year if you have not done it yet
Onion sets in areas with mild winters
Bare-rooted trees and fruit bushes
Rhubarb

If you have not yet experienced the first frost you should still be enjoying dahlia flowers; this one is 'Arabian Night'.

'When I go into the garden with a spade, and dig a bed, I feel such an exhilaration and health that I discover that I have been defrauding myself all this time in letting others do for me what I should have done with my own hands.'
Ralph Waldo Emerson

DO NOW

Artichokes Protect from frost by mulching around the base. Better safe than sorry.

Salads and pak choi (bok choy) Protect with fleece (cover cloth) to extend the season.

If you are expecting a severe frost, make sure you lift all root vegetables or cover beds with fleece or cloche.

Mint Pot up runners and bring into the kitchen for fresh supplies during the winter.

Figs Pick off larger figlets, leaving only pea-sized fruit.

Rhubarb Clear away debris to prevent slugs hiding there for the winter.

Fruit trees Mulch.

Dahlias Store after the foliage has been browned by the first frost.

Dig beds, adding organic matter.

Pumpkins and squashes in storage Check, and remove any rotten ones.

HARVEST NOW

Brussels sprouts
Winter cabbages
Celeriac (celery root)
Kale
Leeks
Parsnips, after first frost
Winter radishes and mooli
Welsh onions
Winter savory
Autumn raspberries

Rocket (arugula)
Spinach
Bay
Chives
Parsley
Rosemary
Sage

In mild areas or under cloches
Chard
Oriental leaves (salad greens)
Pak choi (bok choy)

If you have not yet had the first frost of winter, these flowers might still be in bloom:
Calendula
Cosmos
Dahlias
French marigolds

> 'We dug so much that when I got up my arms ached and ached and ached.'
> Matthew, aged eight

EAT NOW

Carrot and ginger soup

Perfect to warm up old and young alike after a cold session in the garden. For a variation, try using pumpkin flesh instead of carrots.

Serves 4
1 onion, diced
2 garlic cloves, crushed
1 tablespoon olive oil
1kg/2¼lb carrots, sliced
1 thumb-sized piece of ginger, peeled and thinly sliced (see below)
1 litre/1½ UK pints organic chicken stock (4 cups) – see below
salt and freshly ground pepper
country-style baguette, to serve
shavings of Parmesan cheese, to serve

If the ginger is woody, use thicker slices and remove them before blending the soup. Make sure you use a good stock, as this will make a difference to your soup and limit the need for any extra seasoning at the end.

50g/1¾oz pumpkin seeds (⅓ cup)
100g/3½oz coarse oatmeal (¾ cup steel-cut oats)
100g/3½oz chopped peanuts, unsalted (1 cup)
50g/2oz raisins (⅓ cup)
25cm/10in-long logs of birch wood
drill
cookie cutters, pine cones and/or 25cm/10in long logs of birch wood
string

In a saucepan gently melt the vegetable oil. In the meantime, put the seeds, oatmeal, nuts and raisins into a bowl and mix well. Pour the melted oil over them and mix with a wooden spoon. Leave in a cool place until the mixture becomes thicker but is still malleable, stirring from time to time so that the ingredients combine well. This may take 2–3 hours.

If you are using a log, drill some 2cm/1in diameter holes through them at random (approximately 5cm/2in) intervals. Both the log and the pine cones will need string attached by which to hang them.

Fill the holes in the log, the cookie cutters (laid out flat on a baking tray) and/or the scales of the pine cones with the bird feed. Pop the bird feeders in the freezer for a couple of hours to make sure the mixture sets firmly.

Attach string to them – carefully make a hole for this with a metal skewer at one end of the cookies – hang them up and watch the birds enjoy them.

Sweat the onion and garlic with the ginger in some olive oil at medium heat. After 2 minutes add the sliced carrots and coat them in the mixture. Pour in the chicken stock and let it simmer gently for approximately 25 minutes or until the carrots are tender. Remove the soup from the heat and whizz it, either in a food processor or using a hand blender, until smooth.

Adjust the seasoning if necessary. Serve with the baguette and top with thin shavings of Parmesan.

CREATE NOW

Bird feeders

Birds are an important part of wildlife and gardening, and we can help them survive winter and rear their young. Children will enjoy doing this project, and also watching the birds eat.

You can make bird feeders in a variety of containers and shapes. Hide tasty snacks in a log, fill pine cones with food or use cookie cutters to make fun shapes.

You will need:

500g/18oz solid pure vegetable oil (2¼ cups) (stocked in shops' butter and margarine sections)
120g/4oz sunflower seeds (¾ cup)

DECEMBER

early winter

Time to pick comfort food, make thick warming soups and raid the freezer for those surpluses of rhubarb or apple purée that seemed so annoying at the time. And to plant trees and shrubs and dream of fruit and flowers to come. Next year's garden is always better . . .

Chard: stalwart winter vegetable.

SOW NOW

In mild areas
Broad (fava) beans

PLANT NOW

In mild areas
Shallots
Rhubarb – divide and replant
Bare-rooted fruit bushes and trees

DO NOW

Brussels sprouts Stake against wind rock.
Figs Protect from frost.
Fruit bushes Prune and then make cuttings with the prunings from red and black currants.
Raspberries Cut down autumn raspberry canes once they have finished fruiting.
Fruit trees Prune apples, pears (but not stone fruit, plums, cherries). Pick off any mummified fruit, such as plums, and destroy.
Prune vines Young vines need formative pruning to reach their eventual shape; on mature vines remove shoots that fruited this year and tie in new growth. Use cuttings to propagate new plants.
Dig and weed.
Compost.
Check bird feeders.
Order seeds.
Dream.

'Then I wanted to dig. I dag a rilly deep hole, then we made a long but deep hole, and then I was sad because I rilly liked it.'
Matthew, aged seven

HARVEST NOW

Brussels sprouts
Cabbages
Kale
Leeks
Parsnips, after first frost
Sage
Thyme
Welsh onions
Winter savory

In mild areas or under cloches
Chard
Oriental leaves (salad greens)
Pak choi (bok choy)
Winter spinach
Spring onions (scallions)
Bay
Parsley
Rosemary

Sage (above) and winter cabbage (below).

Celeriac, onion and sage stuffing

This aromatic stuffing is filled with goodness from your garden and should not be used solely on special occasions. It is simple to make and could be used to stuff duck or chicken, or as a side dish with everyday meat dishes.

Serves 4
1 large onion
2 slices of bread
1 large celeriac (celery root)
100g/3½oz butter
1 handful of chopped fresh sage (scant ½ cup)
1 handful of vacuum-packed chestnuts, chopped
salt and pepper

Finely chop the onion and cut the bread and celeriac into 1cm/½in cubes.

In a large frying pan melt the butter at a moderate heat and sweat the onions in the melted butter for a few minutes. Stir occasionally, making sure they do not burn. Add the celeriac and let them cook for 4 minutes before adding the bread, sage and chestnuts.

Stir from time to time, making sure you keep the mixture moist. You may need to add a bit more butter. Season lightly with salt and pepper and continue to cook until the celeriac is cooked. At this stage the stuffing should be moist and will smell very inviting. Give it a taste and adjust any seasoning.

Set the stuffing aside and let it cool before using it to stuff duck or chicken.

> *'The garden of the mind's eye.'*
> Karen

A–Z OF PLANTS

VEGETABLES

Vegetables form the backbone of the productive kitchen garden. Most are easy to grow and repay the space allocated to them with fresh, tasty produce. With a bit of planning and enthusiasm you should be able to supply your family with vegetables pretty well all year round.

The days when growing vegetables meant an ugly plot at the bottom of the garden are long since past. There is no need for anything unsightly to enter a vegetable plot, whether in terms of plants or equipment. There is no need even for a dedicated vegetable bed, unless you wish: you could just as well grow vegetables amongst the rest of your plants. A vegetable plot can be productive and attractive even in the depths of winter. A row of dark burgundy crinkled kale puts a gleam in the glummest January day, while from the late spring to autumn a bursting vegetable plot can be as pleasing to the eye – let alone the palate – as any herbaceous border.

Children can participate fully in nearly all aspects of vegetable growing, from sowing to weeding, harvesting and preparing. If they have been involved in growing the vegetables themselves they are far more likely to eat them happily. Some vegetables are particularly suitable for younger children (older toddlers and infants) to grow and these we have marked with the symbol ☺.

ANNUALS, BIENNIALS AND PERENNIALS

- **Annuals** These vegetables are done and dusted in one season, from seed to harvest.
- **Biennials** Some vegetables, such as broccoli and chard, are biennial, meaning that they would like to flower in their second year. If you are gardening in a mild area, you will be able to harvest from these plants throughout the winter; in cold areas unfortunately they will die in a hard frost, so are treated as annuals.
- **Perennials** These vegetables stay growing on the same spot for years.

Kohl rabi 'Azur Star' (left);
calabrese broccoli heads (right).

ARTICHOKES, GLOBE

Cynara scolymus • Daisy family
* • half-hardy • perennial

Attractive, thistle-like plants with huge silvery leaves which remain evergreen in mild winters. You can also use them in herbaceous borders, where they look spectacular, but bear in mind that they need a lot of space: plants will be around 2m/7ft high and 1m/3ft in diameter.

Although the plants themselves are spiky, dipping and eating each leaf makes for an interestingly messy first course that children should enjoy.

Not to be confused with Jerusalem artichokes, which are tall yellow daisy-like plants, producing edible tubers. These are invasive in the garden and cause tremendous flatulence. Although some top chefs use them very successfully, after a few bad experiences we avoid them.

Soil and position
- Sunny, sheltered position.
- Good garden soil, well drained.
- Dig in half-rotted manure or compost the autumn before planting; alternatively rake in 150g per sq. m/5oz per sq. yd of blood, fish and bone 2–3 weeks before planting.

Sowing, planting and spacing
- Sowing seed in March/April in modules is possible, but seedling quality is very variable.
- Planting offsets is much more practical. Plant two or three of them as one plant, from mid-April. Offsets should be about 20cm/9in high.
- Cut back the tips of the leaves so that the plant can focus on making roots, not losing moisture from large leaves.
- Plant slightly deeper than they were before.
- 1m/40in between plants.
- Mulch with half-rotted compost or well-rotted manure.
- In cold areas protect with fleece or cover cloth after planting until all danger of frost is over.
- Seed can be stored for up to 4 years.

Aftercare
- Water regularly until established.
- Top up mulch after cropping. If not available, top dress plants with 150g per sq. m/5oz per sq. yd of blood, fish and bone.
- Protect from frost in winter in cold areas: cover the crowns with leaves or straw; remove in April. Or take offsets in autumn just in case, pot up and overwinter under cover, plant out in spring.
- After about 4 years: dig up the old plants, take offsets and plant on a fresh site.

Problems
- Slugs love the young shoots.
- Aphids and greenfly while the flower heads are developing – spray off with a powerful jet of water. Encourage ladybugs and be patient.

Harvesting and uses
- In the first year in autumn, from the second year in June/July.
- Unopened flower buds are the edible parts; pick them just before the scales start to open.
- Cut the stem about 10cm/4in below the flower head – it will keep better cut this way.
- If your artichoke is starting to flower, it is too late to eat it; enjoy the glorious purple flower, but remove before seeds develop.
- Boil whole heads in water with half a lemon until the base of an outer leaf is soft (20–40 minutes, depending on size). Remove the leaf scales with fingers one by one and dip the stem end in vinaigrette. After you have removed all the scales, carefully cut off the choke (the fluffy bit, so called because you will choke if you eat it) and enjoy the heart.

Varieties
- 'Imperial Star' – large heads with an excellent flavour, recommended for colder areas, green.
- 'Green Globe' – most common variety, green.
- 'Violetto' – excellent variety, very pretty purple.

RELATIVES
CARDOON *(Cynara cardunculus)*
Looks very similar to an artichoke, but it is the stalks rather than the heads that are eaten. They must be blanched before harvesting and there are mixed reports about the taste, 'wet cardboard' being one verdict.

ASPARAGUS

Asparagus officinalis
Asparagus family
*** • hardy • perennial

Many people eagerly look forward to the asparagus season. The taste of freshly cut asparagus spears is not comparable to that of supermarket ones.

Asparagus is one of the oldest cultivated vegetables, particularly enjoyed by the Romans. It is a perennial vegetable, so – if planted right – it can stay in the same spot for 15–20 years.

Growing white asparagus spears is trickier; the green varieties contain more vitamins and are arguably more delicious. After you have prepared the bed properly and planted them, asparagus are not very demanding. The two most important things are patience – you have to wait two years for the first harvest – and a bit of space.

Soil and position
- Sunny position.
- Well-drained but moisture-retentive soil. Hates heavy clay.
- Do not plant in a frost pocket.
- The autumn before planting dig in plenty of half-rotted compost or manure.
- Asparagus likes a pH between 6.5 and 7.5. Add lime if necessary.
- The plot must be free of perennial weeds, since it will be difficult to dig up weed roots once the asparagus has established.

Sowing, planting and spacing
- From the beginning of April. Plant 1-year-old crowns. Sowing seeds is possible, but then a long process will take even longer.
- Plant as soon as possible after buying.
- Before planting, dig a trench, 30cm/1ft wide and 15cm/6in

deep, and work in a layer 10cm/4in deep of well-rotted manure or compost.
- Form a ridge along the middle of the trench, place the crowns on top and spread out the roots.
- 40cm/17in between plants; 1m/3ft between single rows or 50cm/20in between each staggered double row.
- Fill in the trench. Water in and mulch with 5cm/2in layer of well-rotted manure or compost.

Aftercare
- Water thoroughly for the first weeks after planting.
- In cold areas: protect plants with fleece or cover cloth from late frosts.
- Keep clear of weeds, but be careful – the roots are very shallow.
- Cut down the fern when it turns yellow in October/November, but leave about 10cm/4in of stem.
- Early spring: cover with 5cm/2in of half-rotted compost or feed with 50g per sq. m/1½oz per sq. yd of organic chicken manure pellets.
- Feed again in the same way after harvesting.

Problems
- Slugs and snails on the young shoots.
- Asparagus beetles: black beetles with yellow blotches, 6–8mm long. They and their grubs feed on the foliage and stems. Pick them off by hand. Burn the foliage in autumn to destroy overwintering beetles.

Harvesting and uses
- From the second year, harvest by cutting a few spears per plant. From the third year onwards harvest fully: 15–20 spears per plant, but always leave a few spears to allow the plant to recover and gain strength for next year.
- Harvest from late April. The traditional day of the last crop is 21 June, Midsummer's Day, after which the plants need a rest.
- Harvest when spears are 15cm/6in above ground, cutting 3–5cm/1–2in *below* the soil surface

with a sharp knife.
- Steam, serve with vinaigrette or butter, cook with risotto.
- See recipe on page 73.

Varieties
There are male and female plants: female plants carry lovely red berries in autumn, but male plants are usually more productive.
- 'Connover's Colossal' – male and female plants, widely available, AGM.
- 'Guelph Millenium' F1 – male plants, from Canada, good for colder regions, also tolerates poorer soils.
- 'Martha Washington' – long straight, early, mid-green spears with purple tips, excellent flavour, high resistance to rust.
- 'Purple Passion' – purple spears, very sweet and tender, with a nutty flavour.

Young asparagus eaters can carry out an interesting genetic experiment. 40–50 per cent of the population notice that very soon after eating asparagus their urine smells very different. The ability to produce smelly urine is inherited. The ability to smell asparagus urine is also inherited, so some people just can't smell it, even though they make it! Children may enjoy mapping the two genes.

BEANS, BROAD (FAVA BEANS)

Vicia faba • Legume family
** • half-hardy • ☺

Broad beans, also called fava beans, have been a Mediterranean staple since ancient times and formed part of the medieval diet in Britain, being particularly valued since they could be stored dried.

All the bean family are fun to grow with children, because the seeds are satisfyingly large for small fingers to handle and they germinate and grow quickly. The flowers are fragrant.

Soil and position
- Sunny position.
- Good and humus-rich, well-drained (especially for growing in winter) soil in a bed where manure was dug in for the previous crop.
- Hardy to about –5°C/23°F, so in areas with mild winters you can sow them in autumn or even early winter to get an early crop the following year.

Sowing, planting and spacing
- Spring sowing: February–end of May, for June–September cropping.
- Autumn sowing: October–December, for cropping in the following May–June.
- About 5cm/2in deep. Either sow directly into the soil, or sow in small pots and plant out when they are about 5cm/2in tall. This gives more control regarding mice and slugs.
- 25cm/10in between plants. In staggered double rows, 30cm/1ft between rows, 1m/39in to the next double row.
- Seed can be stored for up to 2 years.

Aftercare
- Feed autumn-sown plants in spring with a low-nitrogen fertilizer such as liquid seaweed.
- Support tall varieties with stakes and twine.
- Pinch out tops after pods have set: this helps the pods to mature as well as reducing aphids.

- After harvesting leave the roots in the soil and dig them in, or add them to the compost heap, where they will be very beneficial.

Companion planting
- Plant lettuces and spinach seedlings between bean rows; neither should mind a bit of shade.

Problems
- Mice and pigeons love the seeds and seedlings, so you may need to protect them with netting or fleece or cover cloth when small.
- Aphids, especially on the growing tips in late spring. Pinch out tips. Autumn and winter sowings are usually less affected. If the damage is too great, consider planting only in autumn and winter next year.
- Chocolate spot, a fungus that can occur in warm humid weather; late crops are more prone to it. Brown spots are visible on the leaves and when it is really serious the plant will die.
- Bean seed weevil – if you find little holes in your self-collected broad bean seeds. Bin them.

Harvesting and uses
- Harvest the beans young; if they are too big they tend to be bitter.
- If picking with children, make sure they do not rip the plant out as they pick; show them how to hold the plant and pick off the bean pod.
- Use very young pods whole, sliced, like French beans.
- Shell more mature pods and cook the beans. If you leave them on the plant for too long, you will need to peel the outer skin off each bean, which is a drag. So the earlier, the better.
- Beans freeze well, as long as they are not too big. Blanch for 2 minutes and freeze in bags.

Varieties
The different varieties have different pod sizes. There are Longpods, with 8–10 beans in each pod, Windsor varieties, which have only 4–7 beans per pod but apparently a better flavour; and dwarf varieties, also with 4–7 beans per pod on shorter plants.

For autumn sowing, October–December:
- 'Aquadulce Claudia' – Longpod, compact plants, 90–100cm/36–40in, AGM.
- 'The Sutton' – good flavour, dwarf plants, good for windswept areas or under cloches, 40cm/16in, AGM.

Sow in early spring, February–April:
- 'Express' – Longpod, quick maturing, 90cm/36in, AGM.
- 'Red Epicure' – lovely dark red flowers, red beans turn yellow after cooking, 90cm/36in.

Sow in late spring, March–end of May:
- 'Green Windsor' – stubby pods, deep green, good flavour, 90cm/36in.
- 'Jubilee Hysor' – early maturing, light green beans, 90cm/36in, AGM.

EXTRA BENEFITS
Broad beans and other plants in the legume family fix nitrogen from the air and store it in their roots, which grow very deeply and open up the soil, acting as a kind of green manure, but with the added advantage that you also get a crop.

BEANS, FRENCH (STRING BEANS)

Phaseolus vulgaris • Legume family
** • 🪴 • tender • ☺

French beans are easy to grow and do not require much space. Colours and shapes vary, and there are flat or round pods. They come in dwarf and climbing forms, so if you would like to add some height and structure to your garden, grow the taller varieties. You can sow every four weeks up to the beginning of August to ensure a constant supply until October.

Once summer is warm enough they grow quickly and are very prolific, as long as you keep picking them. The dwarf varieties are also nicely at child level, so they are a good thing for children to sow, plant out and harvest.

Soil and position
- Sunny position.
- Warm, sheltered, humus-rich soil, preferably manured for a previous crop.
- Tolerate drier conditions than runner beans.

Sowing, planting and spacing
- Inside from mid-April (3–4 weeks before last frosts), in small pots.
- Outside from after the last frost until the beginning of August; temperature should be at least 13°C/56°F. Should there be an unexpected cold spell, cover them with cloches or fleece, as they will not grow in cold weather.
- 2.5cm/1in deep.
- Dwarf beans: 40cm/16in between rows, 15cm/6in between plants.
- Climbing French beans: As for runner beans (see page 122).
- Seed can be stored for up to 2 years.

Aftercare
- Mulch with half-rotted compost or well-rotted manure once plants are about 20cm/8in tall.
- Check for moisture; water especially when flowering starts.
- Make sure you pick continuously. Once the beans in the pods start to mature, the plant stops producing new beans.
- At the end of the season, let some pods ripen and collect your own seeds for next year.

Companion planting
- Nasturtiums, which attract aphids even more than beans, so should keep the beans free of them. Plant non-climbing nasturtiums in alternating rows with dwarf beans.

Problems
- Slugs – keep an eye on seedlings.
- Aphids – encourage ladybugs.

Harvesting and uses
- From August to October. Do not wait too long to pick – they are best when they still snap when bent.
- If picking with children, make sure they do not rip the plant out as they pick, but show them how to hold the plant and pick off the bean pod.
- Cook with a twig of summer savory – delicious, and should reduce wind after eating.
- Good for freezing; blanch first.

Varieties
Dwarf:
- 'Ferrari' – dark green pencil pods, good disease resistance, very quick to mature, AGM.
- 'Masterpiece' – large, flat, bright green pods, early.
- 'Purple Tepee' – dark purple pods that turn green after cooking, well flavoured.
- 'Sonesta' – bright yellow pods, long, slightly flat, compact plants, AGM.

Climbing:
- 'Blauhilde' – dark purple pods that turn green when cooked, resistant to virus diseases, good for freezing.
- 'Borlotto di Lingua di Fuoco' – pods are speckled red and look spectacular; also available as dwarf variety.
- 'Cobra' – green round pods, long, tender and tasty, very high yields, violet flowers, AGM.
- 'Kingston Gold' – flat yellow pods, slow maturing, AGM.

Left to right: 'Masterpiece', 'Borlotto', 'Sonesta', 'Canadian Wonder' and 'Blauhilde'.

BEAN VOCABULARY
This can be slightly confusing, so in an effort to shed some light on the murky bean world:

Borlotti beans (cranberry beans) A type of haricot (see below) with medium–large seeds for drying. Their pods are quite spectacular – yellow speckled with red.

Cannellini beans Haricots with white seeds. The main ingredient of minestrone.

Flageolets If you leave the pods a little longer on the French bean plant, rather than eating them as a flattish pod, you can shell them and eat the little beans inside. Beans come in white, yellow and green; popular in France.

Haricots Let French bean pods and beans dry, shell them and store them. Cook after soaking.

Kidney beans A type of haricot with red beans.

Pencil pods Type of French beans with thin round pods, also known as 'Kenya' or 'filet' types. Best eaten fresh.

Runner beans (flatpole beans) These are a different species of bean (*P. coccineus*). They have higher yields than climbing French beans. Common opinion is that the French climbers taste better, but runners can withstand rougher climates than French beans.

Wax podded beans (yellow wax beans) French beans with yellow pods, often with a buttery flavour.

BEANS, RUNNER (FLAT POLE BEANS)

Phaseolus coccineus • Legume family
** • 🌱 • tender • ☺

Runner beans originate in the cool mountain regions of Mexico and Guatemala and they actually dislike warm summers so much that they drop their flowers if the nights are too warm. So if you live in an area with cool summers, runner beans are a better bet than French climbing beans, and can be stunningly productive. They are useful for bringing structure and height into your garden and with their coloured flowers make a pretty feature. Ingenious parents could even structure a frame that gradually turns into a bean Wendy house as the season progresses.

Eating runner beans uncooked is not recommended, as raw they contain lectins that can cause stomach pains.

Soil and position
- Sunny site, but cooler than for French beans; they prefer nights that are no warmer than 14°C/57°F throughout the growing season.
- Humus-rich, water-retentive and moist soil, ideally manured for a previous crop.
- If growing them in a light soil, dig in plenty of compost before planting. Since beans store nitrogen from the air, they do not require extra fertilizer.

Sowing, planting and spacing
- Inside from mid-April, in small pots. Outside after the last frost until the end of June, two per bean pole, 2cm/1in deep. Bean poles should be about 30cm/1ft apart.
- Wait until you are sure that the last frosts are over. Harden plants off before planting out.
- Seed can be stored for up to 2 years.

Aftercare
- Mulch with half-rotted compost or well-rotted manure once plants are about 20cm/8in tall to provide nutrients and to retain moisture.

- If you have an exceptionally warm summer, try to water the soil around the beans (but not the leaves) in the evening and hope that the evaporation will be enough to keep the plants cool.
- When they have reached the tops of their supports, pinch out the tips; otherwise they will continue to grow, waving around in the air and eventually overbalancing the whole structure.
- At the end of the season, leave several bean pods to mature and dry: these will be your seeds for next year.

Companion planting
- As for French beans (see page 121).

Problems
- Slugs – especially on young plants.
- Aphids – encourage ladybugs and plant nasturtiums as close to the beans as possible.

Harvesting and uses
- From about mid-summer, depending on the climate.
- Do not wait too long with picking; the smaller, the more tender.
- As soon as the first beans are ready, pick continuously – about every 2 days. As soon as the plant produces seeds, productivity will be reduced.
- If picking with children, make sure they do not rip the plant out as they pick; show them how to hold the plant and pick off the bean pod. Leave the lower beans for them to pick.
- Blanch and freeze, chopped into 2cm/1in-long portions.

Varieties
- 'Desiree' – broad stringless pods, huge crops, white flowers, AGM.
- 'Enorma' – very long smooth beans, heavy yields, red flowers, AGM.
- 'Painted Lady Improved' – early crops, good flavour, pretty red and white flowers.
- 'Sunset' – lovely pale apricot-coloured flowers.
- 'White Lady' – smooth and stringless, copes better with warmer temperatures, white flowers, AGM.

SUPPORTS FOR CLIMBING BEANS
The classic method Two rows of poles, erected sloping inwards and crossing each other at the top, with a horizontal bar tied along the ridge. This has worked well for centuries, generally with sturdy canes thicker than bamboo canes.

Wigwams These do not need as much space and bamboo canes can be used. A wigwam is decorative and does not cast a huge shadow, unlike the traditional bean support. But it has a disadvantage in that it is hard to get at the beans at the top inside the wigwam. These unreachable pods will develop into seeds and as soon as that happens the plant will be less productive.

Be creative Bear in mind that the plants can produce a lot of heavy leaf mass, so whatever you come up with needs to be sturdy.

- 'Hestia' – a dwarf runner. Red and white flowers, good for areas where it is too cool for French dwarf beans. Also good for containers.

BEETROOT (BEETS)

Beta vulgaris • Beet family
* • 🌱 • half-hardy

Beetroot is one of the easiest vegetables to grow. There is only one thing to emphasize: they need a regular water supply. As well as the red classics, try yellow or striped ones for a change.

Soil and position
- Sunny.
- Any good garden soil, well drained, free of stones.
- Does not like fresh manure, so ideally grow in a bed that was manured for a previous crop. If this is not possible, rake in a thin layer of well-rotted compost, or 75g per sq. m/2½oz per sq. yd of blood, fish and bone.

Sowing, planting and spacing
- Early, bolt-resistant ones: from mid-March to mid-April. Maincrop: from mid-April to mid-May (about 4 weeks before the last frosts). Late ones: late May to June.
- Temperature must be above 10°C/50°F; germination is generally rather slow.
- Inside: sow them in small pots or modules. Outside: sow directly in rows, 2cm/1in deep.
- Seed can be stored for up to 3 years.
- If you have sown in modules, plant out seedlings carefully. Beetroot is one of the few root crops that accept transplantation, but it still does not like it.
- 30cm/1ft between rows, 15cm/6in between plants.

Aftercare
- Thin out directly sown beetroot when seedlings are about 5cm/2in tall.
- If you want to eat baby beet, thin to about 7cm/3in between each plant. Then you can harvest alternate ones as baby beet and let the others grow on.
- Water regularly and moderately. If it is too dry, the roots will be woody; if watering is too irregular, they will split.

Companion planting
- Summer savory improves the taste of the plants; dill improves their health.

Problems
- Bolting – if plants are exposed to lower temperatures than 10°C/50°F, they usually bolt. Use bolt-resistant varieties if you want to start early.
- Leaf miners – pick off affected leaves.

Harvesting and uses
Start when they are as big as a golf ball; you can let them grow bigger, but then they will taste more earthy and take longer to cook. Tennis-ball size is the maximum recommended size.
- Tiny leaves can be picked for salads; larger ones can be used like chard.
- If picking leaves for salad or stir-fries, twist the foliage off and leave a few leaves in the middle. If you cut them off, they will bleed.
- Take care of clothing, as the juice stains.
- Baby beetroot is good raw, peeled and sliced.
- When you cook larger roots, only wash them: do not peel them – and leave the stalks on too. Peel after cooking, when the skin should just slip off. Take into account that cooking will take at least an hour.
- You can also roast them in the

(see page 137).

CLUSTER SEEDS
One beetroot seed is actually a little cluster of 2–4 seeds. If you sow them directly outside, you will have to thin them, so that each little plant has enough space to grow good roots. There are some varieties available that are 'monogerm'; this means there is less thinning to do.

oven, with olive oil and herbs. Cover them with aluminium foil to prevent drying out.

Varieties
Early – with good bolting resistance:
- 'Boltardy' – AGM.

Maincrop:
- 'Bull's Blood' – dark red leaves, stunning. Also good as micro-greens (see page 137).
- 'Burpee's Golden' – interesting orange skin, does not bleed (illustrated below). Sow thicker, as has a lower germination rate.
- 'Chioggia' – light red on the outside, red and white alternating rings on the inside (illustrated below). Does not bleed, looks spectacular and is good eaten raw.
- 'Red Ace' F1 – doesn't mind dry weather as much as the others, AGM.
- 'Solo' F1 – monogerm variety, sweet flavour, AGM.

Late (can be stored):
- 'Cylindra' – long roots, stores well.

BROCCOLI: CALABRESE AND SPROUTING BROCCOLI

Brassica oleracea Italica Group
Cabbage family
*** • half-hardy • ☺

Brocco means sprout in Italian and *broccoli* are the diminutives. They come in two forms: the familiar large heads, known as calabrese, and sprouting broccoli. Children are generally happy to eat both and can be encouraged by the shape of the little broccoli trees.

Calabrese is much quicker to grow than the sprouting version. The plants themselves are not as large as other cabbage plants and are practical for small gardens.

Sprouting broccoli, on the other hand, takes up a lot of space for a long time, so for smaller gardens plant only one or two plants, but the flower heads are a welcome treat at a time when there is not much else to harvest.

Soil and position
- Sunny position.
- Humus-rich, deeply dug and well-drained soil.
- Dig in half-rotted compost or half-rotted manure in late autumn or winter, and lime. Let the soil settle for at least 3 months before planting.
- 1–2 weeks before planting, rake in chicken pellets, 50g per sq. m/ 1½oz per sq. yd. Do not fork over.

Sowing, planting and spacing
Calabrese:
- April–June – directly into rows, 2–3 seeds every 20cm/8in.
- Thin to the strongest seedling, leaving 40cm/17in between each plant.

Sprouting broccoli:
- May–June, outside into a seed bed or into modules.
- Plant out in June–July.
- Plant deeply, down to the first leaves. Ensure seedling is firmly anchored by watering in well.

- 75cm/30in between rows; 75cm/30in between plants.
- Seeds of both can be stored for up to 4 years.

Aftercare
- Net against pigeons.
- When plants have settled in, mulch with half-rotted compost or well-rotted manure.

Calabrese:
- Always water well; otherwise plants will be woody and produce hollow stems.
- After cutting off the central head to eat, feed several times with tomato fertilizer to encourage more flower development.

Sprouting broccoli:
- Stake in autumn.
- Remove yellowing leaves immediately to prevent the spread of pests and diseases.

Companion planting
- Celeriac, tomatoes, basil, coriander, dill, French and pot marigolds, which confuse cabbage root fly and cabbage white caterpillar with their scent.
- Intercrop with lettuces and spinach.
- Do not plant with potatoes or onions, as they inhibit each other's growth.

Problems
- See Brassica problems, page 126.
- Earwigs love calabrese heads.

Harvesting and uses
Calabrese:
- From summer until the first frosts.
- Pay attention to the right moment of harvesting: when the head is formed, do not wait too long, as the heads will loosen quickly and start to flower.
- Always cut the main flower head first in order to encourage the production of side shoots.

Sprouting broccoli:
- From February to late spring, depending on variety; most March–April.
- Pick when little heads are formed, before they start to loosen.

Both:
- Most nutritious eaten raw.
- As a side dish with melted butter,

> **BRASSICAS OR CABBAGE FAMILY**
> Plant family that includes turnips, cauliflower, broccoli, mustard, Brussels sprouts, oriental leaves, radishes and cabbage.

for stir-fries, steamed, with pasta.
- Freeze on the day of harvest after blanching.
- Use first seedling leaves as micro-greens (see page 137).

Varieties
Calabrese:
- 'Arcadia' – late, very slow to bolt, AGM.
- 'Belstar' F1 – mid-season, produces many side shoots, AGM.
- 'Trixie' F1 – early, first clubroot-resistant variety, AGM.

Sprouting broccoli:
Purple varieties are particularly hardy, while white ones are better flavoured but not as prolific. Plants are between 90–100cm/36–39in tall.
- 'White Eye' – tight white buds, early (from March), AGM.
- 'White Star' – white, big buds, late (from April), AGM.
- 'Red Arrow' – purple, vigorous, good winter hardiness, early–mid season (late February–March), AGM.
- 'Redhead' – very tall, large spears in a pretty purple, March through April, AGM (illustrated below).

RELATIVES
Broccoli rabe 'Cima di Rapa'
More spicy than broccoli, but grown and used in similar fashion.

BRUSSELS SPROUTS

Brassica oleracea Gemnifera Group
Cabbage family
*** • hardy

Traditionally Christmas requires Brussels sprouts, so it makes sense to grow a few of your own. If they are one of your favourites, you do not have to restrict yourself to a harvest in December: with the right varieties you can pick them from October to March.

This is one of the hardiest vegetables and withstands cold down to −10°C/14°F. The sprouts are actually leaf buds that grow all the way up the main stem. If you do not pick them, little branches will eventually grow there, to flower the following spring.

Soil and position
As for broccoli (see opposite).

Sowing, planting and spacing
- Sow indoors from March into trays for early varieties, outdoors from April for late varieties.
- Plant out from mid-May to mid-June at the latest, plant firmly and water in well.
- 75cm/30in between rows; 75cm/30in between plants.

Aftercare
As for broccoli (see opposite).

Companion planting
As for broccoli (see opposite).

Problems
- See Brassica problems, page 126.
- Loose, open sprouts (known as 'blown') – planted out too early or given too much fertilizer.

Harvesting and uses
- From October to December; late varieties from January, sometimes until March.
- Some say frost enhances sweetness, so they taste better after a cold spell.
- Start to pick from the bottom, working upwards.
- Do not let sprouts get too big, as they will not taste as nice and there is a danger they might blow.
- One plant is productive for about 8 weeks.
- Before cooking, check for aphids – soak in salted water for 15 minutes.
- Freeze small firm sprouts after blanching for 3 minutes.

Varieties
All modern varieties are F1 varieties, mostly around 75–100cm/2–3ft tall. These have the advantage of producing uniform sprouts of the same size that do not blow as quickly as the old varieties. Some of the old varieties have special features, so it is also worth trying them.
- 'Cascade' F1 – good uniform plants, round sprouts, resistant to mildew, late, AGM.
- 'Falstaff' – purple red sprouts, mid–late season, very decorative but not hugely productive, only 60cm/24in tall. The colour is supposed to stay throughout cooking – add a splash of vinegar to the cooking water to be sure.
- 'Maximus' F1 – harvest from autumn to Christmas, AGM.
- 'Noisette' – said to be the most delicious variety, with a nutty flavour, mid-season.
- 'Sanda' – good cold resistance, December–March.

> ### 'PLANT BRASSICAS IN WELL-TRODDEN SOIL'
> This rather puzzling advice is always given by old timers at the common. The reasoning is that many of the brassicas grow quite tall and have a tendency to be top-heavy when mature. If they are not properly anchored in the soil, they will simply be blown over in the first autumn gale. However, if you already have compacted soil and are desperate to make it more workable, it seems counter-intuitive to trample it down again. After digging, the bed should settle for a couple of months. Forking it over just before planting would compromise the stability of the plants.

BRASSICA PROBLEMS

Before you have a heart attack reading this: most of these problems will probably not happen (or at least not all at the same time)! Only clubroot is really serious, and in the worst case you could always abandon the brassica family and concentrate on growing other vegetables.

- **Mealy cabbage aphid** Greyish greenfly. The plant looks as though it has been dusted with flour, usually from mid-spring to autumn. Affected leaves have pale blotches and are distorted and crumpled; shoot tips can be destroyed. It lays its black eggs in autumn on brassica remnants, so keep your cabbage beds tidy. As a last resort, spray with pyrethrum or other organic insecticide.

- **Cabbage maggot** An insect that looks like a house fly. It lays its eggs close to the stem of the cabbage, and the creamy white maggots then eat the roots of the plants. Plants take on a bluish colour and stop growing. This usually happens by the end of April, in July and then again in late summer. Most susceptible are white and savoy cabbages, as are cauliflowers and kohl rabi. Protect newly planted cabbages with collars, which you can buy in garden centres, or mulch after planting with strong-scented herb cuttings like lavender or sage.

- **Cabbage white caterpillar (looper)** Check regularly for small groups of sulphur yellow eggs on the underside of the leaves and rub them off. Or try to catch the caterpillars and put them on the bird table. Try companion planting: the butterflies are less attracted when there is not much open soil between the cabbages. Or plant nasturtiums somewhere else in your garden, as these attract the butterflies even more and you can collect the caterpillars conveniently. You could also cover plants with fine netting (Enviromesh).

- **Clubroot** A soil-borne fungus that affects the roots and causes plants to wilt. When you lift the plant, you find swollen roots. Prevent the disease by crop rotation and regular liming before planting brassicas – the fungus does not thrive if your soil pH is above 7. Make sure the soil for brassicas is not compacted and is always well drained. Kale and rocket are the least susceptible brassicas. In the unfortunate event that you do have clubroot, do not put affected plants on the compost and be aware that you can transmit the disease via gardening tools as well, so observe strict hygiene. Sow new brassica seedlings in shop-bought (and thus sterilized) compost only and plant them as far as possible from the affected spot. Do not plant any other member of the cabbage family on the same spot for at least 7–10 years. Since the cabbage family is large (see page 211), it is worth trying to avoid this disease. But since clubroot is a big problem for commercial growers, research on breeding resistant varieties is ongoing.

- **Flea beetles** Blackish little beetles 1–3mm (about 1/16 –1/8in) long, which hop away when they are disturbed. They make lots of tiny holes in the young leaves of all brassicas. Larvae can damage germinating seedlings. With most plants, once they are over the 3–4 leaf stage, flea beetles are less of a problem. Flea beetles love stable dry spring weather, which is usually from April to May. There are several ways to annoy them, and hopefully interrupt their breeding patterns:
  - Keep soil around plants damp – flea beetles hate this – and hoe regularly to irritate them even more.
  - Protect directly sown seedlings with fleece or cover cloth until plants are tall enough.
  - Sow in modules and plant out when tall enough.
  - Grow rows of lettuce and spinach between brassicas – flea beetles do not like these.

- **Whitefly** These live on the underside of plants, usually from late summer and especially on kale. Shake the plants regularly and spray the whitefly off with a jet of water. Unfortunately they seem unaffected by frost. Treat with organic pesticides if it is too bad.

The most important rule for growing brassicas is: keep your beds tidy, especially in autumn and winter, to reduce the habitat of pests and diseases. Pull out old cabbage stalks immediately and do not put any diseased or pest-infected material on your compost heap.

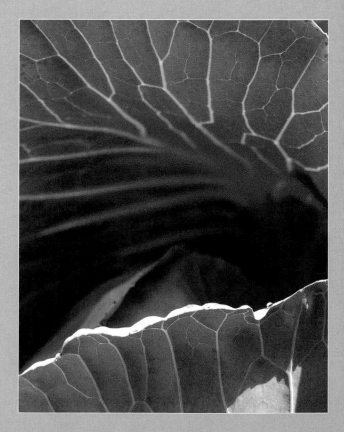

CABBAGES

Brassica oleracea Capitata Group
Cabbage family
*** • half-hardy

Undeniably cabbages take up a lot of space in a garden for quite a while, but they can be delicious and the leaf textures are often spectacular. They are not very difficult to look after, although they can be affected by some pests and diseases. Cabbages are happy in cooler climates and will not be affected by a bad summer.

Forget the mushy over-cooked cabbage that the older generation had at school. Pulling up a huge cabbage can be very satisfying for a small gardener, while a crispy raw leaf, or an easy stir-fry tempts young palates. Fresh shredded cabbage contains quantities of vitamin C and fibre, and so provides a good source of nutrients in autumn and winter.

Soil and position
As for broccoli (see page 124).

Sowing, planting and spacing
- Sow in trays or modules.
- Prick seedlings out into individual small pots when they are large enough to handle: then they will be less likely to be devastated by slugs. Make sure you plant them deep, with the lower leaves just above soil level.
- Seedlings are ready for planting out when they have at least 3–4 real leaves.
- Seed can be stored for up to 4 years.

Aftercare
- As for broccoli (see page 124).
- For spring cabbages: in cold areas cover with cloches over winter. Top dress in early spring with chicken pellets.

Companion planting
- As for broccoli (see page 124).

Problems
- See Brassica problems, opposite.

Harvesting and uses
- Cut the heads with a sharp knife, close to ground level.
- Spring cabbages: pick every second plant from early spring and use as spring greens; let others form heads for harvesting from about May.
- Red cabbages and winter white cabbages can be stored for 2–3 months. Cut off the stem, remove the outer leaves and store in a cool dry place.

Cabbage timetable

Cabbage type	Variety	Sowing	Planting out	Spacing	Harvesting	Time to maturity
Summer	'Greyhound' – pointed, green, AGM 'Primo' – round, green, very tender	February–March, indoors (late winter–early spring)	Mid-April–May (spring–late spring)	45 x 45cm/ 18 x 18in	From mid-June (early summer)	5 months
Autumn	'Kilaton' – round, green, clubroot resistant. 'Winningstadt' – white, large pointed heads. 'Ruby Ball' – red cabbage, early, AGM 'Savoy King' F1 – savoy, early (illustrated above).	April (spring)	May–June (late spring–early summer)	45 x 45cm/ 18 x 18in	From September (early autumn)	5–8 months
Winter	'January King' – round heads, slightly red, very decorative. 'Tundra' – very hardy, long cropping time, AGM.	May (late spring)	June–July (early–mid-summer)	60 x 60cm/ 24 x 24in	From November (late autumn)	6–8 months
Spring	'Pixie' – small heads for smaller gardens, AGM.	July–August (mid–late summer)	October (autumn)	15 x 45cm/ 6 x 18in	From March (early spring) as spring greens, from May (late spring) as heads.	8–10 months

CARROTS

Daucus carota subsp. *sativus*
Parsley family
** • 🪴 • half-hardy • ☺

Carrots originated in Asia Minor, where they grew in white, yellow, red, green and purple forms. The Romans were especially fond of white and purple ones. The orange carrots we all know derived from a particularly successful seventeenth-century PR stunt: patriotic plant breeders in the Netherlands created orange ones – the colour of the House of Orange.

Rare is the child who will not eat a self-pulled carrot, usually right there in the garden. Carrots are one of the vegetables that best retains residues of pesticides, so it is one of the most appealing to grow organically yourself so that you know what is in them. But eating lots of carrots is not enough to make a difference to seeing in the dark: that was a propaganda myth put about in the Second World War to keep the invention of radar secret. Nevertheless carrots do contain healthy beta-carotene and vitamin A.

Soil and position
- Sunny, sheltered and warm position.
- Soil preferably on the sandy side, well drained, free of big stones. If the growing point of a carrot meets a stone, it will divide, creating forked roots.
- Hates fresh manure. Ideally grow after hungry feeders such as brassicas, or on ground vacated by early potatoes.
- On new ground, spread a thin layer of well-rotted compost or fertilize with 75g per sq. m/2½oz per sq. yd of blood, fish and bone.

Sowing, planting and spacing
- Early varieties: March and April at at least 7°C/45°F. The soil should have warmed up already.
- Maincrop varieties: May and June.
- Late varieties: August.
- Sow every 4 weeks for a continuous crop.
- Sow 1–2cm/½–1in deep, very thinly. Carrot flies are attracted by the smell of the leaves, so the less

thinning you have to do later, the better.
- 20–30cm/8–12in between rows; 5cm/2in between plants.
- Make sure you keep soil moist during germination.
- Seed can be stored for up to 3 years.

Aftercare
- Thin to about 5cm/2in between each plant – preferably on a wet day to reduce scent. Smooth back disturbed soil.

Companion planting
- Onions, shallots, chives and garlic – they keep carrot flies away, but only as long as they are in the bed with the carrots. So if you harvest your onions earlier, the protection will be gone.

Problems
- Carrot fly appears in late spring to early summer. It travels at a height of maximum 45cm/18in. It lays its eggs in the carrot, and then when you harvest your carrot you find it is full of disgusting little black wormy tunnels. Apply protection as soon as you sow your seeds: these flies are very smart.
- Choose resistant varieties and use companion planting.
- Sowing in June and July avoids the worst of the carrot fly attacks.
- Build a physical barrier around your carrots using fine netting (polypropylene, Enviromesh), open at the top, supported by sticks. You can also cover your crop with fleece or cover cloth, but the plants can get a bit stuffy underneath as the temperature heats up.
- Try mulching the soil with strong-smelling plant materials, such as herb clippings.
- In autumn, make sure that no carrot fly maggot is able to overwinter in your garden: lift carrots by mid-October, and bin or burn infected parts.

Harvesting and uses
- Use a fork or trowel to help ease the carrots out. Try not to tug the foliage too much, as this alerts hovering carrot flies to the

CARROTS IN CONTAINERS
If you are not lucky with carrots in your garden – because you have heavy or stony soil, or are bothered by carrot fly – try them in containers. Whatever kind of container you use, it should be at least 45cm/18in high. Use good garden compost, sow sparsely, thin to about 7cm/3in between each plant and keep well watered.

remainder of the harvest.
- See recipe on page 108.

Varieties
Recently seeds of 'novelty' varieties in all kinds of shades have again become available. Carrots also come in different shapes, from long via intermediate to stump rooted.

Early (sow March–April):
- 'Amsterdam Forcing 3' – smooth, good colour, little core, AGM.
- 'Earlibird Nantes' – early, stubby.

Maincrop (sow May–June):
- 'Purple Haze' – purple with an orange core (illustrated below).
- 'Rainbow' – all shades between white and orange.
- 'Sugarsnax 54' F1 – very sweet, long smooth roots, AGM.
- 'Sytan' – less attractive to carrot fly, AGM.

Late (sow August):
- For late sowings use early varieties – they mature more quickly and this is what they must do before the first frost.

CELERIAC (CELERY ROOT)

Apium graveolens var. *rapaceum*
Parsley family
** • half-hardy

Unlike the closely related (and similarly named) celery, celeriac makes large whitish knobbly bulbs. It is a winter vegetable rich in vitamins and minerals and widely used in Continental Europe, but for some reason it has not really made it across the Channel. There are rumours that it is difficult to grow, but it is certainly easier than celery. Celeriac's main requirement is good soil and regular watering.

Note that you have to sow quite early and the seedlings cannot go outside until mid-May – which is perhaps not a problem in a greenhouse, but may prove tricky at home, especially if there is strong competition for the best windowsill from tomatoes and others.

Soil and position
- Sunny position.
- Humus-rich, moisture-retentive soil.
- Dig in half-rotted compost or half-rotted manure in autumn.

Sowing, planting and spacing
- In March indoors in trays (about 10 weeks before you expect the last frosts).
- Prick out when large enough to handle, in cells or small pots.
- Harden off before planting – and do not start too early. If late frosts occur, the plants will bolt and you will miss out on large roots.
- 30cm/1ft between plants, 40cm/17in between rows.
- Plant out from mid-May to mid-June, once the seedlings have at least 5–6 true leaves.
- Do not plant too deep or else the roots will not grow big and fat.
- Seeds can be stored for up to 5 years.

Aftercare
- Hoe regularly until early summer.
- After plants have recovered from transplantation, mulch the bed with half-rotted compost to nourish and improve water retention, but make sure you do not cover the plant.
- Needs regular watering.
- Remove oldest leaves to expose the swelling root.
- Celeriac loves potassium, so feed it with tomato fertilizer in summer.

Companion planting
- Autumn cabbages – share the same planting time and the scent of celeriac is supposed to deter cabbage white (looper) butterflies.

Problems
- Slugs love seedlings, but are less problematic with older plants.
- Celery leaf miner (celery fly) – pick off affected leaves.
- Carrot fly (see opposite) – in gardens plagued with them, they can also attack celeriac.

Harvesting and uses
- From October, in mild areas they can stay in the beds until you need them; a light frost once in a while does not harm them.
- In areas with colder winters make sure you harvest before a heavy frost.
- Use in stews and stuffings (see page 113), mix with other vegetables for roasting, mash with potatoes.
- Peel off the skin generously and cut out all brown bits. If you do not use it straight away, put in a bowl of water with a squeeze of lemon juice.
- In summer, try using the young leaves for flavouring like parsley, and for bouquet garni.
- To freeze, cut into cubes and blanch first.

Varieties
- 'Giant Prague' – introduced in 1885 and still going strong.
- 'Monarch' – very large roots with firm white flesh.

RELATIVES
Celery requires lots of watering and a certain amount of fiddling around trenching and blanching with wrapping paper or cardboard around the stalks, so we think it is not worth the effort.

CHARD AND SPINACH BEET

Beta vulgaris subsp. *cicla*
Beet family
* • 🪴 • half-hardy

These are some of the prettiest and easiest to grow of all vegetables. A good alternative to spinach, but even better because it does not bolt in hot weather and withstands cold temperatures better. The big leaves accumulate minerals, which are good not only for you but for your compost heap as well.

These are such tough plants that even the clumsiest child will find it difficult to destroy them, and the colours of the leaves brighten up the garden, especially in winter.

Soil and position
- Sunny position.
- Any good garden soil.
- Rake in a thin layer of well-rotted compost, or organic chicken pellets, 50g per sq. m/1½oz per sq. yd.

Sowing, planting and spacing
- Sow inside in modules from mid-March; or outside, not before mid-April.
- Not too deep – 1cm/½in.
- Germination time: 10–14 days.
- Thin plants to 40cm/17in between plants, 40cm/17in between rows.
- Seed can be stored for up to 3 years.

Aftercare
- When sown directly, thin the plants when they are large enough to handle. Eat the thinnings.

THINNINGS
These are the seedlings you have to remove as plants grow and need more space. You might thin every second and third seedling, leaving only every fourth plant to grow to maturity. If you need more plants or are really soft-hearted, you may be able to transplant the thinnings. Or just eat them: infanticide is acceptable in this case and many vegetables taste even better when young.

- Bolting is rare, but if it happens, just remove flower shoots.

Companion planting
- Happy next to all other plants, except beetroot and spinach, which are from the same family.

Problems
- Slugs – especially for the seedlings.
- Pigeons – net.

Harvesting and uses
- When large enough for kitchen use – do not wait until the leaves have reached their full size. Twist off as many outer leaves as you need without pulling out the whole plant. Pick a big bag full, because chard cooks down to a surprisingly meagre quantity.
- Late-sown plants can be harvested throughout winter (protect with fleece or cover cloth if it gets too cold – below freezing).

CONFUSED? SO WERE WE ...
Swiss chard or leaf beet Alternative names for chard. Has white fleshy leaf stalks, which are said to taste best of all chards.
Ruby chard A variety of Swiss chard, with slim red stalks.
Spinach beet or perpetual spinach Looks like spinach, though with larger and fleshier leaves, but it is not: in fact it is closely related to Swiss chard.

- Use like spinach, but cook stalks longer than leaves. Stir-fry over garlic (see recipe on page 61); use in quiche.

Varieties
- 'Swiss Chard' – white stalks, good flavour.
- 'Bright Lights' – stalks show a variety of colours between white-yellow-red – gorgeous..

COURGETTES (ZUCCHINI) AND MARROWS

Cucurbita pepo • Cucumber family
* • 🌱 • tender • ☺

Courgettes (or zucchini) and marrows come from the same plant, the only difference being that plant breeders call 'courgette plants' those which will produce lots of small fruits rather than a few large fruits, which are then known as marrows. Courgettes have a more delicate flavour; marrows tend to rely on a good stuffing. Botanically speaking they are summer squashes; for these, see page 149.

Two plants should be enough for a household for a whole summer. The large seeds and quick seedling growth along with bright, large fruit make these ideal children's plants.

Soil and position
- Sunny site, protected from strong winds.
- Well-drained soil, very rich in humus.
- Mix two trowels of well-rotted garden compost or well-rotted manure into each hole while planting; alternatively rake 100g per sq. m/3oz per sq. yd of blood, fish and bone into the bed.

Sowing, planting and spacing
- Indoors: late April, about a month before the last frost is expected.
- Outdoors: late May or early June; cover with a cloche in colder areas for a few weeks.
- Germination time: 5–8 days.
- Plant out indoor seedlings after hardening off when danger of frost has passed, and when 2 leaves have formed and a third is starting to develop.
- Build a little wall of soil to form a ridge round the base of each plant to retain water.
- Trailing varieties: 1.2m/4ft between rows and plants.
- Bush varieties: 60cm/24in between rows and plants.
- Seed can be stored for up to 5 years.

Aftercare
- Mulch after planting with half-rotted compost.
- While the plants are young, look out for slugs.
- Keep the soil moist, but do not wet the leaves – plants are easily scorched.
- When the plants start flowering, feed with a seaweed-based or other potassium-rich fertilizer such as liquid tomato food.
- Pinch out the tips of main shoots of trailing varieties when they reach 60cm/24in long.

Companion planting
- Borage, French and pot marigolds to encourage pollinating insects.

Problems
- Powdery mildew – very common on older leaves when short of water, but the plant still continues to crop well until frost, so generally can be ignored.
- Cucumber mosaic virus – leaves are mottled dark and light green, and plants are stunted. The virus is spread by aphids, so attract aphid predators to prevent damage, and if plants are affected, discard them.
- Fruits only swelling at the top, and then rotting off. Two possibilities: either there are too many fruits on one plant, which can lead to the smaller fruits rotting; or pollination has been incomplete, because of a lack of visiting insects, often due to cold temperatures – wait for the weather to improve.

Harvesting and uses
- From July onwards; twice weekly for courgettes.
- Expected yield per plant: about 16 courgettes. Or 2–3 marrows.
- Do not let courgettes grow longer than about 15cm/6in, as younger fruits taste much better. Round varieties should be about 6cm/2½in (tennis-ball size) in diameter.
- Cut through the stalks with a sharp knife or pruning shears; otherwise you might damage the plant and make it prone to disease.
- Continued cropping is essential to prolong fruiting; once the fruits are marrow-sized, productivity slows down.
- Salads when picked young. Grilled or roasted.
- Courgettes should be eaten fresh, but marrows can be stored for weeks.

Varieties
Trailing courgettes:
- 'Genovese' – light green speckled fruits, early maturing, tasty.
- 'Gold Rush' F1 – yellow, vigorous, also good raw in salads.

Bush courgettes:
- 'Jemmer' F1 – yellow, AGM.
- 'Supremo' F1 – dark green little fruits, high yields, some mosaic virus tolerance, AGM.

Round fruits:
- 'Eight Ball' F1 – dark green, bush type (illustrated below).

For courgettes and marrows:
- 'Tiger Cross' F1 – pale striped fruits, high yields, some mosaic virus tolerance, AGM.

> ### TRAILING OR BUSH
> There are two different growth models. Bush varieties remain neat and compact with fruits forming around the centre. Trailing varieties can go all over the place, up trees and on to paths, unless carefully controlled. You need to stop these by pinching off the top, or else quality of fruit will be affected.

CUCUMBERS

Cucumis sativus • Cucumber family
** • 🪴 • tender • ☺

Believed to originate in India, cucumbers later spread throughout Europe, probably, as with so many other fruits and vegetables, via the Romans. Emperor Tiberius is supposed to have eaten cucumbers every day.

Throughout this book we assume that you do not have a greenhouse, so we only discuss outdoor cucumbers here. Anyhow, not only are they supposedly sweeter than greenhouse varieties, but there is some complicated business about sexing your flowers and removing the male ones when growing cucumbers in greenhouses, whereas outside plants generally just get on with it. Outdoor cucumbers are also known as 'ridge' cucumbers.

The thrill for children is seeing how an everyday vegetable actually grows. Hunting for hidden cucumbers under the foliage is very satisfying, as they have a tendency to lurk and only emerge when they are huge and over-ripe.

Soil and position
- Sunny and warm site, sheltered from wind.

- In cold areas you can grow them in a cold frame, without support, trailing along the ground.
- Well-drained soil, rich in humus. Dig in half-rotted compost or well-rotted manure 4–6 weeks before planting; alternatively rake in organic chicken manure pellets, 50g per sq. m/1½ oz per sq. yd.

Sowing, planting and spacing
- Sow April–May in pots indoors, or end of May–June outdoors.
- Temperatures below 16°C/61°F make cucumbers unhappy.
- Soak the seeds overnight before sowing.
- Place seeds edgeways 2.5cm/1in deep, indoors or outdoors, covered with a cloche. Consider investing in biodegradable pots because cucumbers hate root disturbance.
- After gradually hardening off, plant out, disturbing the roots as little as possible. Any damage to the stem will make the plant collapse.
- Build a little wall of soil to form a ridge round the base of each plant to retain water.
- 30cm/12in between plants, 45cm/18in between rows.
- Seed can be stored for up to 5 years.

Aftercare
- Train them up a trellis or a tripod, to about 1.2m/4ft.
- Water regularly, but be careful to water around the plants, not over the leaves. In cold periods, water less.
- When the plants reach the top of the canes or trellis, pinch out the growing tip.
- Once the first fruits have started to swell, feed with organic liquid tomato fertilizer every 2 weeks.

Companion planting
- Borage, French and pot marigolds to encourage pollinating insects. Basil is said to reduce powdery mildew; dill is good for plant health in general.

Problems
- Powdery mildew – do not plant cucumbers too close together, as

CUCUMBERS IN POTS
Plant them in large deep pots, with a good drainage layer. Use a rich, loamy potting soil. Add plenty of vermiculite and provide a tripod of canes for the plant to scramble up. Water twice a day in hot weather.

air should circulate.
- Cucumber mosaic virus – mottled yellow leaves, deformed fruit. Rip out and bin.

Harvesting and uses
- End of July–September.
- About 10 cucumbers per plant.
- Cut before they get too big, or else they will begin to turn yellowish.
- Cut off with sharp knife or pruning shears; be careful not to damage the rest of the plant.

Varieties
- 'Burpless Tasty Green' F1 – splendid name, as well as being juicy, disease resistant and smooth skinned. Pick fruits at 20–25cm/8–10in.
- 'Bush Champion' F1 – short stumpy fruits, bushy plants, especially for containers or cold frames, AGM.
- 'Marketmore' – masses of dark green fruit, fairly smooth but still needs peeling, good disease resistance, reliable, AGM.
- 'Crystal Apple' (aka 'Crystal Lemon') – tasty round yellow fruits. Something a bit different.

'A cucumber should be well sliced, and dressed with pepper and vinegar, and then thrown out, as good for nothing.'
Samuel Johnson, quoted in Boswell's *Tour to the Hebrides*, 1785

KALE

Brassica oleracea Acephala Group
Cabbage family
* • hardy

Kale (or borecole) is the easiest of all the brassicas to grow. It is very hardy and completely unphased by sharp frosts. As a good source of vitamins and iron it is a valuable winter vegetable. You will not need to grow many plants, since many recipes require only a few leaves.

And it is easily the most handsome of all brassicas, the deep burgundy leaves of some varieties adding a much-needed note of colour and texture to a winter plot.

Soil and position
- Sunny position.
- Humus-rich and well-drained soil – but kale tolerates even poor soil.
- Dig in half-rotted compost or half-rotted manure in autumn or winter, and lime. Let the soil settle for at least 3 months before planting.
- Before planting in do not fork over: just rake.
- Rake in organic chicken manure pellets, 50g per sq. m/1½ oz per sq. yd, 1–2 weeks before planting

Sowing, planting and spacing
- If you want to eat it before Christmas, sow in April; for later cropping sow May–June.
- Sow thinly into a seed bed, about 1cm/½in deep, or into modules, 2–3 seeds per cell.
- Germination time: 7–12 days.
- Thin seedlings after germination to about 10cm/4in apart.
- Ready for planting into their final position when they are about 15cm/6in tall. Plant really firmly, pressing the soil down around the seedlings and watering in well. The lowest leaves should be just above the soil surface after planting.
- 45cm/18in between plants, 60cm/24in between rows.
- Seeds can be stored for up to 4 years.

Aftercare
- Net against pigeons.
- Mulch with half-rotted compost or well-rotted manure in early summer.

Companion planting
- Celeriac, tomatoes, basil, coriander, dill, French and pot marigolds, which confuse cabbage root fly and cabbage white caterpillar (looper) with their scent.
- Intercrop with lettuces and spinach.
- Do not plant with potatoes or onions, as they inhibit each other's growth.

Problems
- Particularly susceptible to whitefly, but rarely affected by clubroot, root fly or cabbage white caterpillars (loopers). (See Brassica problems, page 126.)

Harvesting and uses
- From December to early spring.
- Take only young and tender leaves, not the bitter old ones. Cut out the central rib if it is too tough. Pick a few leaves from each plant, rather than stripping one.
- Shredded in soups and stews – add in the last few minutes of cooking.
- As a side dish with onions and melted butter or white sauce.
- Suitable for freezing.
- Also good as micro-greens (see page 137).

Varieties
- 'Cavolo Nero' (aka 'Black Tuscan', 'Tuscan Kale', 'black kale') – narrow, dark green leaves with a purple tinge, great favourite in Italy, becoming more and more popular. Very decorative as well.
- 'Dwarf Blue Curled Vates' – dwarf hybrid, only about 25cm/10in high.
- 'Pentland Brig' – eat young leaves from the crown from November; in spring you can harvest flower heads and cook like sprouting broccoli.
- 'Redbor' – has fabulous purple leaves, very ornamental, AGM (illustrated below)
- 'Red Russian' – blue-green leaves that turn purple when temperatures fall, mild-flavoured; small uncooked leaves can be added to salads.

KOHL RABI

Brassica oleracea var. *gongylodes*
Cabbage family
* • 🌱 • half-hardy

Kohl rabi is not a familiar sight in many gardens yet, but it deserves to be more widely grown. It is an easy plant that does not take up much space and can also be grown in containers. The odd-looking result is a thick, round stem which tastes like something between a turnip and an apple. You can eat it raw, like an apple, so it's also good for lunchboxes. For a constant supply sow some every 2–4 weeks, like lettuces.

Soil and position
- Sunny site and humus-rich, well-drained soil.
- Does not need as many nutrients as the big brassicas; working in a thin layer of compost before planting is sufficient.

Sowing, planting and spacing
- Sow from early March in trays or pots on the windowsill, outdoors from late April until August.
- Plant out in late April after hardening off. Transplant young: do not let them become pot bound.
- 20cm/8in between plants, 25cm/10in between rows.
- Seeds can be stored for up to 4 years.

Aftercare
- Water regularly: then the bulbs will be soft and delicious.
- Keep weed free, but be careful – kohl rabis have shallow roots.
- If there are pigeons around, cover with netting.

Companion planting
- Celery, tomatoes, basil, coriander, dill, French and pot marigolds, which confuse cabbage root fly and cabbage white caterpillar (looper) with their scent.
- Nasturtiums to attract aphids and cabbage white caterpillars (loopers0) away from the kohl rabi.
- Do not plant with potatoes or onions, which would inhibit growth.

Problems
- Clubroot (see Brassica problems, page 126).

Harvesting and uses
- When they are between golf- and tennis-ball size – bigger ones can get woody.
- If you harvest them small, you can eat the skin (if unblemished); otherwise peel.
- Raw for crudités or grated for salads.
- Cooked with béchamel sauce or as an addition to soups and stews.
- The young leaves are also tasty: you can cook them like spinach or add to kohl rabi with béchamel sauce.

Varieties
The old classics 'Green Vienna' and 'Purple Vienna' are widely available but can get a bit tough with size, and there are better alternatives. Blue varieties, with purple skin and pale flesh, grow a bit slower than the white ones but are more tender.

Blue varieties:
- 'Azur Star' – purple bulbs, white mild-flavoured flesh, quick to mature, good resistance to bolting.
- 'Blusta' – purple-blue, resistant against becoming woody, sweet nutty flavour.
- 'Purple Danube' – sweet flavour, very good raw, does not become woody quickly.

White varieties:
- 'Grand Duke' – rather big bulbs, quick to mature.
- 'Early White Vienna' – dwarf, light green.

LEEKS

Allium porrum • Onion family
* • hardy (down to -10°C/14°F) • ☺

The leek is one of the national symbols of Wales, to be worn in the hat on St David's Day, 1 March. It is beautifully easy to grow, and hardy. Recommended especially for beginners.

Leeks are fun to plant out with children, being quite resilient to handling; watering in the seedlings is a satisfying experience for all ages.

Soil and position
- Humus-rich, but not too fussy. Soil should not be waterlogged or compacted.
- Sunny if possible, but will tolerate slight shade.
- Dig in half-rotted compost or half-rotted manure in autumn; lime.
- Rake in organic chicken manure pellets, 50g per sq. m/1½ oz per sq. yd, 1–2 weeks before planting.

Sowing, planting and spacing
- Sow thinly into a nursery bed, 1cm/½in deep, March–May.
- Transplant when they are 20cm/8in long, around June–July. Traditionally they should be 'the size of a pencil' but a little thinner will do.
- Replant using a dibber (or a fattish stick) to make a hole about 10cm/4in deep. Drop one seedling into each hole. Do not push the soil back over the root, but water the hole so that the soil is washed back around the seedling, burying the root in soil. When planted deep they will have substantial blanched white stalks when you come to harvest them.
- 15–20cm/6–9in between plants and rows.
- Seeds can be stored for up to 3 years.

Aftercare
- Hoe if necessary between the rows.
- Pull up soil around the stems with a hoe if you feel like being a perfectionist.

Companion planting
- With brassicas, as they have similar feeding requirements and leeks deter brassica pests with their scent.
- Not next to other plants of the onion family because they can infect each other with rust.

Problems
- Bolting – thick flower stems appear amongst the leaves. Remove stem and eat as soon as possible. Try a bolt-resistant variety next year.
- Rust – orange spots on leaves. Remove and destroy diseased leaves. Grow elsewhere next year.

Harvesting and uses
- Pick as necessary once they reach a decent size.
- Will stand through winter, as frost-hardy.
- By spring they will be threatening to flower, so pick before they start to produce flower stems.
- Soups, stir-fries, bakes.

Varieties
- 'Bleu de Solaise' – dark blue leaves, turning darker after frost. Attractive and tasty; happily stands over winter.
- 'Giant Musselburgh' ('American Flag') – very popular, reliable, thick stems, mid-season.
- 'Lincoln' – giant type that can be harvested early as a baby leek.
- 'Lyon Prize-taker' – dark green leaves, mild flavour, early.
- 'Swiss Giant Jolant' – medium to dark green, bolt- and rust-resistant, mid-season. AGM.

LETTUCE

Latuca sativa • Daisy family
* for cut-and-come-again • ** for
heads • 🪴 • half-hardy

Lettuces can be grown in two ways: as full-sized lettuces with heads or as leaves to cut-and-come-again. Grown as the latter, lettuce is amongst the easiest vegetables to grow, and particularly handy for small gardens.

Lettuces come in different leaf types and shades. They are very decorative, both in your garden and on your plate, and perfect for growing in containers, even on a windowsill. So there should be no need to buy chlorine-washed salad bags from the supermarket any more.

You do not have to fit lettuces into the crop rotation; they are perfect for intercropping between slower-growing plants.

Soil and position
- Sunny position, but prefers light shade in summer.
- Humus-rich, moisture-retentive soil – tends to bolt when too dry.
- Before planting, rake in a thin layer of compost.

Sowing, planting and spacing
Sow from February inside, in a cold frame or on a cool windowsill, at about 10–15°C/50-60°F. Outside from late March to July; August to September for autumn and winter varieties.
- For cut-and-come-again crops, sow thinly in rows.
- For heads, sow a small number of plants every 2 weeks – this should give you a steady supply throughout the season.
- Seed germination can be a bit erratic in hot weather.
- Plant out from mid-March, with a sheet of fleece or cover cloth to hand until the last frosts are over.
- In mild areas, plant winter varieties in September in a cold

WHAT IS 'CUT-AND-COME-AGAIN'?
This is a technique where you pick or cut the leaves of a plant instead of a whole head. The plant regenerates quickly and you can pick a few times from the same plant.

frame or protect them with cloches or fleece or cover cloth.
- Heads: 30cm/12in between plants, cut-and-come-again: 15cm/6in between rows.
- Seed can be stored for up to 3 years.

Aftercare
- Lettuces need sufficient water while they are growing. Water in the morning so that the leaves can dry off through the day and they will be less susceptible to fungi; try to water the roots, not the leaves.
- There is no need for extra feeding – too much nitrogen makes the leaves bitter.
- In autumn, as long as there are only light frosts, you can cover them with fleece or cover cloth.

Companion planting
- Chervil is said to deter snails, mildew and aphids from lettuces.
- Lettuces should deter flea beetles from brassicas.
- Lettuces are happy with almost every other plant, except parsley and celeriac (the heads won't form as well), and cucumbers because they share diseases.

Problems
- Slugs – the major problem. Surround plants with a wide strip of used coffee grounds.
- Aphids.
- Bolting – avoid by regular watering and choosing varieties which are appropriate for the time of year.
- Downy mildew – prevent by planting spaciously enough and not watering on the leaves.
- Birds picking the edges of leaves. Apparently red varieties are less susceptible.

Harvesting and uses
- When harvesting leaf lettuce there are two schools of thought: pinch off outer leaves continuously, leaving 3–4 small leaves in the centre of the plant. Or more radical: wait until the plants are about 10–15 cm/4–6in high and chop all leaves off with scissors. The remaining stumps should be at least 2.5cm/1in high. After a

LOTS OF DIFFERENT LETTUCES . . .
Butterhead or Boston lettuce These are the light green ones with tender and floppy leaves which form round heads. The epitome of spring.

Loose leaf Make heads like the butterheads, but not as tightly packed. Can also be grown as a cut-and-come-again crop.

Iceberg Crisp lettuces with large hearts; slower to mature and to bolt, so better in warmer weather.

Batavia or escarole Loose leaf; texture of the leaves is somewhere between butterheads and icebergs, and they can also have reddish leaves. Quite hardy.

Cos/romaine Large, longish heads with crispy leaves. Since the leaves are coarser, they are not as susceptible to mildew in the wet as the soft leaves of butterheads.

Semi-cos Like cos, but the leaves are more tender.

Mesclun or misticanza Mixture of salad leaves of different types, usually bought as ready-made seed mix. Grown as cut-and-come-again crop.

few weeks the plants should have reached the original size again.
- For heads there is only a short span of about 1 week between the ideal head and bolting, so be punctual.
- To brighten up a lettuce salad, add oriental leaves, herbs such as mint, chervil, chives, edible flowers (see list on page 202) or baby leaves and micro-greens (see box opposite).
- Wash leaf by leaf – there's nothing like grit or a slug to spoil your appetite. Particularly hard to detect on reddish varieties.

Varieties

With lettuces it is important to choose the right variety for the right time. There is an enormous choice of varieties on the market. Here are some to try.

For spring and summer:
- 'All Year Round' – butterhead, crisp green leaves.
- 'Bijou' – Batavian, dark red, frilled and glossy leaves, AGM.
- 'Little Gem' – well known and one of the best semi-cos varieties, AGM.
- 'Little Leprechaun' – semi-cos, leaves with brownish edges, very reliable, slow to bolt, AGM.
- 'Lollo Rosso' – loose-leaf type, also good as cut-and-come-again crop, frilled leaves, centre of plants green, outer leaves bronze, AGM.
- 'Salad Bowl' – oakleaf type, good for cut-and-come-again, available in green and red, AGM.
- 'Tom Thumb' – butterhead, one of the first ones to harvest, small heads, tender leaves; do not sow later than April.
- 'Webb's Wonderful' – iceberg, slow to bolt in hot weather, sow until end of July.

For autumn and winter (these varieties are especially hardy and withstand temperatures down to –5°C/23°F):
- 'All Year Round' – butterhead, crisp green leaves.
- 'Marvel of Four Seasons' – butterhead, green with red edges, good taste.
- 'Rouge d'Hiver' – semi-cos, bronze red leaves with green veins.

WINTER CROPS WITHOUT A GARDEN

From September, sow a few seeds of winter lettuce (see above) in pots or windowsill containers. These containers can look very pretty if you combine different varieties. Keep them on a light cool windowsill or – weather permitting – outside. This will give you a nice crop of cut-and-come-again lettuce – how big depends on the space available. It will take about 6–8 weeks until your first harvest.

MORE VARIATIONS FOR YOUR SALAD BOWL

Baby leaves are leaves picked when smaller than 5cm/2in.
Micro-greens are basically grown and used like cress. You need only 2cm/1in of vermiculite as growing medium, in a seed tray. Place on a warm, light windowsill, let the seeds germinate and cut the first leaves that develop.

Many different plants can be grown as baby leaves or micro-greens, or to cut-and-come-again, providing different tastes and colours. Here are some to try.

For baby leaves	For micro-greens
Beetroot	Thai basil
Chard	Beetroot 'Bull's Blood'
Red and green mustard	Broccoli
Kale 'Red Russian'	Coriander (cilantro)
Lettuce	Kale
Mibuna	Radish, red-stemmed
Mizuna	Rocket (arugula)
Pak choi	
Rocket (arugula)	
Spinach	

ONIONS

Allium species • Onion family
* from sets • ** from seed • half-hardy
• ☺

This staple in the kitchen, introduced by the Romans, is cheap to buy, but nevertheless very satisfying to grow, and easy too. There is still something about plaiting your own onions and hanging them in the kitchen ready to use that makes you feel very smug about your local food-growing credentials.

Onions can be grown from seed. However, a common shortcut is to grow them from 'sets', which are tiny onions, in mild areas planted traditionally before Christmas on the shortest day of the year, and harvested on the longest. These – unlike seeds – are very satisfying to plant with children because they can see exactly that *this* little onion will grow into *that* big onion.

Soil and position
- Sunny site.
- Well-drained soil.
- Grow after hungry feeders such as brassicas. No fertilizer needed.

Sowing, planting and spacing
- Seeds and sets: 30cm/12in between rows, 10cm/4in between plants.

Sets:
- Plant in autumn or early spring.
- Plant each with the tip sticking out. The tips are very tempting for birds, who do not even eat them but just yank them out, so net for the first few weeks. As they grow, the roots can push them out of the soil, so keep an eye on them and push them back in if necessary.

Seeds:
- Sow in modules under glass from February or directly from late February to early April, depending on your climate.
- Sow 1cm/½in deep. Thin as they grow and eat the thinnings.

> '*Mine eyes smell onions: I shall weep anon.*'
> William Shakespeare,
> *All's Well That Ends Well*

Aftercare
- Hoe carefully between the rows to keep down competition from weeds.
- Water if very dry, but try not to wet the leaves.

Companion planting
- Carrots: the onion smell distracts carrot fly from the carrots.
- Parsley to distract onion flies.

Problems
- Bolting – if the onions throw up thick flower stems, snap them off. If the soil was too rich when they were planted, this may have encouraged them to bolt.
- Downy mildew. Choose a better-drained spot next year.
- Onion fly – maggots in the base. Next time grow from sets rather than seed.
- White rot – yellow foliage, rotten fluffy white base. Sadly, give up growing onions in that area for a decade.
- Rust. A sprinkling of wood ash worked gently into the soil between the bulbs in February may help; keep plants well watered.

Harvesting and uses
- When the foliage begins to turn yellow and die down, the plants are nearly ready. Traditionally gardeners used to bend the tops over, but this prevents the bulb maturing properly.

SETS OR SEED?

Sets:
- Easier to plant.
- More satisfying with children.
- Good for areas with mild winters (planted in autumn) or short growing seasons (planted in spring).
- 5 months to maturity.

Seeds:
- Cheaper and more varieties available.
- Have less tendency to bolt.
- Store better.
- 6 months to maturity.

- Harvest on a dry day and spread them out to dry completely. In theory this is done outside on wire trays for a week, but in the real world this ends up being on newspaper in a corner of the kitchen.
- Set aside any bulbs that were about to flower (check for thick hard necks and/or a flower stem) or are damaged in any way for use as soon as possible.
- When onions are sliced they release a sulphur compound that makes eyes weep but turns into sulphuric acid when it comes into contact with water. Slicing onions under cold running water dilutes the compound but is not very practical. Chilling the onion in the fridge for an hour before slicing it may help to mitigate the weeping.

Storage

- Autumn-planted sets keep for only a few months. Spring-sown or -planted onions store better, for 6–9 months.
- Dried onions can be plaited (braided) together and hung until used. This allows air to circulate and prevents rotting. This sounds easier than it is, and can involve much swearing and dextrous manipulation. Any practice you can get plaiting small restless children's hair beforehand will stand you in good stead.
- An alternative to traditional plaiting: using a central string, tie two onions on to the lower end, winding the leaves around the string with each bulb resting on the one below. Continue tying the bulbs on up the string. At the top, tie a knot and hang to dry.
- Do not store near potatoes, as they cause each other to rot faster.

Varieties
White and yellow

Some of these are usually available either as seeds or as sets; some come in both forms.

For sowing or planting in spring (Allium cepa):
- 'Hercules' F1 – almost round, but slightly elongated bulbs, golden-brown skin. Slow to bolt. Good storage. AGM.
- 'Sturon' – globe-shaped, yellow-brown, slow to bolt, reliable, AGM.
- 'Walla Walla Sweet Yellow' – light brown with white flesh.
- 'White Sweet Spanish' – bright white.

For planting in autumn (some varieties of A. cepa and the Japanese onion, A. fistulosum):
- 'Radar' – mild taste, good yields.
- 'Senshyu Semi-Globe Yellow' – dark yellow skin.
- 'Swift' – very early, resistant to bolting.

Red

Red varieties tend not to store well, but taste and look lovely, especially in salads.

For planting in spring:
- 'Hyred' F1 – round red globes, late, improved storage.

- 'Red Baron' – attractive purple-red, good colour inside, spring, seeds and sets, AGM.

For planting in autumn:
- 'Electric' – globe-shaped bulbs.

RELATIVES
GARLIC (*Allium sativum*)

Credited with antiseptic and antifungal properties, and beneficial for the cardiovascular system, garlic is recognized as a staple that most kitchens will need in quantity. It is easy to grow and there are more varieties available for growing than you can buy in the supermarket. Chew parsley to mask the smell on the breath. Children can easily help planting the cloves.

- Plant in similar position to onions. Garlic must have a period of cold to break its dormancy, so plant preferably in September/October, or in spring if necessary. Buy fresh cloves at the garden centre or by mail order. Do not use supermarket garlic, as it will probably have been grown somewhere warmer and will not be suitable. It may also harbour viruses.
- Plant individual cloves (peel off the papery skin and break up a bulb into separate slices), making sure the flat plate is downwards, the point upwards.
- 2.5cm/1in deep, with soil the depth of the clove above it.
- 15cm/6in between plants, 30cm/1ft between rows.

Varieties

There are two types, hardneck and softneck. Softnecks store better but the taste is less pronounced; hardnecks produce a tough flower stalk and are rarely found in supermarkets.

Hardneck or 'gourmet garlics':
- 'Early Wight' – early (May/June), white cloves with purple splodges. Use fresh, but keeps for a few months.
- 'Purple Wight' – early, good flavour. Does not store well.

Softneck:
- 'Albigensian Wight' – early (June), prefers autumn planting, purple-tinged cloves, good flavour. Stores well.
- 'White Pearl' – July/August, prefers autumn planting, pink-

> *'There are five elements: earth, air, fire, water and garlic.'*
> Louis Diat

tinged white cloves, good flavour.
- 'Thermidrome' – large white cloves, good flavour, poor storage.
- 'Solent Wight' – mild flavour, large bulbs, good storage.

ELEPHANT GARLIC (*Allium ampeloprasum*)

Recently popular. Satisfying huge cloves, very mild. Excellent for baking and roasting.

SHALLOTS (*Allium cepa aggregatum*)

A more tender, delicately flavoured alternative to onions. Like onions, shallots are grown from sets, planted in winter, or failing that, in spring, early to mid-March, for a slightly smaller harvest. However, whereas each little onion bulb matures into a big fat onion, each shallot set magically multiplies into a bunch of about ten shallots. Otherwise cultivation is similar to that of onions: plant each shallot up to the shoulders,

15–20cm/6–8in apart. Harvest in June/July when leaves start to turn yellow. Allow to dry and then store in a cool dark place for up to several months. Can also be grown in containers, one shallot per 15cm/6in pot.

Varieties
- 'Gray' – purplish-white flesh, strong distinctive flavour.
- 'Jermor' – copper-skinned, with pink flesh, good flavour, long shape, AGM.
- 'Pikant' – reddish-brown skins. Good flavour and storage. AGM.

SPRING OR SALAD ONIONS (SCALLIONS) (hybrid of *A. fistulosum* and *A. cepa*)
JAPANESE BUNCHING ONIONS (*A. fistulosum*)

Japanese varieties are slightly stronger in flavour than spring onions, do not produce bulbs and are usable sooner, but otherwise are grown in the same way.

Soil and position
- Sunny site.
- Well-drained soil.

Sowing, planting and spacing
- From March, sow thinly (1cm/½in) apart. If seedlings are closer together, they will form little bunches of onions that are smaller but even tastier. 30cm/1ft between rows.
- For successional harvesting, sow every few weeks.
- Can be grown as catch or marker crops (see below). For instance, could be sown early into space destined for squashes, or late into space vacated by early potatoes.
- From August, sow onions for the following spring, using winter varieties.

Harvesting and uses
- When about the size of a pencil. If they are left to become too old they coarsen in taste and texture, and may go to seed, especially in hot weather.

Problems
- Very few.

Varieties
Spring and salad:
- 'White Lisbon' – probably the most popular; medium-green leaves with good white blanched stem. Recommended for early and successional sowing. AGM.
- 'Deep Purple' – bright green leaves, purple bases all the way through, AGM.

Overwintering:
- 'Guardsman' F1 – very vigorous, AGM.
- 'Ramrod' – later crops, good white blanched stem, AGM.
- 'Winter White Bunching' – dark green leaves, AGM.

Japanese bunching:
- 'Laser' – no bulbing, white, very straight, AGM.
- 'Summer Isle' – early maturing, good flavour, AGM.
- 'Ishikura' – no bulbing, white stalks, very good flavour. Can overwinter. AGM.

CHIVES AND WELSH ONIONS
See pages 190 and 199.

> *'Shallots are for babies; onions are for men; garlic is for heroes.'*
> Author unknown

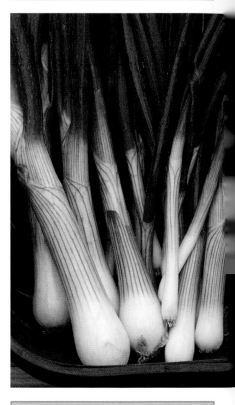

> *'The onion being eaten, yea though it be boyled, causeth head-ache, hurteth the eyes, and maketh a man dimme sighted, dulleth the senses, ingendreth windinesse, and provoketh overmuch sleepe, especially being eaten raw.'*
> John Gerard, *Herball or General Historie of Plantes*, 1597

MARKER CROPS
A vegetable that matures very fast and can be grown in the same place as a slower-maturing, or germinating, crop, to show where the line is. For instance, parsnips germinate slowly, so radishes are often sown in the same line. By the time the radishes are ready to eat, the parsnip seedlings will be revealed.

ORIENTAL LEAVES (SALAD GREENS)

Brassica species • Cabbage family
* • 🪴 • half-hardy • ☺

Oriental leaves became popular in the 1990s, and understandably so. Grown as cut-and-come-again crops (see page 136), these brassicas are some of the easiest vegetables to grow, and they make a tasty addition to stir-fries, salads and sandwiches.

If you live in an area with mild winters and plan well, you can harvest them for almost the whole year.

Oriental leaves are brilliant for gardening with children, because they germinate quickly. You could grow some seeds on the windowsill and your child could pick the leaves for their school sandwich – they are as easy to grow as cress, but much tastier and more varied.

Soil and position
- Sunny position; good, well-drained garden soil.
- Rake in a thin layer of compost before planting; alternatively rake in organic chicken manure pellets, 50g per sq. m/1½oz per sq. yd 1–2 weeks before planting.
- Oriental leaves withstand temperatures down to –5°C/23°F; grow over winter in a cold frame or cover with fleece or cover cloth.

Sowing, planting and spacing
- Sow from mid-March in modules and plant out when large enough to resist flea beetles.
- Sow *in situ* in July and August, when there are fewer flea beetles around.
- For winter crops in mild areas, sow in September and October (possibly with protection).
- Sow directly in rows, thinly, 2cm/½in deep. If you sow sparsely enough, there should be no need to thin.
- Sow in succession, every 2 weeks.
- 30cm/1ft between rows.
- Seeds can be stored for up to 4 years.

Aftercare
- Water regularly.
- If you are growing them over winter, remove any decaying or mouldy leaves regularly to prevent diseases spreading.
- Have some fleece or cover cloth close to hand – either against flea beetle attacks in spring or against cold spells in winter.

Companion planting
- Grow between lettuces and spinach to distract flea beetles, which do not like these.

Problems
- Slugs.
- Flea beetles in spring and early summer; see page 126.

Harvesting and uses
- Start harvesting when the plants are small, but take only a few leaves per plant, so that the plants can recover and produce more leaves.

Varieties
You can buy individual species of oriental brassicas, such as those listed here, but they are often sold as mixtures with names such as 'Oriental Mustards' or 'Salad Leaves Stir Fry Mixed'.
- Komatsuna 'Tendergreen' (*Brassica rapa* var. *komatsuna*) – can be used like spinach.
- Mibuna (*B. rapa* var. *nipposinica*) – long thin leaves, mustardy flavour.
- Mizuna (*B. rapa* var. *nipposinica*) – lacy leaves, similar in flavour to mibuna, but milder.
- Red mustard (*B. juncea*) – reddish green leaves, pick only small leaves – the bigger, the more peppery.
- Red mustard 'Red Frills' (*B. juncea*) – dark red leaves, similar shape to mizuna.

PAK CHOI (BOK CHOY)

Brassica rapa var. *chinensis*
Cabbage family
* • 🌱 • half-hardy annual

A fast-growing type of cabbage originally from the warmer regions of China. It is easy to grow, tasty and healthy, and the plants are very decorative, with wide white or green stems. The latest introduction has purple leaves, and is very pretty in the autumn garden. Pak choi leaves have a slightly mustard flavour and contain many essential minerals.

Soil and position
- Sunny position.
- Good fertile soil with organic matter added.
- Tolerates light frost.
- Rake in a thin layer of well-rotted compost or well-rotted manure; alternatively rake in organic chicken manure pellets, 50g per sq. m/2oz per sq. yd, 1–2 weeks before planting.

Sowing, planting and spacing
- First sowings: early to mid-spring under glass in modules or little pots; plant out in late spring/early summer.
- Best sown directly in late summer, when they are less prone to bolt. 2cm/1in deep. Last sowing 6 weeks before the first frosts are expected.
- 15cm/6in between plants when grown for baby leaves, 30cm/1ft when grown for heads; 30cm/1ft between rows.

Aftercare
- Thin out directly sown plants until you reach the desired spacing; eat the thinnings.
- Keep well watered or else it may bolt.
- Protect with fleece or cover cloth when it begins to get cold.

Companion planting
- Grow between lettuces and spinach to distract flea beetles.

Problems
- Overcrowding or drought cause checks to growth and bolting.
- Snails and slugs love them.
- Protect with netting if your local pigeons look hungry.

Harvesting and uses
- Pick leaves as required and use immediately.
- Or cut off the whole head about 3cm/1in above the ground, since it will re-sprout.
- Young leaves for stir-fries, noodles, soups and salads. Stir-fry with ginger and garlic. Cook stalks slightly longer than leaves.
- See recipe on page 61.

Varieties
There are white-stemmed varieties and green-stemmed.
- 'Joi Choi' F1 – white stem, slight resistance to bolting.
- 'Choko' F1 – green stem, slow bolting.
- 'Pak Choy Purple' F1 – new introduction adding a touch of interesting colour.

PARSNIPS

Pastinaca sativa • Parsley family
* (apart from germination) •
half-hardy annual

Closely related to the carrot – though even healthier, containing more fibre and potassium – parsnips are easy to grow and very tasty roasted. It is essential to buy new fresh seeds each year – more so than for any other crop. Incidentally, the Russian for parsnip is Pasternak . . .

Soil and position
- Sun or partial shade.
- Sandy, loamy soils are ideal, preferably manured for a previous crop. Stony soils are not suitable, since roots will fork if they meet a stone.
- On new ground, spread a thin layer of well-rotted compost or fertilize with 75g per sq. m/2½oz per sq. yd of blood, fish and bone.

Sowing, planting and spacing
- Sow outside in March.
- Germination rate unreliable and potentially slow. Sow a marker row of carrots or lettuce along the same row to remind you where they are while you wait.
- Sow 1cm/½in deep. Thin to 15cm/6in between plants. Hates being transplanted, so discard thinnings and do not try growing in modules or trays.
- 30cm/1ft between rows.

Aftercare
- Hoe carefully between rows.
- Only water in case of prolonged drought.

Companion planting
- Plant lettuces or spinach between parsnip rows to use the space, as parsnips develop very slowly.

Problems
- Shares some problems with carrots (see page 128).
- Parsnip canker – goes black and rotten around the crown. Discard affected plants. Next year lime soil in winter and sow resistant variety.

Harvesting and uses
- In late autumn or winter after the first frost, when foliage begins to die down.
- Lift as required; leave the rest in the ground until needed, or until end of February before they start to re-grow.
- Roasted, boiled and mashed with sprinkle of nutmeg.
- Can be frozen, once cleaned, chopped and then blanched.
- See recipe on page 57.

> *'Fine words butter
> no parsnips.'*
> Traditional saying

Varieties
- 'Cobham Improved Marrow' – smooth skin, canker resistant, AGM.
- 'Gladiator' F1 – smooth skin, good yield, AGM.
- 'Tender and True' – long roots, some canker resistance, AGM.

PEAS

Pisum sativum • Legume family
*** • half-hardy • ☺

Peas are one of the most popular of vegetables, although eating 'green peas', in other words fresh peas, only became popular in the seventeenth century. Louis XIV, creator of one of the largest and most stylish vegetable gardens in the world at Versailles, was obsessed with peas, regularly over-eating them.

They are a great crop to sow with children, because the seeds are large enough to handle easily, and they look similar enough to the finished crop for children to understand exactly what they are sowing.

Soil and position
- Sunny.
- Good garden soil, preferably manured for a previous crop.
- On new ground, spread a thin layer of well-rotted compost or fertilize with 75g per sq m/2½ oz per sq. yd of blood, fish and bone.

Sowing, planting and spacing
- From February (depending on your climate) to mid-July. In mild areas sow in October to overwinter.
- Make a flat-bottomed drill about 15cm/6in wide, 5cm/2in deep, and sow seeds zigzag in two rows every 9cm/3in.
- Place pea sticks – irregular twiggy sticks – along the rows to support the seedlings.
- A support of bamboo poles and/ or netting will help taller peas.
- Distance between rows: as much space as the plants are to be high. So for 1m/3ft peas, for instance, leave 1m/3ft between rows.
- Seeds can be stored for up to 2 years.

Aftercare
- Protect young plants against birds with netting.
- Keep well watered.
- Mulch with compost in early summer to help retain moisture.
- Peas store nitrogen in their roots, which they collect from the air. After harvesting leave the roots in the soil and dig them in; alternatively add them to the compost heap.

Problems
- Mildews – downy and powdery. Powdery is particularly prevalent in dry summers. Peas can still be eaten, even when the plant is affected, but discard or burn the plant as soon as the peas are picked.
- Pea moth – little green caterpillars in the peas. You can still eat the unaffected peas, but the whole experience is unnerving. Throw out the whole crop.

Harvesting and uses
- The lower pods mature earlier, so pick them first. Hold on to the plant while you pick the pod to avoid damaging it. Child pickers need this to be explained or else they may rip out the whole plant.
- Pick pods regularly; if pods are left on the plant, it will stop producing more.
- See recipe on page 80.
- Frozen peas are nutritionally the same as fresh ones, so freeze any surplus immediately after picking. Boil for 1½ minutes, and then run them quickly under a cold tap. Let them dry, spread them out on a baking tray and freeze; then bag them up into freezer bags or plastic containers.

Varieties
Peas can be divided into three main types:

Classic/standard shelling peas
The old-fashioned 'princess and the pea' type of pea: round and green. These are divided into round peas and wrinkled varieties, which just refers to the state of the pea when dried as a seed (in other words this is completely irrelevant if you will be eating the pea fresh).
First earlies, sow in October or February onwards:
- 'Feltham First' – 45cm/18in tall. Very early crops, short sturdy plants. Pods about 10cm/4in long.
- 'Kelvedon Wonder' – 45cm/18in. Heavy cropper, small peas, mildew resistant, AGM.

> 'We lived very simply – but with all the essentials of life well understood and provided for – hot baths, cold champagne, new peas and old brandy.'
> Winston Churchill

Second earlies, sow end of March onwards:
- 'Hurst Green Shaft' – 75cm/30in. Reliable, heavy cropper, sweet flavour, mildew resistant, AGM.
- 'Little Marvel' – 45cm/18in. May need cloche for early sowings. AGM.

Maincrop, sow mid-April onwards:
- 'Rondo' – 60–75cm/24–30in. Heavy cropper, plump peas, AGM.
- 'Senator' – 75cm/30in, heavy cropper, good flavour.

Mangetout
Eat the whole pod early, when it is about 7cm/3in long, embryo peas and all, while pods are still flat.
- 'Oregon Sugar Pod' – 1m/39in tall. Sweet flavour, resistant to powdery mildew. Sow in succession, March–June. AGM.

Sugar snaps
Eat the whole pod and the developed pea within.
- 'Delikett' – 75cm/30in tall. Pick young as sugar snap or mature as normal pea. AGM.
- 'Sugar Ann' – 75cm/30in. Compact bushes, requiring minimal staking. Very sweet pods. AGM.

PEPPERS, SWEET (CAPSICUM/ BELL) AND CHILLI

Capsicum species
Nightshade family
** • 🪴 • tender

Sweet peppers – bell peppers in the United States – are used mostly as a salad or cooking vegetable, and also as a dried spice, called paprika.

Chilli peppers are eaten raw or dried to spice up dishes. The hotness factor is measured in Scoville Heat Units (SHU) with big sweet peppers at 0 and the hottest pepper, the Ghost Chilli, coming in at 1,001,304.

Peppers of both kinds are very decorative and easy to grow outdoors in milder climates, as long as you can start them off indoors. Further north, they should be grown in containers and may need to be brought back into protection at the end of the season to ripen fully.

Soil and position
- Sunny position, south-facing wall or well-protected patio.
- Hungry feeder, so dig in half-rotted compost or well-rotted manure a few months before planting.
- Alternatively plant each plant with two trowels of well-rotted compost or manure or rake 100g per sq. m/3oz per sq. yd of blood, fish and bone into the bed.

Sowing, planting and spacing
- Sow seeds on a warm windowsill in spring (March), into modules or a seed tray on the windowsill. Do not start too early. Packet instructions often tell you to start in late winter or early spring, but then your plants will be too lanky before you can plant them out.
- Chilli pepper seeds are the peppery part, so do not let children help sow them, and use gloves or a pencil point. Immediately afterwards wash your hands and do not touch your eyes.
- Germination time is longer than usual, 2–3 weeks, so do not despair if nothing appears at first.
- Transplant seedlings when large enough to handle into 9cm/3½in pots. Once the roots have filled the pot, transplant into a larger container.
- Seeds can be stored for up to 5 years.

Aftercare
- Pinch out when 16–20cm/6–8in tall.
- Once all risk of frost has passed, plant out in the garden in a warm sheltered spot, 45cm/18in between plants and rows, or keep outside in big pots.
- Stake for support.
- Mulch with half-rotted compost or well-rotted manure.
- Once fruits appear, feed with tomato food each week. Keep well watered, especially if in containers.

Harvesting and uses
- August to October when green, or left on the bush to turn yellow or red. They will taste sweeter or hotter depending on which kind of pepper they are.
- Sweet peppers: fresh in salads, ratatouille, stuffed peppers, ketchup (see recipe on page 100).
- Chilli peppers: for spice and decoration.
- If you want to douse the flames in your mouth, eat bread, rice or yoghurt; water doesn't help.
- Chilli peppers can be dried by hanging them on a string.

Varieties
Sweet peppers
- 'Big Banana' F1 – 25cm/10in long, scarlet. Very crisp and juicy, good for eating raw.
- 'Jupiter' – 12cm/ 4½in long, sweet, high-yielding, early.
- 'Topgirl' – compact bush, 50cm/20in high, early crop of little fat red peppers. Good for stuffing and salads.

Chilli peppers
These vary in hotness, size (of fruit and bush) and colour of fruit, including black, red, purple, yellow, orange and green.

Moderately hot:
- 'Hungarian Hot Wax' – largeish, conical, tapering fruits, red and yellow, easy and reliable, AGM.

Hot:
- 'Jalapeno Summer Heat' F1 hybrid – early ripening, tapered fruit, stripey scars on the skin, AGM.

Very hot – cayenne:
- 'Albertos Locoto' or 'Rocoto Pepper' – spreading bush, purple flowers, slightly furry leaves.
- 'Demon Red' – small attractive plants, for a windowsill or containers. Classic elongated chilli pepper shape, red. Recommended for Thai cooking. AGM.

Extremely hot:
- 'Lemon Drop' – good-size bush (60cm/24in), bright yellow, citrus taste. Very early and productive.
- 'Prairie Fire' – short spreading plant, with hundreds of tiny colourful chilli peppers. AGM.
- 'Tabasco' – used to make the famous hot sauce. Yellow-green classic-shaped chilli peppers.
- 'Thai Dragon' – very long (9cm/3½in) red fruits. Prolific cropper, but plants need staking. AGM.
- 'Pretty in Purple' – small bush (25cm/10in) covered in small bright purple chilli peppers, ripening to red and yellow.

POTATOES

Solanum tuberosum
Nightshade family
** • 🌿 • tender • ☺

The potato originated in South America and the first recorded usage of it in Europe dates from 1573. It survived a rumour that it caused leprosy, and today average annual US consumption stands at some 64kg/142lb per person. In recent years potatoes have received a bad press, but their nutritional (and calorific) value all depends on how you serve them.

They are often chosen as a soil-clearing crop, the first crop to go in a patch that has been problematic for weeds, leaving pleasantly loose soil for following crops. This is partly because potatoes are tough, but mainly because in planting them and then digging them up you do a lot of weed-clearing work – sadly not because they magically clear the weeds.

There is something deeply satisfying about harvesting – lifting - potatoes. Searching through the soil looking for potato treasure is one of the most fun things that children can do in the garden.

Soil and position
* Sunny.
* Humus-rich, deeply dug and well-drained soil.
* Dig in half-rotted compost or half-rotted manure in winter.
* Alternatively work in a good layer of well-rotted compost or well-rotted manure before planting. Sprinkling seaweed meal into the trenches makes potatoes extra happy (100g per sq. m/3½oz per sq. yd).

Buying seed potatoes
* On sale around January in garden centres, or by mail order. Several specialist nurseries offer dozens of varieties via the Internet.
* Do not grow any old potatoes from the supermarket: buy seed potatoes that are certified free of blight.
* Set them out in an egg-box or tray with their eyes – the little dots that will become shoots – upwards. Leave them in a cool light place

for the eyes to start shooting. This is called 'chitting', a sort of pre-sprouting.

Sowing, planting and spacing
* Plant out traditionally after St Patrick's Day in mid-March.
* If you are not superstitious and do not live too far north, earlies could go in at the end of February.
* The leaves are susceptible to frost damage, so you must time planting so that the potato can be growing underground but the leaves won't emerge too far until the risk of frost has receded.
* Dig a trench about 15cm/6in deep and put a layer of well-rotted compost along the bottom. Place your potatoes along the trench, about 10cm/4in deep, little sprouted leaves facing upwards, each tuber 30cm/12in apart from the next.
* Before you cover your trench, put a stick at each end, so that you know where they are. Then cover the trench.
* 30cm/1ft between plants, 75cm/30in between rows.

Aftercare
* As the first leaves appear, earth them up: scrape the soil from between the rows into ridges to cover most of the plants except the tips of the leaves, so that you have a triangular heaped row with a valley between each row. This prevents the potato tubers from growing too near the sun, and therefore turning green.
* Weed if infested; water (in the valleys) if it is exceptionally dry.

Companion planting
* Do not plant potatoes near your tomatoes. Being from the same

> '*My favourite bit of all was digging up the potatoes because digging up the soil was the best thing.*'
> Alya, aged seven

TO CHIT OR NOT TO CHIT
There is a school of thought that says you need not bother chitting and this could well be true. But since potatoes may be offered for sale in January and February, and you can't plant them out until around March, you might as well.

If you have a potato with eyes going both up and down, choose whichever end seems most hopeful. If you got it wrong and the bottom ones shoot more, you can always turn the potato the other way up. Leaving them in a cool light place is important: you are aiming for little fat greenish buds, not the etiolated white string that you might get growing from your potatoes left too long in a dark cupboard.

family, they suffer from the same diseases, so may infect one another.

Problems
* Green potatoes. If the potatoes get too close to the surface and turn green they will become poisonous. Always make sure you mound up the plants as they grow.
* Potato scab. Can be a problem in soils with a pH greater than 5.5. Choose resistant varieties.
* Blight (*Phytophthora infestans*) – brown or pale spots on the foliage, usually towards the end of the season, responsible for the Irish potato famine of 1845. Remove infected foliage immediately and

do not add it to your compost – burn or discard. The potatoes should still be OK underground, as long as less than 75 per cent of the leaves were infected. Choose resistant varieties.

- Volunteer potatoes. These are the ones you missed, but they'll be back next year. Try to clear the bed properly, because these may well harbour disease for next year.
- Crop rotation is a must to avoid potato diseases. Never plant in the same place as last year; leave a 3-year gap.

Harvesting and uses

- Harvest on a dry day, and leave them in the sun for a couple of hours to dry out as you dig them up.
- When you are lifting them, be very careful not to spear them on the fork.
- Store them in a cool dark place, ideally at 6–9°C/43–48°F. Too cold

and the starch turns to sugar, too warm and they start to sprout. They do not store well with apples.

Varieties

As well as having different ripening periods, potatoes come in different textures – waxy for salads, floury for mash, creamy for taste – for different purposes: roasting, frying, baking. Lots of exciting choices to make.

- 'All Blue – deep blue skin and blue flesh, fine flavour, good keeper, midseason.
- 'Bintje' – yellow flesh, excellent

texture and flavour, drought resistant, late season.

- 'Charlotte' – slug resistant. Hot or as a salad. Lovely waxy nutty taste. Very popular potato, extra early.
- 'Fingerling' – yellow-fleshed salad potato, delicious fried or boiled, late season.
- 'Irish Cobbler' – said to be named for an Irish shoemaker from New Jersey. White flesh, good for boiling or baking, very high yields, not good for storing, early.
- 'German Butterball' – yellow-fleshed all-purpose potato with excellent flavor, late season.
- 'Kennebec' – smooth white skin, smooth-textured white flesh, long-keeping all-purpose potato, especially good for boiling, disease resistant, midseason to late.
- 'Norland' – red skin, fine white flesh, excellent cooking quality, heavy yielder, extra early.
- 'Pontiac' – thin reddish skin, crisp white flesh, does particularly well in heavy soils, excellent keeper, late season.
- 'Russet Burbank' – one of the best known varieties, an Idaho baking type with heavy brown skin and white flesh, bred by the American horticulturist Luther Burbank in 1874. Late season.
- 'Russian Banana' – small banana-shaped tubers with buff-yellow skin and light yellow flesh, waxy texture, good for salads, stores well, developed in the Baltic

region. Midseason.

- 'Yellow Finn' – yellow flesh, tubers shaped like a dumpling, delicious flavour, good for boiling or baking, early to midseason.
- 'Yukon Gold' – extremely popular, yellow flesh, very high yielder, good for storage, early.

PUMPKINS AND SQUASHES

Cucurbis species • Cucumber family
* • tender • ☺

Pumpkins and squashes are easy and satisfying to grow. Anything that can grow from a seed to a massive great vegetable within a very few months with nothing but the addition of water and muck has a great deal going for it.

A bright orange pumpkin is the absolute image of autumn, and the plants are one of the coolest things to grow, as well as providing a Hallowe'en fright and a tasty and healthy soup. Plant one seedling and within a few weeks a plant with enormous leaves will be rambling through your garden (if you let it), producing fruits which can weigh more than your children.

The seeds are large and easy for small hands to sow, and the speed of growth is encouraging for beginners and experts alike.

Soil and position
- Sunny, warm, protected from strong winds.
- Well-drained soil, rich in humus and nutrients.
- Hungry feeder, so dig in half-rotted compost or well-rotted manure a few months before planting.
- Alternatively plant each seedling with two trowels of well-rotted compost or manure or rake 150g per sq. m/5 oz per sq. yd of blood, fish and bone into the bed.

Sowing, planting and spacing
- Sow indoors: late April. Outdoors: late May or early June. In colder areas cover seeds/seedlings with cloches for a few weeks.
- Place seeds edgeways 2cm/1in deep.
- Germination time: 5–8 days.
- Plant out seedlings in late May or early June.
- Growth will be checked if plants become pot bound, so do not delay.
- Build a little wall of soil to form a ridge round the base of each plant to retain water.
- Trailing varieties: 1.2m/4ft between rows and plants.
- Bush varieties: 60cm/24in between rows and plants.
- Life expectancy of stored seed: 6 years.

Aftercare
- Young plants: look out for slugs.
- In summer mulch plants with half-rotted compost or well-rotted manure to retain moisture and provide nutrients.
- Keep well watered, but do not wet the leaves.
- Pinch out the tips of main shoots of trailing varieties when they reach 60cm/2ft long, or else they will put all their energy into length, rather than size of fruit.
- Feed with liquid seaweed if leaves look at all yellowish.
- When squash and pumpkins have formed, lay them gently on an old tile or a plate to keep them off wet soil and prevent rotting and slug damage. Be careful not to damage the stems.

Companion planting
- Any flowers that attract pollinating insects.

Problems
- Powdery mildew – very often on older leaves, but the plant will still continue to crop well until the first frost, so it can be ignored.
- Virus infection – the plant is stunted and fails to produce any fruit. Dig it out promptly and bin.

Harvesting and uses
- Harvest summer squashes continuously. Cut the stem back to just above the next leaf. Make a clean cut to protect plant against infection.
- Harvest winter squashes once the skins have had a chance to bake hard in the sun: otherwise they will store poorly over winter.
- All squashes and pumpkins must be harvested before frost, or else you will end up with mush. Do not risk this for the sake of a day or two's more growth.
- Harvest by cutting through the stalk with a sharp knife. Leave a short stem (or 'handle') on the fruit of about 10cm/4in to prevent rotting.

> ### SQUASHES
> The term squash includes an enormous variety of shapes, colours and tastes. The squashes divide into pumpkins and winter and summer squashes.
> **Pumpkins** Basically winter squashes that are bright orange, large and round, probably with a slightly coarser flavour than winter squash. Purists may disagree, but …
> **Summer squashes** are harvested while the skin is still soft and edible. They have pale flesh and should be eaten straight away. Zucchini and marrows belong to this group (see Courgettes/zucchini, page 131).
> **Winter squashes** are harvested when the rind has become tough and hard and offers protection against rotting. The season may be too short in some areas for the sun to bake the skin properly for good storage.

- Store winter squashes in a cool room or shed – they should easily keep until Christmas.

Varieties
As a rule of thumb, the smaller the fruit the sweeter the taste. When space is limited, choose bush instead of trailing varieties. Trailing squash like to climb: varieties with small fruit benefit from scrambling up a wigwam or even a nearby tree or fence. Climbing for larger-fruited varieties spells disaster: they climb while light, and then grow …

Pumpkins
For eating:
- 'Baby Bear' – cute-looking (as the name implies) miniature orange pumpkins. Compact plants, good for cooking with bright orange flesh. Seeds are shell-less and can

be eaten roasted. Trailing; once five fruits have started to form, pinch out the tip. Good storer.

- 'Jack Be Little' – even cuter than 'Baby Bear' (aah …), being only 8cm/3in diameter when fully grown. 8–20 fruits per plant. Good for baking and stuffing. Boil for 5 minutes before baking and the skin will be edible too. Trailing.
- 'Musquée de Provence' – very vigorous, trailing, 2–5 pumpkins each. Large flat green fruit ripen to ochre and can weigh 8–9kg/17–19lb. Very sweet firm flesh, keeps well.

For Hallowe'en and carving:
- 'Aladdin' F1 – bright orange, easy to carve, strong handle. Large (10–20kg/22–44lb). Not bad to eat.
- 'Atlantic Giant' – holds the Canadian and American records for size and weight. Big orange ribbed fruit. If you are going for big, ensure only one per plant.
- 'Ghost Rider' – oval with dark orange skin, hard and ridged, inside yellow-orange. Striking dark green stem. 5–10kg/11–22lb.
- 'Hundredweight' – enormous, heavy fruits, dark orange with paler non-prominent ribs. Over 50kg/110lb.

Summer squash
Pattypan or custard:
- Flat, scallop-edged fruits: available in white ('Polo' F1), orange-yellow ('Sunburst' F1) and green ('Green Buttons' F1). Pick when tiny.

Crook and straight neck:
- 'Early Golden Crookneck' – vigorous bush producing warty club-shaped fruits, buttery flavour.
- 'Summer Crookneck' – knobbly and bulbous with a curved neck. Pick early and use like a courgette. Interesting and attractive addition to the crop.
- 'Tromba d'Albenga' – long greenish-yellow squashes, up to an extraordinary 1m/39in long, but growing curved like a French horn, with a bulb at the end. Can be picked when young, 25cm/10in, and cooked like a courgette, or mature and roasted. Delicate taste, trailing. Can be stored for a short time.

- 'Zephyr F1' – straight-necked, looking like a yellow club that has had its tip dipped in pale green paint. Nutty taste.

Round:
- See Courgettes/zucchini, page 131.

Winter squash
Acorn:
Handy small size; each half is one neat portion. Split in two, scoop out the seeds, fill with butter before baking in the oven. Cutting can be hard work, as the rind is tough.
- 'Table Ace' – green skin, orange flesh.

Butternut:
Usually pear-shaped with beige skin. Nutty moist and tasty flesh; firm but thin rind that can be peeled off with a potato peeler or mandolin.
- 'Barbara' F1 – hybrid bush. Orange flesh but, unusually, stripy green skin.

Hubbard:
Very large, tasty, irregular or teardrop shaped and often warty. Very hard skins that make them tricky to open, but also very good storers. In the United States these are often sold by the slice. Possibly named after a Mrs Elizabeth Hubbard, who first pointed out how good they were in 1857.

- 'Blue Hubbard' – rated very highly for flavour, pale blue-grey, very vigorous.
- 'Red Kuri' – small, teardrop-shaped, very vigorous.
- 'Kabocha' – Orange flesh, stripy rind. Dryer than butternut squash. Taste a bit like sweet potatoes.

One-offs:
- 'Marina di Chioggia' – old Venetian variety. Very thick warty green skin, which also makes it a good keeper, and succulent yellow flesh.
- 'Tivoli' – spaghetti squash/ vegetable spaghetti. Bush or semi-bush type. Boil for 25 minutes and cut in half, remove seeds, scrape out spaghetti-like strands with a fork, season with butter, sea salt and freshly ground pepper.
- 'Turk's Turban' – stunning orange-and-green-striped double squash. Tough to get into and not really worth it when you do, but looks great and stores very well (illustrated on page 2).

RADISHES

Raphanus sativus • Cabbage family
* • 🌠 • half-hardy annual • ☺

Radishes are the classic children's vegetable, the one on which everyone lost their gardening virginity. And the plant does indeed have many advantages, including large cheap seed and usually lots in the packet, and a very quick germination period. They are usually a very satisfying red colour too, although in fact there are little yellow ones, big white ones, black ones, summer ones and winter ones from which to choose.

Soil and position
- Spring crops prefer sun, summer crops prefer dappled shade.
- Prefers fertile and well-drained soil.

Sowing, planting and spacing
- Sow summer radishes *in situ* from March to June every few weeks, and from September to October. Sow winter radishes in July/August.
- Thinly 1cm/½in deep, one seed every 1cm/½in for small varieties. For larger varieties thin to one every 5–10cm/2–4in for winter radishes and one every 15cm/6in for large winter radishes.
- 25cm/10in between rows.
- Seed can be stored for up to 5 years.

Aftercare
- Water regularly if necessary.

Problems
- Woodiness – if grown too long, too hot, too dry.
- Splitting – irregular watering.
- Gone to seed – too long, too hot, too dry.
- Flea leaf beetle, tiny holes in the leaves – see page 126.
- Slugs.

> 'The salad was nice, I wasn't so fond of the radish.'
> Alex, aged eight

Harvesting and uses
- For summer radishes, pull the whole plant up when the shoulders look ready (scrape a bit of soil away and have a peep). Do not leave them in too long or else they will get woody or run to seed.
- For winter radishes, pick when needed. They can stand cold weather, although not a hard frost.
- Winter radishes can be eaten raw, stir-fried or grated in salads.

Varieties
Spring or summer:
- 'Cherry Belle' – round red roots, AGM.
- 'French Breakfast' – long red with a white tip, AGM.
- 'Scarlet Globe' – round, medium-sized, AGM.

> 'The radish was very firery.'
> Katie, aged nine

Winter (Japanese radish, daikon, mooli):
- Mooli 'Monaco Beer' – sow June–September, long (23cm/9in) white crunchy root.
- Mooli 'White Icicle' – sow February–June and September–October. Long white root.
- Chinese radish 'Mantanghong' F1 – tennis-ball sized, green and white, with bright pink inner and white rim. Visually stunning.
- 'Black Spanish' – round or long root radishes, black-skinned with white flesh.

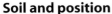

ROCKET (ARUGULA)

Eruca sativa • Cabbage family
* • 🪴 • half-hardy • ☺

Rocket (arugula) became fashionable during the 1990s and has maintained its position as a slightly peppery leaf to be added to blander salads to provide a bite or served in its own right. Also known as rucola or roquette. It is quite hardy, so will outlast nearly all other green leaf salad plants.

Rocket seeds are cheap, a packet usually holds a good quantity and it doesn't matter too much if it is sown too thickly, so children can sow a row on their own. Rocket also grows satisfying fast, and a leaf can be picked and chewed *in situ* for a quick peppery snack.

Soil and position
- Full sunshine when sown in spring and autumn, dappled shade in summer.
- Any good garden soil.

Sowing, planting and spacing
- Sow *in situ* from March to late September every 4 weeks, thinly, 1cm/½in deep.
- Thin to 15cm/6in apart, or use as cut-and-come-again (see page 136).
- Sow every couple of weeks for continuous crops.
- Can be grown as a catch crop.
- Seed can be stored for up to 3 years.

Aftercare
- Water if very dry; otherwise self-sufficient.

Problems
- Flea beetles can make tiny round holes in the leaves, but although unsightly, the leaves are still perfectly edible and the beetle – small and shiny black – doesn't hang around to revolt the cook or the diners. More about flea beetles on page 126.
- Bolting in summer. You can eat the flowers, but bolted rocket leaves are very peppery. The advantage is that it self-seeds prolifically, although the offspring can have smaller leaves.

Harvesting and uses
- Start picking outer leaves and keep picking. Once the flowers have formed the leaves become small and extremely peppery, so move on to the next batch.

Varieties
- Cultivated rocket – the standard variety.
- 'Apollo' – rounded leaves, no bitterness.
- Wild rocket – leaves are darker and taste is more intense.

SPINACH

Spinacia oleracea • Beet family
** • half-hardy • ☺

Spinach was traditionally guzzled by Popeye (albeit from a can) whenever he needed an extra muscular boost to increase his iron thews, fight off his nemesis and save his girl. Unfortunately the data on iron content in spinach had been wrong by a crucial decimal point since 1870. Popeye was clearly benefiting from a psychosomatic muscular surge – or perhaps he was just a poorly researched cartoon character.

Anyhow, come the 1990s and spinach took another blow when research showed that the iron it does contain is poorly absorbed by the body, unless served with a squirt of lemon. But no matter, it is still healthy and tasty and fairly easy to grow. The seeds are large enough for even very young children to handle.

Soil and position
- Full sunshine; tolerates a bit of shade in summer.
- Good, humus-rich and water-retentive soil, not acidic.
- Fork in well-rotted compost before planting; alternatively organic chicken manure pellets, 50g per sq. m/2oz per sq. yd.

Sowing, planting and spacing
- From February if you have cloches or can start seedlings off under glass. March–May for summer crops; August for autumn crops.
- In mild areas sow in September for winter or following spring crops.

- Sow thinly, 1cm/½in deep. Repeat sow every 3 weeks for continual crops.
- For true spinach: 25cm/10in between rows. Thin seedlings to 15cm/6in between plants. Eat the thinnings.
- For New Zealand spinach: sow later in the season, late April–May, as it is not hardy. Soak the seed the day before sowing. Thin plants to 75cm/30in apart. Eat the thinnings.
- Seed can be stored for up to 4 years.

Aftercare
- Water in very hot weather.

Companion planting
- Good companion for brassica seedlings, as it deters flea beetles.
- Plant between taller crops that can provide mid-summer shade, such as beans, sweetcorn or tomatoes.
- Not with cucumbers, as they share diseases.

Problems
- Bolting – plants run to seed prematurely, producing little greenish flowers and very small leaves. Probably not enough water, weather too hot and sunny.
- Aphids – wait for ladybugs to catch up.
- Mildew – can be problematic in late summer and autumn. Plant resistant varieties. Space plants further apart.
- Slugs and snails.

Harvesting and uses
- Pick spring-sown spinach from May, autumn-sown from March.

> ### WHAT IS 'BOLTING'?
> When a plant rushes into flower. Once it is in flower, the leaves produced are very small and often taste bitter. A plant may bolt if, for instance, the weather is very dry and it feels it needs to set seed quickly before dying. Plants susceptible to bolting include fennel, spinach and rocket. Also called 'running to seed'.

- Pick a few outer leaves from each plant; do not pull up the whole plant. You should get several picks.
- Spinach is one of the plants that cooks down the most. Harvest an armful and you will be left with not much more than a thimbleful after boiling.
- Young leaves as salad, boiled for a few moments as a vegetable, stir-fries, soup, quiche.

Varieties
True spinach varieties include:
- 'Matador' F1 – dark green smooth leaves, slow to bolt, mildew resistant, AGM.
- 'Medania' – bumpy roundish leaves, mildew resistant, reliable, AGM.
- 'Giant Winter' – withstands cold and damp. Autumn sowing only.

RELATIVES
NEW ZEALAND SPINACH
(*Tertragonia expansa*)
Half-hardy perennial. More drought tolerant than spinach.

> ### SPINACH TYPES
> There are two types of spinach and another that gets confused as spinach:
> Spinach or true spinach – annual, prefers cool seasons (spring and autumn/mild winters). A good catch crop.
> New Zealand spinach – a relative (see right).
> And the confused one – spinach beet or perpetual spinach: this is really chard. See Chard, page 130.

SWEETCORN (CORN)

Zea mays • Grass family
** • tender • ☺

This is one of those crops that you haven't really eaten until you have grown your own. The saying goes that before picking your cob, you should prepare the boiling water, so that once you have picked it you can sprint back to the kitchen and cook it immediately. Once picked the sugar starts to turn to starch, so get your running shoes on …

Sweetcorn takes up quite a bit of room to ensure pollination and productivity. But the seeds are so satisfyingly enormous and look so like the finished edible product that it is an ideal plant to grow with very young children. Also, they germinate quite quickly and come up fast and large, so providing a great deal of child satisfaction. Even for the grown-up children amongst us.

Soil and position
- Sunny position.
- Hungry feeder, so work in lots of garden compost before planting.
- Remember that corn is very tall and will shade plants near it, so choose neighbours carefully.

Sowing, planting and spacing
- Sow in late March, into pots or large modules under glass. Corn needs a long season to ripen, so get started as early as possible, but remember you will need to keep seedlings protected until they can go out, but not too late or else you will have to deal with enormous plants on your windowsill or in your cold frame. Late March is probably realistically the earliest you can sow.
- Harden off and transplant out after all risk of frost has passed.
- Sow outside in May, two seeds to each station, and remove the weaker if both germinate.
- 45cm/18in between rows, 45cm/18in between plants.
- Sweetcorn is wind-pollinated, and the plants must be pollinated to form cobs, so grow in a block, not a row to assist pollination.
- Seed can be stored for 2 years.

Aftercare
- A few weeks after planting, mulch with half-rotted compost or well-rotted manure.
- Feed a few times with liquid organic tomato food (potassium-rich) when cobs begin to swell.
- May need staking, as can reach 1.8m/6ft.

Companion planting
- Spinach and lettuce in the shade of corn in summer.
- Traditionally squash can be grown to meander through the stems, but we are not convinced, having ended up with a jungly muddle in the past.

Problems
- Failure to ripen – blame the weather.
- Some kernels not filled – poor pollination. Plant more next time, in a slightly draftier spot.
- Birds and rodents like the cobs.

Harvesting and uses
- Pick when the tassel turns brown, usually in August. Peel back the leaves and stick your fingernail

into a kernel, and if milk oozes forth, it is ready. Twist off the cob and run to the kitchen.

Varieties
In theory you should grow only one variety in a season, unless you have a very large garden – otherwise they will cross-pollinate, and the end product is not guaranteed. (Mind you, nothing is guaranteed in gardening.)

From the 1980s supersweet hybrids became popular, having been discovered in Illinois in 1953. They store less starch and far more sugar than the standard varieties.
- 'Butter and Sugar' – bicolor kernels, medium size ears, popular with home gardeners, early.
- 'Illini Gold' – supersweet variety, medium size ears, midseason.
- 'Silver Queen' – standard, high-quality white corn, large ears, disease resistant, late.
- 'Spring Snow' – very tender white kernels, medium size ears, extra early.

Different corn varieties from Peru.

TOMATOES

Lycopersicon esculentum
Nightshade family
** • 🍃 • tender • ☺

Tomatoes originate in South and Central America; the word *tomatl* comes from the Nahuatl language as spoken by the Aztecs. They were brought to Europe after the Spanish Conquest; the first European mention of *pomi d'oro*, golden apples, comes in a herbal of 1544. English sources of the late sixteenth century, worried perhaps by their relationship to deadly nightshade and their bright colour, referred to them as ornamentals, rather than edible plants. Nowadays it is hard to imagine a kitchen, let alone the entire Italian and Spanish national cuisines, without them.

Home-grown tomatoes taste infinitely superior to supermarket ones. There is even something evocative and specific about the scent of the foliage (which by the way is mildly poisonous). Many people who have only a small patio decide that if they can grow only one thing, it must be tomatoes.

The seeds are familiar to children from their own experiences of eating tomatoes, and they can be shown how to pinch out shoots. Judging by people's reported childhood memories of gardening, the pleasure of picking and eating your own tomatoes off the vine is a lasting one.

Soil and position
- Sunny spot, sheltered from strong wind.
- Humus-rich, well-drained soil.
- Hungry feeder, so dig in half-rotted compost or well-rotted manure several weeks before planting.
- Alternatively plant each seedling with two trowels of well-rotted compost or manure or rake 150g per sq m/5 oz per sq. yd of blood, fish and bone into the bed.

Sowing, planting and spacing
- Sow seeds under glass in mid-spring (mid-March–early April), into modules or a seed tray. Do not start too early. Packet instructions often tell you to start in late winter or early spring, but then your tomatoes will be too long and lanky before you can plant them out. Start them off about 6 weeks before they can go outdoors. Seeds are fairly large, so children can help sowing.
- If grown in a tray, transplant seedlings when large enough to handle into 9cm/3½in pots. Do not wait too long or else plants will become competitive and spindly.
- Harden off before planting out.
- Plant out when about 30cm/15in tall, after all risk of frost has passed. Make your hole quite a bit deeper than the depth of the pot; tomatoes are able to grow extra roots along the buried stem, giving additional stability. Provide a strong, well-fixed cane for support.
- Distance between plants: 45cm/18in.
- Seed can be stored for up to 3 years.

Aftercare
- Look out for side shoots (see below) and remove regularly.
- As soon as the first fruits begin to form, start to feed regularly with organic liquid tomato food.
- As the fruit ripens and the leaves begin to look old and used, peel some off, allowing more sun and air around the ripening fruit.
- Keep them well watered, but

TOMATO TYPES

Cordon, also called vine or indeterminate
- Most amateur-grown varieties fall into this category. The plants keep on growing upwards until stopped.
- The fruit is carried on shortish shoots coming off the main stem.
- The extra side shoots that very frequently form in the axils (between the leaves and the main stem, as illustrated right; if you imagine the tomato leaves as arms, then these are any new shoots growing in the armpits) should be pinched out or else the plant will become too overcrowded, becoming susceptible to disease and producing too much leaf and little fruit.
- Each plant should be stopped by removing the top shoot after the fifth truss (cluster of flowers/fruits) or by the end of July, whichever comes first.
- They need a stout stake or some kind of supporting structure that holds sticks or strings for a whole row of vine tomatoes. This must be built before they get too big.

Bush
- Although books always mention these, very few of the varieties available are bush tomatoes. They form compact plants, and are easier to control than vines as the plants naturally form bushes. Do not remove side shoots from bush plants, as these are the fruiting shoots.
- All fruit tends to ripen at the same time, so they are more appealing to the commercial grower.

Semi-determinate
- The best and worst of bush and vine. In other words, they grow bushy but still need support and shoot removal.

Tumbling
- These are small plants that are grown to cascade over the side of containers. Generally these are cherry tomatoes to keep the crop in proportion.

try to avoid spraying the leaves, directing any water to the base of the plant.

- Tomatoes can respond very acutely to watering. Too much and they may be watery and tasteless; too much too suddenly and the skins may split.

Companion planting

- Plant with marigolds to deter harmful nematodes, basil to repel flies (and for convenience when you eat them together). Parsley grows happily in the shade of tomatoes.
- Apparently tomatoes do not flourish if planted close to sweetcorn or dill.
- Potatoes are susceptible to similar diseases, so do not plant them close if possible, or in the same spot the following year.

Problems

- Blight. This is the bane of gardeners' lives. Brown lesions on stems and fruit expand quickly in humid weather. Fruit that is not affected can be eaten, so you may be able to rescue some if you pick quickly, but otherwise bin or burn affected plants. Choose more resistant varieties, and make sure you plant somewhere else next year. And comfort yourself with the thought that most gardeners suffer from it at some point.
- Blossom end rot – black/brown patch at the base of the fruit. Can be caused by irregular water supply.
- Curly leaves. Too cold.
- Greenback – hard green bit on the top of the fruit. You probably failed to provide consistent sun and water. One of these you can

do something about next time.
- Few fruits. Poor pollination; it was probably too cold when they flowered and the bees were chilled. Blame the weather.

Harvesting and uses

- August to October.
- Each plant could produce around 1.5kg/3lb.
- Place any tomatoes that are only slightly ripe at the end of the season in a bowl with a banana to speed up the process.
- Chutney with green unripe tomatoes at the end of the season.
- Homemade ketchup: see recipe on page 100.

Varieties

Tomatoes used to be 'red, round and eight to the pound' but nowadays there is a huge variety of shapes and colours from which to choose. We have limited our recommendations to outdoor varieties (and you will be disappointed if you try to grow greenhouse varieties outdoors, so check the packet). Unless otherwise stated all are cordon types.

- 'Ferline' F1 – large deep red fruits. Happiest indoors, but can be pushed outdoors. Supposedly the most blight-resistant tomato, but not top for taste.

- 'Tigerella' – normal size tomato, red with yellowish stripes, AGM.
- 'Sungold' – yellow cherry. Sweet flavour, disease resistant.
- 'Sweet Million' F1 – cherry. Round red, good yield and flavour, AGM.
- 'Tumbler' F1 – bush for growing in containers. Largish cherries.
- 'Brandywine' – large beefsteak renowned for its flavour. Large, rather soft fruit, outstanding flavor. Unsuited to very humid hot areas where disease is a problem.
- 'Mortgage Lifter' – extremely large, furrowed, red beefsteak. In good conditions it can be exceptionally productive.
- 'Early Girl' – starts maturing fruit early and carries on producing to relatively late in the season. Moderate sweetness, medium to high acidity. A good all season tomato.

FRUIT

From Eden onwards fruit trees have played a major role in the history of gardens. In return for minimal maintenance they offer blossom in spring, shade in summer, fruit in early autumn, colour as the leaves turn and structure in winter. Fruit bushes too repay minimal attention with berries for browsing as you pass, and jams and preserves for the more organized. Fruit trees and bushes are a marvellous – we would even go so far as to say essential – addition to your garden. Children enjoy picking and eating the fruit and, unless your garden is sold to developers, chances are your fruit trees will outlast you.

How to choose a tree

Buying berry bushes is a fairly straightforward thing to do, but choosing a fruit tree needs some thought beforehand. After deciding which fruit you would like to grow, assess your garden. Is there enough room for one or even several free-standing trees? Fruit trees can now be grown as very small trees, so even if you have only a small patio, there may still be room. Fruit production is at its peak when a tree is mature (around 5–10 years old) but not ancient. Most fruit trees can be grown in a whole range of shapes:

Tree shapes

- **Standard** A proper tree with a stem of 1.8m/6ft before any branches.
- **Half standard** Looks like a proper little tree with a stem of 1.2m/4ft before any branches.
- **Bushes** have just a trunk of about 60cm/24in and look like a miniature tree.
- An **espalier** is a central stem with horizontal branches coming out either side, grown along a wall or a wire structure. Particularly attractive and appropriate if you are short of space. Needs special pruning, so you may be better off buying a tree that is already shaped into an espalier, which makes the ongoing pruning much easier.
- **Fans,** like espaliers, are grown flat against a wall, but instead of a central main stem, the branches split outwards at the base, like the struts of a fan. Can be bought ready trained.

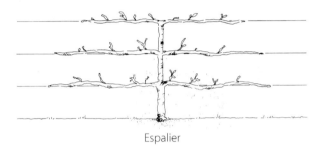

Espalier

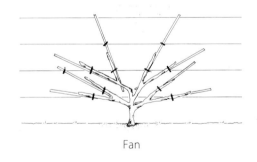

Fan

> 'The great French Marshall Lyautey once asked his gardener to plant a tree. The gardener objected that the tree was slow growing, and would not reach maturity for 100 years. The Marshall replied, "In that case, there is no time to lose; plant it this afternoon."'
> As told by John F. Kennedy

GRAFTING
If you were to plant a seed, in several years' time you should get an apple tree, but it would not come true and would produce fruit of unpredictable quality. Because of the time and effort involved, a better method was developed. Grafting is the technical term for sticking two halves of a woody plant together – a top half with the flowers or fruit you want, and a bottom half with a strong root that controls the eventual size and yield of the tree. This is the job of the nursery.

The graft union is the point where the rootstock meets the fruiting stock – you can see a kind of knuckle on the stem.

- **Cordons** These are single stems trained at a 45-degree angle. Not recommended for beginners.
- **Stepover cordons** Clever little trees trained to grow parallel at shin height. Also known as trip-over cordons for obvious reasons …
- **Ballerinas or minarettes** One single stem with fruit all the way up, so in theory good for growing up a pole or gatepost. We remain to be convinced.
- **Family trees** These are trees with three different types of fruit on the same stem. Tricky to prune. Not recommended for beginners.

Tree size

Fruit trees are grafted on a rootstock, which will produce a tree of the size and vigour you want. Depending on the shape you want, choose a tree grafted on the appropriate rootstock:

Dwarfing rootstock:
- For small trees (up to 2m/7ft tall) and espaliers.
- Crops soon after planting.
- Needs more care and pruning than a larger tree.
- Usually needs staking because the roots are too small to support a cropping tree.
- Has a shorter life span.

Vigorous rootstock:
- Half standard and standard trees up to 5m/16½ft tall.
- Crowns will be at least 5m/16½ft in diameter.
- Needs more time until first crop.
- More robust than a smaller tree, and needs less care.
- Pruning and picking can be tricky in a big tree.

Semi-dwarfing rootstock:
- A good compromise between the two.

A fruit tree is a long-term investment, so it really is worth spending time to get the choice right.

For more information on suitable rootstocks, see individual fruit entries.

Tree age

Try to order a two-year-old tree; this cuts a year off the waiting time for your first taste. If the tree has already received formative pruning in the nursery, ongoing training will be much easier.

Tree ages and advantages

1 year old	Maiden whip (basically one thin twig); feathered maiden (a twig with side twiglets – the first branches).	Least expensive.	You must carry out all the formative pruning.
2 years old	Tree.	Mid-price.	Partly trained.
3–5 years old	Tree.	Expensive.	Already trained into a basic shape.

Planting fruit trees and bushes

Fruit trees and bushes have similar planting requirements, so the following applies to both. All the fruit trees and bushes in this book, except figs, are hardy (although the blossom is not).

Where?
- In full sunshine.
- Good soil of a reasonable depth, not waterlogged.
- Protected from strong winds.
- With enough room for the tree or bush to reach its eventual size.
- Never replace fruit with the same type, as the new plant may be susceptible to replant disease.

When?
- When dormant in autumn or in early spring. It's best not to plant too late in autumn, so that they can settle in before spring growth. Never plant into frozen soil.

FROST PROTECTION
Fruit trees will cope with being frozen in winter, but if the flower blossoms get frosted, your crop for the year will be directly affected. Fruit trees produce flowers at different times, so the earlier the flowering period, the more sensitive they are to frost.
Avoid growing them in shady and colder parts of your garden (see page 21). There are a few methods of protecting against frost:
- Sunny walls protect against cold winds and absorb heat during the day that they give off at night when temperatures fall and the plant needs a few extra degrees.
- Horticultural fleece – have a few metres of this handy, and if you see that a sudden late frost is forecast on the evening news rush out to protect your blossom. Clipping it on properly, or folding it over as a double layer, offers more protection.

- If you order from a nursery, they may arrive bare rooted – in other words with no soil – and should be planted immediately.
- If you have impulse-bought from your local garden centre, then your tree will probably be in a pot and you can plant throughout the year, bearing in mind that if planted in hotter months it will need lots of watering to get established.

How?
- Remove all perennial weeds very thoroughly, because once you have planted your tree or bush, it will be really hard to remove deep-seated weeds. Annual weeds can be hoed off as they grow.
- Cut back damaged roots to healthy wood. Soak the roots in a bucket of water for about an hour before planting.
- Make a hole the size of the width of the roots plus 15cm/6in in diameter. The latest research recommends that a square hole is best, rather than a round one in which the roots may continue to grow in a circle. The idea is that if the roots reach a corner they will force their way onwards.
- Mix the soil from your hole in equal parts with well-rotted manure or garden compost.
- Add a sprinkle of bone meal and lots of compost to the hole. If you have foxes around, make sure the bone meal is right at the bottom.
- Put a stake in before you fill the hole (or else you might stake through the roots). Drive it in firmly to at least 30cm/1ft below the bottom of the planting hole.
- Place the tree in the hole to the same level as it was in at the nursery; you can usually see a line showing the soil level. The stem should be about 8cm/3in away from the stake.
- If planting in poor soil or in a recently built or landscaped garden, sprinkle mycorrhizal fungi gel (see box on page 160) on to the damp roots.
- Fill up with the soil mixture, gently firming each layer of soil with your foot, but carefully, without

> **MYCORRHIZAL FUNGI**
> In the wild, nearly all plants live in symbiosis with the fungi around their roots, supplying them with sugar in return for nutrients and water, which the fungi are more efficient at collecting. Recent research shows that plants with mycorrhizal fungi can resist drought, stress and disease better. Buy it in packet form from a garden centre.

damaging the roots.

- Tie the trunk of the tree to the stake, so that the tie supports the tree but does not strangle or damage the trunk. Use a proper tree tie, not wire or thin string, and make a figure of eight around trunk and stake, ensuring that the trunk will not rub on the stake if the tree moves in the wind.
- Water well.
- Mulch with more compost, or a mulch mat from the garden centre, a kind of circular carpet to fit around the stem, which you could hide with a layer of shredded bark.
- If you have rabbits or deer, protect trunks.

How for espaliers and fans

- Prepare your wall or fence first with horizontal wires every 45cm/18in (for an espalier) held 15cm/6in out from the wall with vine eyes, or canes (for a fan) in an angled position as required. Once that framework is in, training a tree is much easier.
- If planting by a wall, make the hole about 30cm/1ft in, and lean the tree towards the wall. The soil right by the wall will be too dry for a tree to be happy.
- Follow the planting instructions under **How?**

Aftercare

- Water in dry periods for the first 2 years.
- Keep the soil around the tree's base clear of weeds or grass (a circle of about 90cm/36in), especially for the first couple of years, to avoid competition and facilitate feeding and watering.
- Check the tie occasionally to make sure that it is still supportive but not strangling the tree.
- Some fruit trees may do a 'June drop' when, of their own accord, they get rid of small and diseased fruit. Do not panic.

Feeding and mulching

- Feeding is not necessary in the first growing season, as roots should be encouraged to grow out into the surrounding soil; from the second year on you can start if necessary.
- Mulch trees and bushes in spring. Keep the mulch away from the stem to prevent rotting. Berry bushes in particular appreciate compost or leaf mould, since most of these plants originated around the woodland edge. Apply after the soil has warmed up.
- Fruit bushes and trees are not usually heavy feeders, but fruit trees on dwarfing or very dwarfing rootstock or any fruit planted in poor soil will need yearly feeding. Mulch with well-rotted manure or half-rotted compost. If you cannot supply either of these, or if your plants need a boost, you can also use blood, fish and bone (100–150g per sq. m/3½–5oz per sq. yd). Fruit in good soil and fruit trees on vigorous rootstocks can be fed similarly every second or third year. In general avoid nitrogen-rich fertilizers.
- Fruit bushes (including raspberry canes) may need to be replaced every ten years or so. Keep an eye on productivity and if they begin to fail for

reasons other than poor cultivation, you may need to replace them. Do not replant in the same spot.

Any special feeding requirements that differ from this are described in individual entries in the A–Z.

Pruning – a few basics
Why?

A tree or a shrub grows happily without any pruning, but the result is often not exactly what the gardener had in mind. The natural tendency would be towards an overgrown plant with a lot of tiny fruit; the plant's aim is not to reward us with big apples or large blooms, but rather to produce as much seed as possible. But with a bit of knowledge we can modify that. Other aims of pruning are:

- To create a pleasing shape, especially in the early years.
- To increase sunlight on fruit, thereby making the fruit ripen quicker and taste sweeter.
- To increase air flow, thereby discouraging pests and disease.
- To achieve a good balance between fruiting shoots and leaf growth.

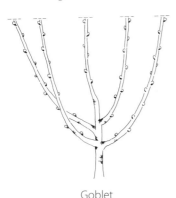

Goblet

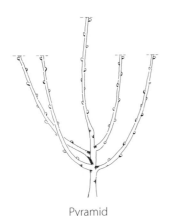

Pyramid

The shapes that best favour these aims are:
- An **open goblet**, in other words, with branches round the outside and an airy space in the middle, e.g. apple, currants, gooseberry.
- A **pyramid**, with a wider base rising to a triangular shape, e.g. pear.
- A flat **fan** or **espalier** against a wall.

When?

Most plants prefer **early spring treatment**, when they are dormant. These include:
- currants
- grapes (with another light trim in summer)
- apples and other cored fruit (with some light work in summer).

Some plants become infected when pruned in early spring, and prefer **summer treatment**, including:
- plums, cherries and other stone fruit.

What equipment?
- Whatever you use – pruning shears, long-handled loppers, pruning saws – must be sharp. Remember to be safe.

The first rules of pruning

These are the basic and most important pieces of advice:

- Start by removing dead or damaged branches. Anything that looks shrivelled, or that has scraped branches or strange callouses – remove. Look for crossing branches and remove the weaker, less favourable one.
- For espalier trees or fans, remove anything sticking directly out, or back into the wall.
- Keep stepping back to look at the overall shape.

Now you can work towards the required shape of your tree or shrub. For pruning details of particular shrubs and trees, see the A–Z of plants.

How?

- Always cut just above a bud.
- Usually cut above an outward-facing bud, so that the new growth will grow outwards, away from the centre of the plant.
- Cuts should slope downwards so that any water can run off away from the bud.

Pruning branches

Stump is likely to die; dead wood attracts diseases | Ideal | Too close to trunk

Pruning twigs

Too far from bud | Ideal | Too close to bud; angle too steep

- Do not damage the bud that you are leaving by going too close; leave just a millimetre or so of stalk above the bud to support it, but do not leave more or else the stalk will die back to the bud and may allow disease to enter. Follow the same principle for cutting back branches. The traditional advice is: 'Do not leave anything you could hang your hat on.'
- Cuts need to be sharp and clean, never ragged. Choose the correct blade for the size of branch you need to cut.

Pruning new vs. pruning established plants

For the **first few years** get your tree to grow in the shape that you want. Anywhere you want a new branch, let it grow; anywhere the growth is in the wrong place, nip it out. You are simply pruning to get the tree or bush into the right shape for its future life.

When it has reached its **desired size or shape**, the pruning shifts gear to keeping the tree more or less the same size but producing more fruit.

If a tree has been **neglected** and needs lots of pruning, involving removing several large branches, spread the work over a few years. A strong tree will react with strong growth; the more you prune, the more it will grow back.

If you would like to learn more than the basics, there are many specialist books available.

Do plants fruit on old wood or new wood?

You need to know this, because if a plant fruits only on old wood, and you keep removing the old wood, then you are going to be continually disappointed. Old wood is darker brown, more knobbly; new wood, produced in the spring and summer, is fresh and greenish. Flower buds (which will develop into fruit) are round and plump; buds bearing only leaves are usually smaller and more elongated. Check the details for each fruit in the A–Z.

Do not be daunted: this is supposed to be fun. Unless you have been 'chainsaw massacre' drastic, then the worst-case scenario is that your plant does not produce fruit next year. Observe your tree and next year you will be more confident about new and old wood. Trees are a long-term project.

Use fruit wood prunings to make sweet-scented fires or practise your carvings.

Problems

Do not be put off. If you buy healthy trees and bushes, plant them well in a favourable position and keep them watered for the first year or two, then you will probably have no problems.

Trees and bushes suffer more problems when they are stressed, for instance when grown in poor soil or not fed or watered enough. In general, remedying these conditions will solve the problem. Removing any diseased twigs, fruit or branches immediately by pruning back to healthy wood, and disposing of the infected material, will help prevent spread of disease. Good hygiene – clearing up leaves and debris under the tree – will remove hiding places for caterpillars and harmful insects, thereby helping to keep moth and maggot populations down.

See also the A–Z for problems affecting specific fruits.

APPLES

Malus domestica · Rose family
*** · 🪴 · tree · ☺

The symbol of love and fruitfulness, an apple tree somehow represents all that is best about having your own fruit in your own garden. No garden is too small for an apple tree. You just have to choose the right variety for you, and then you are assured of blossom in spring and fruit in late summer.

Soil and position
- Sunny, airy site, not shaded by other trees or exposed.
- Good soil, ideally well-drained loam.

Sowing, planting and spacing
- See Planting trees, page 159.
- Distance between trees: the same as the final height of the tree you have chosen (see Rootstock, page 158). As a rule of thumb, these are the minimum distances:
Standards: 6–9m/20–30ft
Half-standards: 4.5–6m/15–20ft
Bush: 2.5–4.5m/8–15ft
Espaliers: 6m/20ft per tree.

Aftercare
- Feeding and mulching are not necessary the first year.
- From the second year onwards mulch in early spring; see also Feeding and mulching, page 160.
- Thin fruit. Apple trees may do a 'June drop' when, of their own accord, they get rid of small and diseased fruit. In July, check whether the tree is producing too much fruit. You can have bigger,

GROWING AN APPLE TREE IN A CONTAINER
- Choose a miniature rootstock (M27).
- Grow in a pot with lots of crocks or gravel at the bottom for good drainage and a rich, loamy potting soil.
- Top up with compost the second year.
- Very little pruning required.
- Needs a lot of regular watering, so not a good idea if you go away in summer.

sweeter apples if you thin them to 10–15cm/4–6in apart (cooking apples: about 18cm/8in). At most you should leave two fruits at each cluster.

Companion planting
- Bees and bumblebees pollinate apples, so plant spring-flowering attractants like rosemary.

Pruning
Winter pruning
- General pruning – see the first rules of pruning on page 162. Do these first.
- If the weather is warm and wet in late summer, the tree may produce water shoots – upwards-growing whippy shoots at the end of each branch. Remove these, unless they are creating new growth for the tree that you would like to keep.
- Spur-pruning. Most apples are spur-bearing. This means that the productive parts of the apple trees are the shoots that are 2 years old or older – little woody clusters called spurs. You can shorten the laterals (the side shoots growing out from the main stem) to encourage fruit and flowers.
- Spur-thinning: remove groups of spurs to prevent fruit being overcrowded.

Summer pruning
- Summer pruning is for espaliers and fans only.
- Get out your pruning shears in late summer – say early to mid-August – when the new shoots are beginning to become woody. It is better to do it too late than too early.
- For the first years, get your tree to grow in the shape that you want. Anywhere you want a new branch, let it grow; anywhere the growth is in the wrong place, nip it out.
- Once your tree has grown to the shape you are aiming for, cut back anything newly grown that is not following the shape you have chosen.

The saying goes, 'You should be able to throw a hat' – some versions say a cat – 'through the centre of your tree.'

> '*A man would have to be an idiot to write a book of laws for an apple tree ...*'
> Martin Luther, *On Secular Authority*, 1523

Problems
You may not have any problems – we have had apple trees for 10 years with none of these, so fingers crossed …
- Poor fruiting. If your apple tree produces small, misshapen fruit, count the seeds. A badly pollinated apple will have five seeds or fewer. Plant another tree from the same pollination group as yours (see pages 166–7).
- Bitter pit – brownish sunken hollows on the surface of the apple late in the season or in storage. Insufficient calcium levels in the fruit, caused by irregular water supply; avoid it the following year by regular watering, especially in late spring and early summer. Do not feed your tree with additional potash, as it reduces calcium absorption.
- Scab – brown hard patches on the leaves and fruit, spread by rain splash and wind. The fruit is still edible, if not beautiful, but the scab can then crack and let worse infections enter. Choose resistant varieties. Clear up under trees during winter, and prune out infected branches.

Harvesting and uses
- When the apple comes away in your hand with a gentle twist, it is ready. If you have to tug at it, leave it another few days.
- Let your mind dwell for a moment on a fruit that is perfect as a quick fresh healthy snack or as a warm comforting crumble; your salivary glands are probably telling you to hurry up and order a few trees.
- You will need good storage conditions: a dark, unheated, frost-free room such as a shed or garage. Apples are best stored on racks off the ground to deter mice and must not touch one another.

Choosing your tree

The initial choice of variety, rootstock and pollination times can sound very daunting, but stay with us here. You have to make three initial choices:

- **Shape** Do you prefer a standard tree or an espalier?
- **Rootstock** This determines the size of the tree. For apples there are several different kinds of rootstock, many named M plus a number, after the East Malling Research Station. These are widely available in the UK and the US.
- **Pollination times** Your apple tree blossoms must have a chance to be pollinated by insects that have visited the blossoms of another apple tree. Apples have different flowering seasons and hence are divided into different pollination groups. So buy trees from the same pollination group, but if you live close to other gardens, you can cross your fingers and hope that your neighbours have a tree within a bee's flight of your own. If you want only one apple tree and you are not sure about other trees in the neighbourhood, try a self-fertile one. Self-fertile trees will be able to produce some fruit; however, they will do much better when there are other pollinators around. For areas that are prone to late frost, choose late-flowering trees.

	Height	First fruits at	
M27 very dwarfing	1.2–1.5m/4–5ft	2–3 years old	For dwarf bushes, cordons and stepovers, containers. Needs good soil, regular watering, feeding and permanent staking.
M26 dwarfing	About 2.5m/8ft	3–4 years old	For bushes, cordons, small espaliers. Average soil conditions, staking needed for the first 5 years.
MM106 semi-dwarfing	About 4m/14ft	4–5 years old	For half-standards, bushes, espaliers. Copes with poor soil.
M25, MM111 vigorous	6–7m/20–22ft	6–7 years old	Serious orchard-sized big tree. Good on poor soil; not practical for the average garden. Drought tolerant.

> *'With an apple I will astonish Paris.'*
> Paul Cézanne

diseases. Descriptions of taste are so subjective and personal we have hesitated to make recommendations. We suggest you go to an apple tasting day – usually held around the end of October – and pick your favourite.

> *'Stay me with flagons, comfort me with apples, for I am sick of love.'*
> The Song of Solomon 2:5

Buy from a good nursery, and ask their advice.

Varieties

This is the interesting bit. Ideally aim for a selection of trees to ensure they all pollinate one another but do not all fruit at the same time. Some varieties should be eaten early and may drop from the tree if not picked, others can stay on until you need them before picking; some store well, others do not.

In the list below we suggest varieties that are usually healthy and resistant to common apple

Picking	Eating	Name and description	Type	Attributes	Flowering time
August	August–September	'Discovery' AGM Red, juicy and crisp. Better keeping quality than other earlies. Moderate growth.	Dessert	Disease resistant, frost tolerant.	Mid-season
Mid-August	August–September	'Grenadier' AGM Yellowish green. Crops heavily, compact growth.	Cooking	Good disease resistance, hardy.	Mid-season
Mid-August	August–September	'Laxton's Epicure' AGM Yellow with red stripes, Cox-like flavour. Small tree. Heavy crops, needs thinning.	Dessert	Prone to bitter pit, canker.	Mid-season, self-fertile
Early September	Sept–Oct	'James Grieve' AGM Yellow, orange speckles and stripes. Juicy and tangy. Prolific, reliable. Good for juice, stewing and eating.	Dessert and cooking	Hardy, resistant to mildew, bruises easily.	Mid-season, partly self-fertile
Mid-September	Oct-Nov	'Lord Lambourne' AGM Greenish yellow with some red stripes. Sweet and juicy fruits. Heavy and regular crops, compact growth.	Dessert	Resistant to mildew.	Early flowering
Late September	Oct-Dec	'Sunset' AGM Golden, flushed with red, 'Cox'-type. Crops heavily and regularly, with small fruit. Compact tree.	Dessert	Good disease resistance, hardy.	Mid-season
Late September	Oct-Dec	'Egremont Russet' AGM Nutty, sweet, crisp. Rough skin. Good regular crops.	Dessert	Scab resistant, hardy.	Early flowering self-fertile
Early October	Oct-March	'Fiesta' (aka 'Red Pippin') AGM Red, crisp. Nutty aroma, Cox-like. Heavy regular crops.	Dessert	Reliable.	Mid-season
Mid-October	December–April	'Winston' AGM Yellowish green, flushed and striped with red. Good regular crops, but rather small apples, so thin in June.	Dessert	Disease resistant.	Late season self-fertile
Mid-October	December–April	'Edward VII' AGM Ideal for purée. Upright growth, good for small gardens.	Cooking	Good scab and mildew resistance. Good for cold areas.	Late season

BLACKBERRIES AND RELATED BERRIES

Rubus fruticosus • Rose family
** • shrub

Blackberries are delicious, but can be invasive (they are a Weed of National Significance in Australia). Usually one can find some growing wild on derelict ground or a hedgerow somewhere, but if you choose carefully, especially from the thornless varieties, and keep the plant under control, there are many who would not be without their own blackberries.

Soil and position
- Sun or partial shade.
- Well-drained soil; can be poor.

Sowing, planting and spacing
- Add compost when planting, ideally between October and March.
- Immediately on planting, cut stalks down to about 18cm/9in above the soil, just above a bud. Provide a trellis or framework for them to grow up (see below).
- Water and mulch.
- Plants 3.6m/12ft apart, rows 2.5m/8ft apart.

Aftercare
- Mulch in early spring.

Companion planting
- Avoid areas where strawberries, potatoes or tomatoes have been grown previously, since they may share diseases.

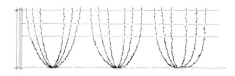

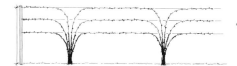

Pruning
- The canes are biennial: in other words they grow one year and fruit the next.
- Remove the old canes after fruiting (these are the ones with the old dead berry stalks on them), in October.
- Select the six best young shoots, cut out any spindly canes and any side shoots, and tie these new canes into a trellis for ease of picking.
- Be strict; any stem that rests on the ground for a few weeks will probably root and begin to take over your garden.

Harvesting and uses
- Pick when the whole berry turns black, around August; there should be several pickings from a bush, as the berries ripen at different times. Each bush could produce around 3kg/10lb.
- If you are taking the family blackberry picking, remember to wear long sleeves against thorns and clothes that you do not mind getting stained.
- According to tradition, blackberries should not be picked after Michaelmas (around 29 September) because when Satan was banished from Heaven he fell into a blackberry bush and either spat or pissed on them. Either way, the late watery ones do not taste good.
- Fresh, cooking, jam.
- Can be frozen very successfully for use in winter apple crumbles and other desserts.

Varieties
- 'Oregon Thornless' – good for obvious reasons. Long easy-to-train canes, pretty incised leaves, with good autumn colour. Not invasive. Can be grown on a trellis or wire support.
- 'Loch Ness' – thornless, easy to train, for smaller gardens, 2.5m/8ft long, requires little support. AGM.
- 'Black Butte' – good if you want absolutely enormous berries, twice the size of the hedgerow ones.

RELATIVES
Blackberries have been crossed with other fruiting berries to create tasty hybrids. All should be planted about 1.8m/6ft apart; otherwise follow the same cultivation instructions as for blackberries.

BOYSENBERRY
Loganberry/blackberry/raspberry hybrid. Originated in the 1920s on the farm of Ralph Boysen in California. Big reddish-purple soft berries. Simon and Garfunkel prefer jam from this berry to all others. Suitable only for milder areas of the US (zone 7 and warmer).

LOGANBERRY
Raspberry × dewberry/blackberry hybrid from nineteenth-century California. Probably too sharp to eat without cooking, vigorous, thorny, can grow 1.5m/5ft in a year. Long dark red conical berries.

TAYBERRY
Blackberry/raspberry from Scotland. Heavy cropper, from July, can produce up to 9kg/20lb of fruit. Deep red, long juicy berries, sweet and aromatic. Good for jam, very vigorous.

WINEBERRY (*Rubus phoenicolasius*)
Its Latin name translates as 'blackberry with purple hairs'. Produces small red fruits, very tasty. Can be invasive.

BLUEBERRIES

Vaccinium corymbosum
Heather family
** • 🪴 • shrub

Blueberries are of American origin – in the United States and Canada, July is National Blueberry Month. They are related to the wild bilberry that grows on acid heaths and moors, and which is smaller and hard to harvest. As well as tasting delicious, recently blueberries have become fashionable superfoods because of their high antioxidant levels; there is even some medical evidence to back up anti-ageing claims, since in experiments old rats fed on blueberries were smarter than blueberry-free – and therefore more senile – rats. So tuck in.

Deciduous blueberries look good in autumn as their leaves change.

Soil and position
- Blueberries need acid soil, pH between 4.5 and 5.5.
- If you have neutral soil you can add lots of ericaceous compost. If your soil is alkaline or neutral and you cannot be bothered with the above, grow them in containers (see box).
- Full sun or partial shade.

Sowing, planting and spacing
- Plant when dormant in autumn or early spring.
- 1.2–1.5m/4–5ft apart.
- Eventual height 1–2m/3–7ft.

Aftercare
- In spring, after pruning, mulch with pine bark or leaf mould. Do not use normal compost.
- Water using rainwater. Do not allow the plant to dry out, nor to get 'wet feet' and become too moist.
- Remove flower buds for the first year, so that the plant concentrates on its roots.
- From the second year when it starts to set fruit, you can feed it

ERICACEOUS COMPOST
Ericaceous composts are specially pre-blended acidic soils for acid-loving plants, available in garden centres. Check that they are peat free.

a few times with organic liquid tomato food, which is potassium-rich and improves fruit.
- Net when the fruit starts to ripen.

Pruning
- No pruning for the first 3 years.
- Fruit is carried on stems that are 1–3 years old.
- Prune in the winter when dormant, removing any dead, damaged or crossing wood.
- Pruning should allow more light into the bush, but do not prune too much.
- After 3 years, take out one or two old stems from the base each year.

Problems
- Dehydrated plants rarely recover.

Harvesting and uses
- When the berries come off easily, the fruit is ready.
- Fresh, jams, with muesli, in smoothies.

Varieties
If you are only buying one bush, choose a self-fertilizing variety such as 'Sunshine Blue'.
- 'Bluecrop' – heavy cropper, very large berries, good flavour. Disease resistant. One of the best

BLUEBERRIES IN A CONTAINER
This is a good way to grow blueberries, although you must never let them dry out.
- Choose a container at least 35cm/15in diameter, filled with ericaceous compost.
- Pot on every couple of years into a bigger tub.

all-rounders. 1.5m/5ft high.
- 'Duke' – mild flavour, good storage, hardy, prolific. Flowers late. Upright, 1.5m/5ft. AGM.
- 'Ozark Blue' – late season, very tasty. Hardy. 1.5m/5ft.
- 'Sunshine Blue' – tangy flavour, self-fertile but happier with a pollinator, evergreen, more tolerant of alkali than the other varieties, only for mild areas. 1m/39in.

RELATIVES
CRANBERRY
Too complicated unless you can provide a lime-free bog with a pH of less than 5.0.

CHERRIES, SWEET AND SOUR

Sweet cherries: *Prunus avium*
Sour cherries: *Prunus cerasus*
Rose family
** • trees

Cherry trees were common throughout the Mediterranean, with the Romans introducing them to northern Europe, and the Europeans to America in the seventeenth century. The beauty of the blossom is renowned, and in Japan picnickers and tourists travel specially to view the trees in season. Less aesthetically sensitive countries have cherry seed-spitting competitions instead.

Soil and position
- Sweet cherries need sunshine; sour cherries tolerate some shade.
- Good, well-drained soil.
- Fan-trained: south or south-west facing wall for sweet cherries, north facing wall is possible for sour cherries.

Sowing, planting and spacing
- See Planting fruit trees, page 159.
- Tree/bush:
  semi-dwarfing rootstock (for rootstocks, see under Choosing your tree, page 158): plant 1.5m/5ft apart; expect to grow to 2m/7ft high.
  semi-vigorous rootstock: plant 4m/14ft apart; expect to grow 5–6m/16½–20ft high.
- Fan-trained:
  semi-dwarfing rootstock: plant 3.6m/12ft apart; expect tree to grow to 2m/7ft high.
  Semi-vigorous rootstock: plant 5–5.5m/16½–18ft apart; expect tree to grow to 2m/7ft high.

Aftercare
- Protect blossoms if frost is threatened.
- Feeding not necessary in the first year.
- From the second year onwards mulch in early spring; see also Feeding and mulching, page 160.
- Requires netting or else birds will eat them all – the buds in spring, remaining fruit in summer.

Pruning
- To avoid the danger of silver leaf disease, never prune in winter.

Sweet cherries:
- Do not usually need pruning. Only remove dead or diseased wood if necessary.

Sour cherries:
- Sour cherries fruit on new wood. After each harvest cut fruited stems back to younger replacement shoots.

Fans require extra work:
- Rub away inward or outward-facing buds in spring.
- In early summer remove over-vigorous shoots, and anything that grows inwards or outwards or weak shoots.

Problems
- Heavy rain just before harvest or irregular watering can cause the skins to crack.

Harvesting and uses
- Early to mid-summer.
- Remember to warn about the pit if eating cherries with small children.
- Sweet cherries: eat fresh. Sour cherries: compote, juice and Black Forest gateau.

Choosing your tree
When deciding on a cherry tree, you need to consider:
- **Type of cherry** This depends on your personal preference and the space you have available. If you only have half shade you will have to make do with a sour cherry.
- **Shape** See Planting fruit trees, page 159.
- **Rootstock**
  'Gisela 5' – semi-dwarfing, recommended for smaller gardens.
  'Colt' – semi-vigorous, useful for fans or large trees, and for sour cherries, which are less vigorous.
- **Pollination period** If your neighbours have cherry trees that might pollinate yours, you will need only one. On the other hand, how many of us are going to know when our neighbour's cherry tree is available for pollination? So if you are only buying one tree, it must be self-fertile.

Varieties
Sweet cherries:
- 'Bing' – the standard for flavour, needs a pollinator, mid-June to early July.
- 'Cherokee' – self-fertile, dark red fruits, good for wet areas as fruit less inclined to split.
- 'Merton Glory' – sweet flavour, white fruit, heavy cropper, late June. Pollinated by 'Morello'.
- 'Stella' – self-fertile, large blackish juicy fruit, late July. Canker-resistant. Probably best for small gardens. AGM.

Sour cherries:
- 'Montmorency' – self-fertile, rich, tangy flavour. A cooking cherry that ripens in late June.

> ### A CHERRY IN A CONTAINER
> Planting in a container is possible, but the plant will require daily regular watering in summer and a few feeds with organic liquid tomato food after fruit has set.

CURRANTS, BLACK

Ribes nigrum • Saxifrage family
* • shrub

According to recent research, blackcurrants are one of the most nutritious of fruits, containing high levels of both antioxidants and vitamin C. Note that blackcurrants are banned in Maine, Massachusetts, and New Hampshire because the plants can serve as vectors for white pine blister rush. The bushes grow 1–1.5m/3–5ft high.

Soil and position
- Full sun, but tolerates slight shade.
- Prefers heavy loamy soil enriched with well-rotted compost.
- Tolerates wet soil, but dislikes sandy.
- Dislikes cold wind.

Sowing, planting and spacing
- Plant in late autumn or when dormant, before spring growth starts.
- Plant with well-rotted compost and a handful of bone meal in the hole, slightly deeper than the plant was in the nursery.
- After planting cut all shoots back to just above the first bud, about 30cm/1ft above soil level, so that the plant can concentrate on producing new branches.
- 1.5m/5ft between plants, 1.8m/6ft between rows.

Aftercare
- Mulch in early spring. On poor soils use half-rotted compost or well-rotted manure. Alternatively feed with blood, fish and bone, 100g per sq. m/3½oz per sq. yd.

Companion planting
- Borage, French and pot marigolds to encourage pollinating insects. Basil is said to reduce powdery mildew; dill is good for plant health in general.

Propagation
Take hardwood cuttings in the winter when the plant is dormant:
- Cut twigs about 25cm/10in long,

thick as a pencil.
- Trim just below leaf joint or bud at the bottom. Make sure you put the cutting in the right way up, in other words with the bottom at the bottom.
- Stick your spade into your garden soil to make a slot, trickle some sand into the base of the slot, and then stick the little pencil cutting in halfway. Leave a few inches between each cutting.
- Water but otherwise ignore for a year.
- Next winter, dig it up and if there are roots it's a new bush.

Pruning
- Hard pruning is not needed for the first 3 years.
- Blackcurrants fruit on 1-year old wood, in other words on the shoots produced during the previous year, so the more new shoots you have, the more fruit there will be.
- After the first few years, each winter cut out one-third of the old branches at the base. The old branches are the ones that look rough, dark and gnarled.
- If the bush is sprawling untidily, trim back the offending branches by a third.

Problems
- Net bushes or else the birds will have the lot.
- Big bud mite – buds become swollen and blackish. No treatment, just burn or bin infected buds, or whole plant if badly infested.
- If the climate continues to warm up and winters become too mild, blackcurrants will fail to flourish. Cut back on driving and flying.

Harvesting and uses
- Each bush should produce a few kilos or pounds of berries.
- Pick when glossy black, around late July.
- Do not expect children to help picking blackcurrants – there is no instant gratification because most people find the taste of them raw nasty, and the leaves also emit a strong odour, which some find off-putting.

- Jam, fruit coulis to add to champagne, ice cream.
- Use leaves for blackcurrant tea.
- Can be frozen.

Varieties
Varieties with the prefix 'Ben' flower late, reducing the risk of frost damage, so they are recommended. As blackcurrants are self-fertile, you can have just one bush.
- 'Ben Lomond' – productive, mildew resistant, medium-size bush, large fruit. AGM.
- 'Ben Hope' – productive, resistant to big bud mite, good fruit.
- 'Ben Sarek' – smaller bush, so plant 1m/39in apart. Heavy crop. Mildew resistant. Berries do not hang well, so pick as soon as ripe. AGM.

RELATIVES
JOSTABERRY
Gooseberry/blackcurrant hybrid. The colour of a blackcurrant but the size of a gooseberry. Use for crisps. If you are feeling adventurous, have plenty of room and like making jam, you might want to try making jostaberry jam.

CURRANTS, RED AND WHITE

Ribes sativum and *R. rubrum*
Saxifrage family
** • shrubs • ☺

Red and white currants are both easy to grow, and require the same conditions. They fruit at child height (bushes grow 1–1.5m/3–5ft high) and can be picked straight to eat. Though a bit fiddly to harvest they have no thorns and are delicious. White currants are rarer and have a slight tendency to look like a very pale little fish with visible stomach contents. In terms of attractive berries, a necklace of bright-red jewelled red currants is hard to beat.

Soil and position
- Sunny position.
- Most soils with the addition of well-rotted compost on planting, and a handful of bone meal in the hole.

Sowing, planting and spacing
- Plant in late autumn or when dormant, before spring growth starts.
- Plant to the same depth as in the nursery.
- 1.5m/5ft between plants, 1.8m/6ft between rows.

Aftercare
- Mulch in early spring. On poor soils use half-rotted compost or well-rotted manure. Alternatively feed with blood, fish and bone, 100g per sq. m/3½oz per sq. yd.

Companion planting
- Poached egg plant (*Limnanthes douglasii*) to attract hoverfly to predate on pests.

Propagation
- Hardwood cuttings are easy to do (see page 171).

Pruning
- Red and white currants fruit on old and new wood. Hard pruning is not necessary. Cut out dead wood and crossing branches, and then take out a couple of the oldest stems at the base.

- Always cut to an outward-facing bud.
- Aim for an open goblet shape to let in air and light.

Problems
- Net bushes or else the birds will have the lot.

Harvesting and uses
- Each bush should produce a few kilos or pounds of berries.
- Pick when glossy red, or for white berries when a test berry is tasty.
- It is easiest to pick the whole strig and then comb out the berries with a fork back in the kitchen, but children will probably prefer to pick individual berries.
- As dessert with a sprinkle of sugar. As jelly or to fill cakes. Fruit juice.
- Can be frozen.

> **STRIG**
> The 'technical' term for a bunch or string of currants.

Varieties
Red:
- 'Jonkheer van Tets' – early, profuse, very bright red fruits, very tasty, AGM.
- 'Stanza' – mid-season, long dark red trusses, AGM.
- 'Red Lake' – mid-season, large bright red fruit, tasty, AGM.
- 'Redstart' – mid-August. Very heavy yield.
- 'Rondom' – Late season (September). Heavy cropper, can cope with windy sites, but fruit not as juicy as the others.

White:
- 'White Versailles' – long strigs, good for dessert.

FIGS

Ficus carica • Mulberry family
** • 🪴 • tree • ☺

The fig is a lovely tree with big glossy lobed leaves and fruit that is considered amongst the tastiest in the world for old and young. It is easy to grow, although slightly more complicated to bring to fruit. Figs are hardy only in zones 7–8 and warmer; in colder areas, grow them in a container and overwinter them in a frost-free spot.

Soil and position

- Being a Mediterranean plant, it needs a sunny and protected spot. Ideally, grow as a rough fan shape, along a sheltered wall, preferably facing south or south-west.
- In their country of origin figs are happiest in poor and stony soil. This should therefore be re-created as far as possible. Mix ordinary garden soil with broken bricks and crocks for drainage. If the soil is too rich, the plant will put on lots of leaf growth at the expense of fruit.
- Will need at least 3–4m/10–13ft space along the wall.

Sowing, planting and spacing

- Fig trees hate root disturbance, so are not sold bare-rooted like most other trees.
- Plant pot-grown fig trees in spring so that they have a season in which to settle before their first winter.
- Dig your planting hole about 15cm/6in away from the wall, and then edge it with four vertical paving slabs 60cm/24in square so that the roots will be restricted within a kind of underground concrete frame. Do not put a slab

across the bottom of the hole. (According to tradition, figs should be planted into an old leather doctor's bag.)

- Use bamboo sticks or a wire framework – horizontal wires, 45cm/18in apart – to train the tree into a flattish shape. Tie in branches to the framework.
- Keep tree pruned to 2m/6ft high so that you can reach the fruit easily.

Aftercare

Feeding and mulching

- Water in the first few months after planting.
- Feed lightly in spring once with a high nitrogen feed such as organic chicken manure pellets, 50g per sq. m/2oz per sq. yd. When fruits begin to develop, change to organic potash.
- Mulch with compost in late autumn.

Winter protection

- Protect with fleece or cover cloth in winter to ensure crop. If you are growing a fig only for its attractive foliage, it will survive down to −11°C/12°F without protection.

Managing fruit development

This is the only complicated part of growing figs. In the Mediterranean, figs have two crops a year, the second crop starting as tiny figlets in late summer and overwintering. In colder climates any larger overwintered figlets do not survive.

- After the leaves fall from the tree, remove any figlets that are larger than a pea.
- Leave the small pea-sized fruit, which will be next summer's maincrop.
- A second crop might ripen by autumn if the summer has been very hot.

Pruning

- Keep tying in branches to the wall framework as they grow.
- In mid-spring (April), cut off any shoots that are growing straight out from the wall or straight back into it.
- Aim for lots of stout branches and shoots, not one or two very long ones. Cut back long shoots in early summer (June).

A FIG IN A CONTAINER

Figs can be grown in containers, but must be kept watered, though not waterlogged.

Use a rich potting soil, or an alternative soil-based compost.

The advantage of containers is that they can be moved for frost protection in winter. If there are a few nearly ripe figs on the tree, a spell in a cool conservatory or a sheltered corner may give them those few extra weeks they need to ripen.

Re-pot every 2 years while dormant in winter.

Once the fig has grown into the size of pot you want, 45cm/18in, cut off 10 per cent of the roots each winter – a few centimetres all round – and replant in fresh compost in the same pot.

Problems

- Birds and squirrels love nearly ripe figs. If you only have a couple on your tree and you are watching and waiting for them to ripen, consider protecting them by wrapping each individual fruit in fleece or cover cloth, or muslin.

Harvesting and uses

- When the fig is very soft and squishy to the touch, it is ripe.
- Fresh; as accompaniment to cheese; warmed with cream.

Varieties

- 'Brown Turkey' – the hardiest variety for colder climates. August/September. Brownish purple when ripe. AGM.
- 'White Marseilles' – originally brought to Lambeth Palace by Cardinal Pole in 1525. Pale fruit, very sweet.
- 'Brunswick' – mid-August. Large, brown figs, red inside. Peel before eating.
- 'Bourjasotte Grise' – pale green fruits, dark red inside. Rich taste.

GOOSEBERRIES

Ribes uva-crispa (syn. *grossularia*)
Saxifrage family
* • shrub

It's not clear why babies should be found under gooseberry bushes; maybe the prickly nature of the bush makes it a safer place to leave the infant. Playing the gooseberry means you are the slightly spiky berry sitting in the way between two loved ones … But since the advent of proper contraception, gooseberry bushes seem to have fallen from favour, which is a pity, because the fruit, picked fresh when really ripe and sweet, can be quite delicious. There are cooking and dessert varieties. Bushes grow 1–2m/3–7ft high.

Gooseberry picking is not a child-friendly activity because the bushes can be very thorny, but gooseberry eating is.

Soil and position
- Good soil, well drained.
- Preferably full sun; can cope with light shade.

Sowing, planting and spacing
- Plant in early spring.
- Enrich soil with well-rotted manure or compost. Sprinkle bone meal in the planting hole.
- 1.2–1.5m/4–5ft between plants.

Aftercare
- Mulch in early spring. On poor soils use half-rotted compost or well-rotted manure. Alternatively feed with blood, fish and bone, 100g per sq. m/3.5oz per sq. yd.

Companion planting
- Undersow with poached egg plant (*Limnanthes douglasii*) to help control gooseberry sawfly.

Propagation
- Whereas other currants are easier to propagate from hardwood cuttings in winter, gooseberries root from similar cuttings in September (early autumn) (see page 171).
- Use cuttings about 30cm/10in long, thick as a pencil.

Pruning
- Aim for an open-centred bush to allow air to circulate and sun to ripen the berries.
- Fruits on older branches.
- Prune in early spring, taking off half the length of each main branch.
- In early summer (early June) prune back extra growth sideways (lateral shoots) on the main branches to five leaves, to avoid the bush becoming overcrowded.

Problems
- Mildew – introduced to Europe from America in the early twentieth century and a real problem: a spattering of greyish sticky powder all over the fruit, which turns into a brown crusty layer. If the plant is not too affected, rub the fruit clean – it is still edible, although having to rub each berry is boring. Choose resistant varieties such as 'Invicta'.
- Gooseberry sawfly – from May onwards, little pale green caterpillars with black spots. If you notice the leaves on your gooseberry disappearing, look closer. Pick them off (and then squash them).

Harvesting and uses
- From July, each bush should produce a few kilos/5–7lb of fruit.
- For dessert, let the berries ripen completely on the bush or else they will be sour.
- For jam-making, pick just before the berries are completely ripe because the pectin levels will be higher then.
- Dessert, straight from the bush, gooseberry fool, cake, granita and jam.
- As a learning aid to avoid explaining the facts of life to your children.

Varieties
All these are mid-season, around late July.
- 'Invicta' – vigorous, prickly, large pale green berries. For cooking. Mildew-resistant. AGM.
- 'Greenfinch' – smooth green cooking variety. Mildew-resistant. AGM.
- 'Leveller' – large pale greenish-yellow, dessert berries. Good taste. AGM.
- 'Pax' – dark red, dessert, few thorns, tasty.

STANDARD GOOSEBERRIES
Gooseberries can be grown as standards, with an initial stem (leg) at least 60cm/2ft tall and then a rounded head on top. In this case, any growth along the leg should be removed, and the head pruned to the desired shape. Yield will be less, but the berries will be at a comfortable height, and the bush will be more attractive.

NUTS

Corylus avellana • Birch family
* • shrub/tree • ☺

A pretty tree with yellow catkins to brighten up the depths of winter. Hazels (*Corylus avellana*), cobs and filberts (*C. maxima*) are basically all types of hazelnut. Supposedly the difference is that in a hazel you can see the snout of the nut poking out, whereas a filbert nut is completely covered by its husk, but this is a discussion best left to botanists. It is important to note that you need two compatible varieties to fertilize one another.

Soil and position
- Sunny site.
- Poor to medium soil, well drained.

Sowing, planting and spacing
- Plant bare-rooted in early spring.
- 5m/16½ft apart.

Aftercare
- Keep the area around the stem clear for the first few years.
- If growing in a grassy area, keep the grass low to make collection of nuts from the ground easier.
- Mulch if you feel generous and have compost to spare.

Companion planting
- Once the tree is mature, underplant with early bulbs, such as snowdrops or daffodils. There is no companion planting benefit, but it looks good. The leaves of the bulbs will have disappeared by harvest time in autumn.

Pruning
- Grow as a bush with many stems. After a few years, remove the largest stems every winter. Remove any crossed branches and try to keep the centre of the bush open.
- In theory you should coppice the whole bush every 7–10 years, in other words chop the whole plant down in winter to 20–30cm/8–12in. This will reduce cropping for a few years, so only carry out this traumatic intervention if you have other bushes to keep you well supplied with nuts in the intervening years.
- Can be grown as a little tree with a single stem. Prune out crossing branches and keep the centre clear and airy.

Problems
- Squirrels.
- Lack of fruit. Check pollination times for your varieties, which must be compatible.

Harvesting and uses
- Pick cobnuts fresh while the husks are still green and the nuts milky and juicy.
- Other hazels (and cobnuts if you missed the chance) can also be harvested later, when they are brown and drop off the tree.
- Each tree could produce 4.5kg/10lb of nuts in a good year.
- Hazels are a pleasant thing to harvest with children, because the nuts just fall off the tree when shaken, and then lie on the ground, where they are easy for short people to scoop up.

> '*I had a little nut tree, nothing would it bear*
> *But a silver nutmeg and a golden pear.*'
> Traditional nursery rhyme

- Fresh, in cookies, with cereal.
- Cobnuts should be stored in the fridge, with loose husks removed.
- All varieties, once brown, will store for months.

Varieties
Nuts are wind-pollinated so need to be close enough to one another for a breeze to float pollen from one to another. These three varieties can pollinate one another:
- 'Cosford Cob' – one of the tastiest, very sweet. Thin-shelled nuts, not prolific.
- 'Gunslebert' – vigorous and productive.
- 'Kentish Cob' – reliable and tasty, very productive.

PEARS

Pyrus communis var. *sativa*
Rose family
** • 🪴 • tender • ☺

Originally from Central Asia. Unless your neighbours have pear trees and promise not to cut them down for as long as you need them to pollinate your tree, you should try to grow at least two. As well as the fruit the tree is a great asset, with attractive blossom and autumn leaf colour. There used to be a saying that you plant pears for heirs, since not only do pear trees take a long time to reach maturity, but they can live for as long as 200 years. But smaller rootstocks (such as quince C) mean that you should be getting a decent crop within 3–4 years.

Pear purée is tasty for the very young, and juicily messy for slightly older children.

Soil and position
- Pears flower a few weeks earlier than apples, so require an even more sheltered position. Cold winds are especially damaging for pear trees, so do not plant in a draught.
- Ideal position for pear trees is therefore against a sunny wall, grown as an espalier. However, they can also be grown successfully as standards.
- If you know there is going to be a late frost, rush out with a sheet of fleece or cover cloth.
- Rich, well-drained soil.

Sowing, planting and spacing
- Add lots of well-rotted compost to the planting area.
- Distance between trees: 2.5–4m/8–12ft apart, the same as the final height of the tree you have chosen, depending on rootstock (see below).
- If you are growing your trees as espaliers, then at least 6m/20ft per tree.

> *'There are only ten minutes in the life of a pear when it is perfect to eat.'*
> Ralph Waldo Emerson

Aftercare
- Feeding and mulching not necessary the first year; from the second year onwards mulch in early spring (see Feeding and mulching, page 160).
- Fruit may need to be thinned once it starts to swell, in midsummer. If you think that the branches may struggle to bear the weight of mature fruits, thin to one or two fruits per cluster.

Pruning
The tendency for pears is to grow as a pyramid shape. Pears fruit on two-year-old wood and on older spurs. Pruning therefore aims to provide lots of two-year-old wood.

Early spring pruning
- While trees are young, only prune in early spring to achieve the desired shape or to remove broken or dead twigs.
- On mature trees, occasionally remove branches to let in light and air to the centre of the tree, or to retain a good espalier shape.
- If the weather is warm and wet in late summer, the tree may produce upwards-growing whippy shoots – water shoots. These should be removed.

Summer pruning
- Only to restrict growth and size if necessary.

Problems
- Young trees flowering but no fruit. Sign of immaturity: just be patient for another year or two.
- Poor flowering on older trees. Feed with organic potash for more flowers next year.
- Yellowing leaves – lack of magnesium. Water with a solution of Epsom salts. Mulch well.
- Fireblight – bacterial disease often spread by pollinating insects. Branches look as though they have been scorched by fire with leaves hanging dead. Late-flowering pears are susceptible. Cut out infected branches 60cm/2ft into healthy wood.

Harvesting and uses
- A standard pear tree can produce over 27kg/60lb of fruit a year, an espalier 11kg/25lb.

A PEAR TREE IN A CONTAINER
Choose a small rootstock. 'Conference' is recommended as a variety. Prune firmly.

- Colour is not a good indication of ripeness and pears should not be allowed to ripen fully on the tree, as they will become floury and gritty. Aim to pick when they are still hard but come away easily when lifted and twisted gently.
- You will need to pick a few times – first those on the sunny side, and then those in the shade and towards the centre of the tree.
- Pears are damaged when they fall, so you cannot rely on windfalls.
- When ready to eat, the fruit should give slightly when you press near the stalk.
- Christopher Lloyd, the famous gardener who died in 2006, pointed out in his very last newspaper column that for a really good pear you also require someone to peel it for you.
- Early varieties do not store well.
- Late pears, if blemish-free, can keep for several months in a cool place such as a dark shed or garage, as long as the temperature does not drop below freezing.

Choosing your tree
- **Shape** Pears can be grown as standard trees or espaliers against a sunny wall.
- **Rootstock and size** Pure pear rootstocks are only appropriate for enormous trees. Smaller trees use quince rootstocks, usually A or C. Quince A: quite vigorous, 5m/16ft for a larger standard tree. Quince C: dwarfing, 3–6m/10–12ft, recommended for smaller gardens and espaliers. Fruit ripens quicker than on larger rootstocks.
- **Pollination** You need to ensure that your pear tree has a pollinator. Even if they flower in the same period, some pear trees will not be useful pollinators for others. The safest option therefore is to plan for two trees and check with the nursery that the two you want will pollinate one another.

'It is, in my view, the duty of an apple to be crisp and crunchable, but a pear should have such a texture as leads to silent consumption.'
Edward Bunyard, *The Anatomy of Dessert*, 1929

Varieties
• See table below.

RELATIVES
ASIAN PEARS (*Pyrus pyrifolia*)
These are sweet watery fruits, often larger and rounder than the more common pears. They are eaten fresh from the tree. They contain too much water to be tasty when cooked. They are grown in the same way as common pears. Varieties include 'Shinseiki', 'Kumoi' and 'Shinsui'. All require pollinators, such as 'Williams', in the vicinity.

Pear variety	Type	Season	Description	Pollinators
'Onward' AGM	Dessert	September	Pale yellow/green, creamy white flesh, good flavour. Reliable. Stores for a couple of months.	Concorde', 'Doyenné du Comice'
'Williams' Bon Chrétien' AGM	Dessert	September	Most popular. Yellow with reddish tinge. Creamy white flesh. Juicy, aromatic. Can be a bit gritty.	'Beth', 'Beurré Hardy', 'Conference'
'Beth' AGM	Dessert	September	Small fruit, high quality, yellow. Sweet and juicy.	'Beurré Hardy', 'Conference', 'Williams' Bon Chrétien'
'Beurré Hardy' AGM	Dessert/cooker	October	Prolific cropper. Reddish fruit. Good autumn foliage. Good flavour. Pick fruit when still hard.	'Beth', 'Conference', 'Williams' Bon Chrétien'
'Concorde' AGM	Dessert	October	Sweet, good flavour. Similar to 'Doyenné du Comice', but less sensitive to cold weather.	Doyenné du Comice', 'Onward'
'Conference' AGM	Dessert	October	Named after the National Pear Conference held at Chiswick in 1885; since we work in the walled gardens at Chiswick we could not ignore this one.	'Beth', 'Beurré Hardy', 'Williams' Bon Chrétien'
'Doyenné du Comice', 'Comice' AGM	Dessert	November	Large golden fruit. 'The quality dessert pear that has never been excelled' – Christopher Lloyd; the sentiment is shared by most other pear growers. Stores for several months.	'Concorde', 'Onward'

PLUMS

Prunus domestica • Rose family
** • tree • ☺

After apples, these are the most popular fruit trees, and when one considers the beauty of the blossom, as well as the tastiness and generosity of the crop, it is easy to see why. Nearly all are sweet and juicy, from tiny greengages to larger more substantial fruit.

Originating in the Caucasus, plums were initially considered cooking fruit, while gages were for eating fresh. Nowadays one can get almost any colour and size of plum and they are very easy and rewarding to grow.

Soil and position
- Free-draining soil.
- Sheltered position, sunny and protected from wind and late frosts.
- If you know there is going to be a late frost, rush out with a sheet of fleece or cover cloth.

Sowing, planting and spacing
- See page 159.
- Plant in late autumn, as trees or fans.
- Trees 6m/20ft apart, 4.5m/15ft between fans.

Aftercare
- Keep the base of the tree free of grass, to a diameter of about 90cm/36in, until the tree is well established.

- From the second year onwards mulch in early spring. On poor soils use half-rotted compost or well-rotted manure. Alternatively feed with blood, fish and bone, 150g per sq. m/5oz per sq. yd.
- Plums tend to overcrop one year and then do nothing the following year. If your tree does this, thin the fruit to one every 5–10cm/2–4in.

Companion planting
- Do not plant anemones next to plums, as both suffer from plum rust.

Pruning
- Standards and half-standards need little pruning; just remove any dead wood and let light and air into the centre of the tree. Always prune in late spring or summer in dry weather.
- With fans, in midsummer prune out anything growing straight out or straight back into the wall. Once the tree has reached the size of its desired framework, simply prune off anything that is growing too long and keep branches to the length of the supporting canes.

Problems
It is very important to start off with healthy, virus-free plants. Check with the vendor to ensure you're getting healthy plants.
- Silver leaf. Always prune in late spring or summer and not while it is raining in order to reduce infection. Prune out diseased branches.
- Yellowing foliage – iron deficiency. Add a dose of sequestrene.
- Aphids. If the new leaves start to curl in early summer, it is aphid damage. The crop will be less, but still viable.
- Plum maggots. You can usually tell a plum has these by the little brownish crumbs of maggot excreta on the skin. The plum moth emerges in late May, and lays her eggs on the fruit in June–July; then the caterpillar tunnels into the plum and feeds around the stone, emerging in late summer, just when you are picking your plums. The caterpillar overwinters under bark flakes and pupates the following spring. Set pheromone traps in late May.
- Brown rot. This is the worst disease. The fruit begins to ripen and then goes brown and pustular. The plums mummify as the season draws to a close. During winter pick off all the mummified corpses and bin or burn; if the twig looks as though it has dried ooze on it, remove that too. In summer, thin fruits and prune the tree to be more airy and well ventilated.

Harvesting and uses
- Plums have a tendency to crop in a 'feast or famine' mode, depending on the lateness of the last frost, and also on whether the fruit was thinned in time. In general a mature standard tree may produce 22kg/48lb, a mature fan 12–14kg/20–30lb.
- Pick when fruit is completely ripe; taste one to check.
- Fruit gums, sorbets, jams, pies, compotes.

Choosing your tree
- **Shapes** Grow as standards, half-standards or fans. Plums are too vigorous for espaliers or cordons.
- **Rootstock and size** 'Pixy', dwarfing, 2–3m/7–10ft. Requires richer soil and better care. Tends to produce smaller fruits.

Plum variety	Type	Season	Description	Pollinators
'Czar' AGM	Cooker	Early August	Heavy cropper. Purple-black.	Self-fertile
'Oullins Gage' AGM	Dessert/jam	Mid-August	Large round yellow fruits. Late flowering, so hardier.	Self-fertile
'Denniston's Superb' (aka 'Imperial Gage') AGM	Dessert	Late August	'Yellow, firm, juicy, rich, sugary and vinous', according to Robert Hogg's fruit manual of 1875. Reliable.	Self-fertile and a good pollinator
'Kirke's Blue'	Dessert	Late August	Blue, with green/yellow flesh. Excellent flavour.	'Ouillins Gage'
'Victoria' AGM	Cooker when under-ripe. Dessert when ripe.	Early September	Oval, red, juicy. A bit boring perhaps, but one of the most reliable self-fertile plums.	Self-fertile
'Coe's Golden Drop'	Dessert	Late September	Oval, bright yellow, apparently heavenly flavour, but very much a 'shy cropper', producing few fruits but delicious.	Partially self-fertile; 'Denniston's Superb'

'St Julien A', semi-dwarfing, 3–4.5m/10–15ft.
'Brompton', very vigorous, 4.5m/15ft.

- **Pollination** If you only plan to get one tree, then one of the self-fertile trees would be recommended. However, even self-fertile trees crop better if they have other pollinators. The aim is to co-ordinate flowering times while spacing out harvesting times. A good nursery will be able to check your choice.

Varieties
- See table above.

RELATIVES

DAMSONS
Good for jams, cakes and damson cheeses.

- 'Farleigh Damson', aka 'Crittenden' or 'Cluster Damson'. Small black/blue round or oval, with greenish/yellow flesh. Earliest damson, early September. Better with a pollinator.
- 'Quetsche' or 'Zwetsche'. October. Oval fruits, good in cakes and delicious fresh. Very prolific. Self-fertile.

MIRABELLES
- 'Mirabelle de Nancy' – comes in yellow or red varieties. Tiny cherry-sized little plums, very sweet, dessert. Popular in Europe. August. Very worthwhile.

GREENGAGES
Sweet and scented but need south- or west-facing wall. For varieties, see table below.

Greengage variety	Type	Season	Description	Pollinators
'Early Transparent Gage'	Dessert/cooker	Early August	Small green fruits with a red flush, very juicy and tasty. Good fan or bush.	Self-fertile
'Cambridge Gage' AGM	Dessert	August	Round green fruit. Wonderful flavour. One of the most prolific of gages.	Partly self-fertile; 'Early Transparent Gage', 'Kirke's Blue', 'Oullins Gage'
'Reine Claude de Bavais'	Dessert	September	'Yellow, tender, melting and very juicy, with a rich, sugary flavour' – Hogg.	Self-fertile

RASPBERRIES

Rubus idaeus • Rose family
* • shrub • ☺

Raspberry originated as a native plant that used to grow on woodland edges, and is now pretty well an essential in any kitchen garden. The taste of a freshly picked raspberry is one of the best things in any productive garden and far outweighs any aesthetic shortcomings. Letting a group of children loose in a raspberry cage and watching them fill themselves up with fruit is a good sight.

Soil and position
- Sunny position, or only a little shade for part of the day.
- Neutral or acidic soil, with good drainage.
- Make sure you remove all perennial weeds before planting; raspberries are shallow rooted and it will be particularly annoying – if not impossible – to weed around them.
- Fork in plenty of compost and organic matter, such as leaf mould, especially into the top 15cm/6in of earth.
- For summer raspberries, use a support system of posts and wires. Raspberries grow up to about 2m/6ft tall, so the posts should be tall enough, strong enough and solidly rooted. Space strong horizontal wires at 30cm/1ft intervals, with the first one about 1m/3ft high.

Sowing, planting and spacing
- Plant in early spring.
- Canes usually arrive bare-rooted in a bundle, and each one should be planted separately. Soak the canes for an hour before planting.
- As you plant, throw a sprinkle of bone meal into the bottom of each hole. Make sure the roots are not cramped in the hole, and firm down the soil around the cane after planting.
- 40–50 cm/16–20in between canes on planting.
- 1.5–1.8m/5–6ft between rows.
- With summer raspberries, when the new growth starts, cut down the stub of the original (bought) cane and tie in the new growth when it reaches the first wire.

AUTUMN RASPBERRIES
There are summer raspberries and autumn raspberries; the main difference is when they fruit and when you cut back the canes. In autumn the fruit has rarity value, whereas summer raspberries appear with all the currants and strawberries, so one can feel a little spoilt. Best thing is to grow both …
- Plant in a row, and pull out any strays that appear too far from the line, but these raspberries do not need a formal support structure.
- These bear fruit – in autumn, obviously, from September – on the current season's canes. Sometimes the crop continues into November and onwards, but it may need some protection.
- Cut the canes down to the ground in late winter (February).
- Otherwise treat the same as summer raspberries.

Aftercare
- After cutting down old canes in summer, mulch with compost.
- Top up mulch in spring.

Companion planting
- Do not plant where there were strawberries, as they share viruses.
- Sow poached egg plant (*Limnanthes douglasii*) near by, as it is helpful for attracting lacewings, which eat aphids.

Pruning
For summer raspberries
- Hoe off any suckers or new canes that appear out of the lines, but be careful, as raspberries have shallow roots. Be disciplined with the suckers, or else you will end up with a raspberry jungle – all leaf and no fruit.
- If the canes reach the top wire, nip them off so that they can focus on fruit production.
- Raspberries fruit on their canes the following summer, in other words on 2-year-old canes. Once a cane has finished fruiting (the little dried husks that show where the berries were, and the stem is brownish) between early July to August, cut it down completely to ground level. Choose strong new canes to tie in. Cut out any thin, weedy canes. You should end up with a new cane every 10cm/4in along the line.

Problems
- Botrytis and grey mould. Pick off affected fruits and bin. If canes turn brown, pull the whole plant out and bin or burn. Grow new ones somewhere else and under more airy conditions.
- Viruses – distorted and mottled leaves. Make sure you buy virus-free plants from a good nursery. Bin or burn affected plants.

Harvesting and uses
- When the fruit is red and the berry comes away from its stem easily.

Varieties
Summer raspberries:
- 'Latham' – mid-season (June/July), large, full-flavoured fruits, highly productive and disease resistant.
- 'Glen Prosen' – mid-late season (July), very good flavour. Spine-free, easy to pick. Firm berries. Virus and aphid resistant. AGM.
- 'Malling Admiral' – late season (August). Resistant to botrytis and mildew. AGM.

Autumn raspberries:
- 'Autumn Bliss' – by far the most reliable and heavy cropper. Short sturdy canes. AGM.
- 'Fallgold' – yellow variety. Vigorous, very sweet.

RHUBARB

Rheum rhabarbarum, R. rhaponticum,
R. x hybridum • Knotweed family
* • perennial

Originating in Mongolia, rhubarb was grown in Europe for medicinal purposes, particularly as a laxative, from the sixteenth century. It is one of the easiest things you can grow and will repay minimal attention with quantities of produce. The leaves are considered poisonous, although it is estimated that you would need to eat about 5kg/11lb to suffer any ill effects. Rhubarb is strictly speaking a vegetable (we use the stalks not the fruit), but since we eat it mostly for dessert, we have put it here in the fruit chapter.

Soil and position
- Prefers full sun, but can cope with short periods of shade each day.
- Deep rich soil, with lots of compost added.

Sowing, planting and spacing
- Can be grown from seed but usually bought as a crown.

- Plant individual crowns 90–100cm/36–39in apart.
- Make sure the soil is very rich when planting, incorporating lots of well-rotted farmyard manure if possible.
- Plant with the buds about 2.5cm/1in below the surface.
- Once planted, do not disturb or dig too close to the roots.

Aftercare
- Mulch with garden compost in winter when the leaves have died down. Top up in spring.
- Occasionally the plant throws off a huge flower spike. This should be cut off at the base unless you are curious to see how it looks or want to try growing some rhubarb seed.
- Dividing: every 5 years, dig up the rhubarb crown in winter and split it into several pieces, hacking it cleanly apart with a spade. Each bit must have a pink nose (the bud) and some roots. Replant at the correct distance to create separate plants.

Problems
Trouble free.

Harvesting and uses
- April–September. Stalks should always be twisted off at the junction with the base, never cut. Choose the thickest stalks first. Discard the leaf, which contains large quantities of oxalic acid.
- Some say that you should not eat rhubarb after mid-summer because the levels of oxalic acid rise, although this is not supported by scientific research. However, the plant needs to keep its later leaves to strengthen it for the following year, so ease off picking the rhubarb late in the season.
- Cooked with a sprinkle of sugar and served with cream or ice cream, crisps, pies, jam, chutney.
- Rhubarb cake: see recipe on page 67.
- Freeze: cut into cubes and freeze straight away.

Varieties
- 'Timperley Early', AGM.
- 'Champagne Early'.

FORCING
Keeping rhubarb shoots completely dark makes them more tender and tasty. This was first done by mistake at Chelsea Physic Garden in 1817 when plants were covered over in a ditch, and since then growers have tried to replicate the experience. At the end of winter cover the rhubarb crown to keep out the light. The official method is to use an attractive specially made terracotta forcer, but the rest of us use a black bucket or big flower pot with the holes blocked out. Stuff the pot with dry straw to help warm up the stalks. After a few weeks, peep inside and pick the stalks in spring when you can't wait any longer. Forced rhubarb will be thinner, paler and more delicate in growth and taste.

STRAWBERRIES

Fragaria x *ananassa* • Rose family
* • 🪴 • perennial • ☺

Little wild strawberries have always grown in the forests, but it was a marriage between sweet red Virginian berries and big juicy Chilean ones ('as big as hen's eggs', commented the Frenchman who brought them back to Europe in 1712) that gave us our now classic fruit. Strawberries are to fruit what radishes are to vegetables – the archetypical children's pick, bright red, tasty and low growing.

Soil and position
- Prefers full sun.
- Strawberries taste best when grown in humus-rich soil. Soil should be well drained, as the plants hate having wet feet.
- Dig in well-rotted compost or well-rotted manure a few weeks before planting.

Sowing, planting and spacing
- Plant new strawberries in August/September. Can be planted later, but the harvest will be smaller.
- Make sure the crowns are neither sticking up from the soil nor covered by it. Plant in a small depression, firm down soil and puddle in.
- Specially frozen runners can be planted in spring or summer theoretically to fruit the same year, but it is more natural to plant untreated runners in the autumn.
- 40cm/16in between plants.

Aftercare
Fruiting
- Strawberries flower early, so may need protection against frost with horticultural fleece or cover cloth.
- After flowering, put a layer of straw around each plant, so that the fruits will rest on the straw, not on the earth.
- As soon as the fruit starts to develop, net to keep birds and squirrels away.
- After fruiting, remove the straw.
Feeding
- Cut back the old leaves, about 7–10cm/3–4in above the plants, leaving the small new central foliage. This prevents fungi spreading.
- After you have cut off the leaves, mulch with half-rotted compost or well-rotted manure.
- Feed twice with potassium-rich fertilizer, such as organic liquid tomato food, within a month of harvesting. The plants are producing the flowers for next year right now.
- Do not feed in spring, as otherwise you will get lush leaves and tiny fruit.
Forcing
- For earlier crops, cover with cloches, or with fleece held over wire hoops, from mid-February. When the plants are flowering, lift off the covers during the day to allow pollination.

Companion planting
- Plants of the onion family are said to ward off fungal diseases; plant perennial alliums such as chives or flowering alliums.
- Do not plant anywhere where strawberries, raspberries, tomatoes or potatoes have been grown in the last 3 years, as they can share pests and diseases.
- Since marigolds deter eelworms, it is a good idea to grow them on the future strawberry bed the year before planting.

Propagation
- Towards the end of the season each plant throws out runners which root to create new plantlets. Runners that appear while the plant is still flowering or fruiting should be snipped off immediately.
- If you want new plants, look out for your best fruiting plants and mark them. Ideally take runners from plants that are fruiting for the second time.
- Peg the plantlet down into the earth or so that it sits in a small pot and can root directly into the pot. Do not let any further plantlets form along the same runner. Once it has rooted properly, sever its umbilical cord back to the mother plant and you

STRAWBERRIES IN CONTAINERS
Strawberries will grow in containers, as long as they can be kept well watered. They require a minimum of 15cm/6in depth of rich potting soil and should be potted up in September. If you want an earlier harvest, you can bring them indoors in February, but you will then need to pollinate them by delicately brushing a small paintbrush in each flower, from blossom to blossom, one after another, collecting some yellow pollen from each and passing it onwards. You can buzz as you do it, but this is optional. Use new plants the following year.

have a new strawberry plant.
- Do not let the mother plant produce more than two or three runners or else it will become exhausted; just snip them off before they have time to grow.
- Throw out plants that have cropped three times and use new runners, planted in a different place.

Problems
- Slugs.
- Birds. Make sure nets are well attached.
- Botrytis – mouldy berries, leaves with little reddish-brown spots. Leave enough space between plants to ensure air circulation. Remove any affected mouldy berries immediately.
- Verticillium wilt – fungal infection, usually in summer: plants wilt, leaves turn brown. Avoid waterlogged areas for planting, remove infected plants and bin or burn them. Don't plant new strawberries in this bed.
- Black eye – if the centre of the strawberry is black, then the flower was hit by frost, and will not produce a fruit. Nip it off, and hope the plant develops more flowers.

Time to maturity
Tough gardeners are supposed to cut off the flowers in the first year to ensure a larger crop the second.

Harvesting and uses

- You can pick berries from one plant for about 2 weeks, but you can extend your strawberry season by planting different varieties.
- Each plant can theoretically produce 500g/over a pound in its second year.
- Only pick when completely red; they will not continue to ripen once picked. Pick with a stalk.

Varieties

Grow a few to spread out the season.

Early:
- 'Cardinal' – large fruits with fine flavour and texture, disease resistant.
- 'Rosie' – aromatic, very early. Can be susceptible to powdery mildew.

Mid:
- 'Cambridge Favourite' – early, reliable, quite disease resistant, AGM.
- 'Hapil' – good taste, tolerates light and dry soils, AGM.
- 'Pegasus' – disease resistant, reliable, AGM.

Late:
- 'Alice' – excellent flavour, heavy crop, good disease resistance, AGM.

- 'Florence' – late. Productive, disease resistant.
- 'Symphony' – very hardy, recommended for colder areas, AGM.
- 'Tenira' – good disease resistance, very good flavour but only average yields.

RELATIVES

PERPETUAL STRAWBERRIES

Perpetual strawberries have a longer cropping time with smaller yields and berries. They usually do not produce runners and can stay in the same bed for a longer time, so you could also use them as edging plants. They usually have an excellent aroma.
- 'Aromel' – very good flavour, AGM.
- 'Mara des Bois' – intense perfume, large berries (for a perpetual), poor storage. Mildew resistant. Crops mid-August to October.
- 'Rapella' – good flavour, heavy cropper for a perpetual.

ALPINE OR WILD STRAWBERRY (*Fragaria vesca*)

These small, delicious strawberries grow in dappled shade, in paving cracks and as edging plants. They fruit from spring to autumn. Tough, easy to grow, slug proof and relatively bird resistant, they are an attractive alternative to the effort of strawing and netting cultivated varieties. Grow them near the path, where children and adults can pick as they pass. They can be left to spread and if happy will quietly increase without any effort on your part.
- 'Baron von Solemacher' – no runners; sow seeds in autumn.

VINES, GRAPE

Vitis vinifera, V. labrusca, V. rotundifolia • Grape family *** • shrub/climber

Traditionally brought to Britain by the Romans, grapes were considered 'the most noble and challenging of fruits'. There is something very satisfying about producing your own bunches of grapes. With warmer summers the harvest is more reliable. In colder climates a decent crop might be a matter of luck. Varieties of *V. labrusca* are hardier than *V. vinifera* varieties, while *V. rotundifolia* thrives only in the South.

Soil and position
- Grape vines can grow in most soils, as long as they are not waterlogged.
- In full sunshine, warm and sheltered.
- Best grown over a pergola, an arch or against a wall.

Sowing, planting and spacing
- Plant in early spring when the vine is dormant.
- Add well-rotted compost or manure, plus a sprinkle of bone meal.
- Plant to the same depth as the plant was in the nursery.
- Do not be afraid that your newly planted vine looks dead; buds burst very late in spring.
- Planting over an arch or pergola: one vine on each side is enough.
- Planting along a wall: fix a series of wires with vine eyes and plant vines 1.2–1.5m/4–5ft apart.

Aftercare
- Mulch in early spring. On poor soils use half-rotted compost or well-rotted manure. Vines root very deeply, and usually thrive without much fertilizer.
- Every few years sprinkle lime around the plant(s) before mulching, 100g per sq. m/3½oz per sq. yd.

Pruning
There are different schools of thought. This is the most basic.

Young plants
- Let one shoot grow straight up. Once the plant starts to grow laterals, let one grow along a horizontal support (such as a wire or a beam of your pergola).
- Young plants should not be allowed to fruit. Vines are usually 1 or 2 years old when purchased. A 3-year old plant should be allowed only three bunches, the next year four or five. Thereafter it is mature.

Late autumn pruning
- Do this as soon as possible after the leaves fall. Leave it too close to spring and the vines will bleed, sap leaking disconcertingly from the cuts and weakening the plant.
- The aim of late autumn pruning is to remove all the growth that fruited this season – in other words, to cut back to two buds. Fruit bunches will grow next season from buds produced from new growth.

Summer pruning
- The aim of summer pruning is to prevent the vines going mad and producing useless metres of growth. It needs to be done throughout the summer.
- Once the vine has flowered, let the shoot produce two more sets of leaves beyond the little bunch. Then cut it off just beyond that second leaf. You are aiming for one bunch of grapes every 25–30cm/10–12in.

Propagating
- In late autumn, when pruning the vine, you can take hardwood cuttings very easily. Cuttings should be the thickness of a pencil and about 30cm/12in long. Cut cleanly just below a node, and at the top about 2.5cm/1in above a node. Each cutting should have about three or four buds along its length.
- Stick the cuttings about 15cm/6in deep into the soil – in a spare bit of earth about 12cm/5in apart, or around the edge of a pot. Once cut it is quite hard to tell which way up the cutting is, but it is crucial that they are planted the right way up.
- You should see signs of success when the cuttings begin to leaf up next spring, but leave

until the following year before transplanting to where you want them.

- A 50 per cent success rate is good going, so if you need new plants for a particular area, make sure you do at least double the number you will require.

Problems

- Yellowing leaves in summer – magnesium deficiency. Feed with Epsom salts in early summer and use dolomitic limestone for next liming (see also page 45).
- Birds. Net the vines from early autumn.
- Powdery mildew. Mulch and water during very dry spells. Get resistant varieties.
- Botrytis – brown spores and rot, especially prevalent in damp weather. Remove affected leaves and grapes. Thin fruit and leaves to allow air circulation. Do not leave mummified fruit to hang over winter.

Harvesting and uses

- When the fruit tastes sweet, from late summer.

Varieties

Assuming that you are not going in for large-scale wine production, we suggest the following for tasty dessert grapes. Children may prefer seedless varieties, but seeds contain healthy antioxidants, so if you can convince them to swallow them with the fruit, it would be better for them, and offer you more varieties from which to choose.

Outdoor whites:
- 'Himrod Seedless' – needs a warm wall.
- 'Madeleine Angevine' – reliable, early. Dessert or wine.
- 'Müller Thurgau' – early–mid-season, German grape. Golden dessert.
- 'Niagara' – tangy and delicate labrusca type, excellent dessert variety.
- 'Précoce de Malingre' – dessert and wine, good flavour.
- 'Seyval' – vigorous, resistant to mildews.

Outdoor blacks:
- 'Black Hamburgh' – probably the

best black indoor grape, but in an exceptionally warm and sheltered situation might cope outside.
- 'Boskoop Glory' – prolific blue-black, very sweet, disease resistant. AGM.
- 'Concord' – well-known bluish black labrusca type, vigorous, hardy, and productive.

HERBS

Herbs have always played an intrinsic role in cultivation and kitchen gardening. Essential since ancient times for medicinal and domestic purposes, they were among the most obvious things to be grown near the house. Being scented and decorative, they also gave pleasure.

Often herbs are not needed in great quantity, but they need to be available for frequent and convenient use. This makes them ideal for container and patio growing, which fits many modern lifestyles.

Many of the herbs we now use in everyday cooking are from the Mediterranean, often introduced by the Romans. When choosing which herbs to grow, decide what you like and need, and then think about the conditions you can offer the plants. Some prefer warm conditions in full sunshine – otherwise their aroma suffers. Some herbs, mint or parsley for instance, prefer cooler areas and a bit of shade.

Children enjoy the different scents, as well as the butterflies that visit herbs, and – as adults do – enjoy the flavouring that fresh herbs provide.

A great advantage of growing your own herbs is that you can experiment with varieties that are not available in your local supermarket, such as purple basil or chocolate mint, as well as less common plants such as savory.

Annual herbs are good to grow amongst your vegetables; some, such as basil, savory or dill, are perfect companion plants and will not only grow well but benefit their neighbours.

Perennial herbs, such as lavender or sage, reach their full potential after two or three years and are best planted in a specific herb bed or used as edging plants.

The shrubby forms of perennial herbs appreciate occasional clipping to keep them in shape. Otherwise they are very undemanding. A top dressing of compost in spring is generally sufficient, but for

some herbs even this is too much: they prefer the poor conditions they are used to on their rocky Mediterranean hillsides.

Whichever selection of herbs you decide to grow, you will have plenty of aromatic and attractive flowers and leaves to use in the house, as well as making your garden welcoming to bees and butterflies, and a place of scent and beauty.

BASIL

Ocimum species • Mint family
** • 🌸 • tender annual • attracts
butterflies and hoverflies

Basil may be associated with Italy, but
the true home of this wonderful herb
is Asia, where it has been grown for
thousands of years.

It is not difficult to grow, although
you need to start it off indoors. There
are only two things basil really dislikes:
cold and wet. Although you should
water it well, you must be careful not
to water too much, because then it will
become susceptible to mildew. In warm
summers, however, you can harvest a
bumper crop of aromatic leaves, which
make every tomato salad an event.

Soil and position
- Sunny site and warm, good, well-
  drained soil.
- In cool summers you could cover
  it with cloches in the evening, but
  raise them in the morning, as basil
  hates humid conditions.

Sowing, planting and spacing
- Sow seeds from mid-March
  indoors on a warm windowsill.
- Sow 7–10 seeds directly into
  9cm/3½in pots; basil dislikes
  being pricked out.
- Leave seeds uncovered, as they
  require light to germinate.
- Make sure seedlings are well
  ventilated, as they are prone to
  damping off.
- Harden off before planting out;
  plant out after the last frosts
  have passed.
- About 20cm/8in apart into beds,

or transplant carefully into
bigger pots.

Aftercare
- Mulch with compost for nutrients
  and moisture retention.
- When watering, try not to wet the
  leaves.
- Aroma suffers in stems that
  produce flowers, and the leaves
  become bitter. Pinch off at least
  half of the flower stems, leaving
  only some to attract beneficial
  insects.

Companion planting
- Plant with tomatoes, eggplants,
  peppers, cucumbers – basil is said
  to improve their fruit growth and
  flavour. Should keep white fly and
  mildew away from cucumbers.
- Do not plant near sage or
  raspberries, as growth of both
  will be hindered.

Problems
- Suffers in cold and damp
  conditions, so make sure you
  avoid them.

Harvesting and uses
- Tastes best before flowering.
- Pinch out the plant tips to eat –
  then the shoots will branch out.
- Eat fresh with tomatoes, make
  pesto with oil, pine nuts and
  Parmesan cheese. Always add at
  the end of cooking.
- Make your own delicious basil
  vinegar (see page 97).
- Best eaten fresh. Only Thai basil
  can be frozen.

Varieties
Green-leaved:
- Bush basil (*Ocinum minimum*)
  – tiny leaves, plant grows only
  about 20cm/8in high.
- Cinnamon basil (*O. basilicum*
  'Cinnamon') – greenish leaves,
  purple stems, small pink flowers,
  from Mexico, about 45cm/18in.
- Genovese basil (*O. basilicum*
  'Genovese') – traditionally best for
  pesto, slow to bolt, 45–50cm/18–
  20in.
- Green ruffles basil (*O. basilicum*
  'Green Ruffles') – large crinkled
  leaves with a mild aniseed flavour,
  45cm/18in.

- Lemon basil (*O. citriodorum*) –
  wonderful lemon scent and taste,
  30cm/12in.
- Lettuce leaf basil (*O. basilicum*
  'Napolitano') – large leaves (hence
  the name), 50cm/20in.
- Thai basil (*O. basilicum* var.
  thyrsiflora) – wonderful scent,
  staple of Asian cuisine; also good
  as micro-greens (see page 137),
  30cm/12in.

Purple-leaved – something different for salads and also good as micro-greens:
- *O. basilicum* var. *purpurascens*
  'Purple Ruffles' – pale pink
  flowers, purple leaves have
  ruffled edges, 30cm/1ft.
- *O. basilicum* var. *purpurascens*
  'Dark Opal' – the tallest of the
  purple ones 45–50cm/18–20in
  (illustrated above).

BAY LAUREL (SWEET BAY)

Laurus nobilis • Laurel family
** • 🪴 • half-hardy shrub

Bays are tall evergreen shrubs that grow very slowly. An uninhibited bay could eventually reach about 10m/30ft in height and width, but before you panic and turn the page, it is very tolerant of pruning and can always be cut back into the required size. It can also be grown in containers and trained in topiary shapes such as cones, balls and pyramids. One of these would make a wonderful focal point in your herb garden, but unfortunately this is only possible if the temperature does not drop below –9°C/15°F. If you grow a male and a female plant you could also harvest berries.

Bay is at home in the Mediterranean and played an important role in classical times. *Laurus* comes from the Latin word *laus*, praise, and bay wreaths were used to crown emperors and poets (laureates).

Soil and position
- Not fussy about soil as long as it is well drained.
- Full sun or partial shade, sheltered from cold wind.

Propagation, planting and spacing
- Buy as plant. Hardy to –9°C/15°F.

Aftercare
- Has very shallow roots, so be careful when weeding.
- Feed container-grown plants from spring to summer with organic liquid fertilizer.
- Plants in containers can remain in their pots for several years. If a new pot is necessary, choose one about 5cm/2in wider.

Problems
- Usually problem-free, with one exception: scale insect. Can attack if you bring your plant in for the winter. Black sooty mould follows. Check your shrub regularly and remove pests by hand as soon as you spot any.

Harvesting and uses
- The leaves can be harvested throughout the year and used for bouquet garni. Also good in soups and stews; it helps the digestion of meat dishes.
- Dried leaves can be stored for up to a year and the flavour is apparently intensified.
- The berries (produced if you have bought a male and a female plant) are very good with venison.

CHIVES

Allium schoenoprasum · Onion family
* · 🌱 · hardy perennial

Chives are tough hardy plants that are very easy to grow. They improve the taste of many dishes with their fresh onion flavour, which is milder than that of onions themselves. Unlike many other herbs, chives like rich and moist soil. They grow 20–25cm/8–10in high.

They die back over winter, but in mild areas chives grow back as early as February.

Soil and position
- Humus-rich and moist soil, and full sunshine.

Propagation, planting and spacing
- From April, sow directly in drills 30cm/1ft apart, or sow 10–20 seeds per 9cm/3½in pot.
- Takes about a month to germinate.
- Division in April of existing clumps gives quicker results.
- Thin to 7cm/3in apart when sown in rows; plant out seedlings 25cm/10in apart.

Aftercare
- For a constant supply of fresh chives, cut back regularly to about 2–5cm/1–2in above soil level. Do this every 4–6 weeks: they grow back quickly.

- Chive flowers come in a pretty purple, but the flower stems are coarse and not really edible. In theory one should not let chives flower, but if you find this is too radical (or you just missed cutting out the buds), at least cut them back before the seed heads develop. Children might enjoy picking the flower heads, thereby deadheading in the process.
- After 3–4 years lift your chive plants in March, divide them and plant anew.

Companion planting
- Chives are often recommended as companion plants because they deter fungi, aphids and carrot flies. Awkward to use between annual vegetables, since the plant is a perennial, but great as an edging plant or planted with more permanent crops such as strawberries.

Problems
- Rust. Cut back to about 2.5cm/1in above the soil; bin affected leaves. Avoid planting too densely and keep plants moist – it attacks plants that are grown too dry.

Harvesting and uses
- Finely chopped fresh chives improve almost any savoury dish: use sprinkled over salads, soups, and sauces, with cheese – or

simply on wholemeal bread with butter.
- Always add just before serving, as the aroma of chives suffers if you cook with them.
- It is possible to freeze chives, but they are best used fresh.

RELATIVES
CHINESE OR GARLIC CHIVES (*Allium tuberosum*)
Flat leaves with an onion/garlic flavour. Leaves and white flowers are edible. Treat the same as chives.

CORIANDER (CILANTRO)

Coriandrum sativum · Parsley family
** · 🌱 · tender annual · attracts bees, bumblebees and hoverflies

Coriander is one of the oldest known cultivated herbs, even rating a mention in the Old Testament. The leaves look similar to those of flat-leaved parsley, but the taste is very distinctive. Like Marmite, people either love it or hate it. Apparently the name coriander comes from that for a Greek bed bug, *koriannon*, which smells similar.

Coriander leaves are used in Middle Eastern, Asian and South American cuisines, as are the seeds, which is just as well, since it has a tendency to bolt. Coriander can also be used as a micro-green (see page 137). Plants are about 20–30cm/8–12in tall without flowers; the flower stalks can reach a height of about 70cm/28in.

Soil and position
- Light and well-drained soil.
- Ideally warm and sunny, but dappled shade in summer delays bolting.

Propagation, planting and spacing
- Sow 5–10 seeds directly in little pots on a warm windowsill. It does not like root disturbance.
- Cover seeds thinly with soil: needs darkness to germinate.
- Keep seedlings moist: once they dry out they are even more likely to bolt.

- Plant in the garden after the last frost.
- For a constant supply, sow every 4 weeks.

Companion planting
- Plant with brassicas; coriander confuses cabbage mealy aphids and cabbage white caterpillars with its scent.

Aftercare
- Keep moist.
- Once your plants have started to flower there is no longer much point in harvesting leaves, but do not rip out your coriander. The flowers attract helpful insects like hoverflies and soon you can harvest the seeds instead.

Problems
- Bolting – coriander is very quick to flower. Slow down the process by keeping plants well watered and growing them in dappled shade in summer.

Harvesting and uses
- For curries and salsas; best added to dishes shortly before serving.
- Flowers can be eaten as well, or used to decorate dishes.
- Seeds are ripe when they develop the typical coriander scent. Let them dry out completely before storing in an airtight container.
- Coriander seeds are good in pickles and chutneys. Ground, they can also be used for cakes and cookies, such as gingerbread. Also soups.

DILL

Anethum graveolens • Parsley family
** • half-hardy annual • attracts bees and hoverflies

Dill originates in Central Asia, but is widely used in Europe, Western and Central Asia. It is a staple in Scandinavian and Baltic countries, where it is used with all kinds of potato and seafood dishes. The herbalist Culpeper wrote in 1653 that it stopped hiccoughs, and was used 'in medicines that serve to expel wind'.

It is a tall herb that will reach at least 60cm/2ft in height. With its feathery foliage it is a striking plant, especially when the lime-green flowers appear. Dill can be used not only in cooking but also in flower arrangements.

Soil and position
- Not fussy about soil, but it should be well drained.
- Full sunshine.

Propagation, planting and spacing
- Sow March–end of June, directly into beds – or into little pots. Does not like root disturbance.
- Rather long germination time: about 3 weeks.
- Sow in succession every 4 weeks; the plants have a short life span.
- 30cm/12in between rows, 20cm/8in between plants.

Companion planting
- Sow with carrots, beetroot, lettuce and onions – dill speeds up germination of these and improves their health.
- Its scent also deters cabbage white caterpillars, carrot fly, onion fly and aphids.

Aftercare
- Plants grow better if well mulched to retain moisture.

Problems
- Dill and fennel grown next to one another hybridize and produce 'Dennel' seeds.

Harvesting and uses
- Taste is most intensive while the plants are in flower.
- With fish dishes, in salads (especially with cucumbers, potatoes and lettuce), with yoghurt and cream cheese. Add to dishes shortly before serving; do not cook.
- Use for herb vinegar (see page 97).
- Dill seeds improve the taste of pickled cucumbers.
- Best eaten fresh, but freezing is possible.

LAVENDER

Lavandula angustifolia • Mint family
* • 🌱 • hardy perennial • attracts
bees

Lavender is one of the most widely known and used herbs from the Mediterranean region. The name originates in the Latin *lavare*, to wash, and the Romans used it in their baths.

It responds well to clipping and can be used as an edging plant. The scent of lavender is considered to be relaxing and soothing, and it is even said to lighten depression. The flowers and oil made from them have antiseptic properties and are also used for cosmetic purposes.

Lavender plants tend to hybridize, so if you want to make sure of getting a certain variety, buy your plants from a nursery that propagates via cuttings and make your own cuttings of these.

Soil and position
- Dry, well-drained soils, preferably alkaline.
- Full sunshine. Some species are hardier than others (see Varieties, below).

Propagation, planting and spacing
- From April, sow directly in drills;

preferably buy as plant.
- Take softwood cuttings from established plants in spring.
- Distance between plants 30–40cm/12–16in.

Aftercare
- Cut back after flowering, as otherwise plants get straggly. Cut back to leaf level. Do not cut into old wood, as it will not re-flower.

Companion planting
- With roses – deters aphids.

Problems
- Usually none.

Harvesting and uses
- Dried flowers can be used for flavouring sugars and teas, and as cake decoration.
- For potpourris and herb pillows, and as moth repellent.

Varieties
- *Lavandula angustifolia* – English lavender. About 50cm/20in tall.
  • 'Hidcote' – dark blue flowers, bushy, strongly scented, AGM.
  • 'Imperial Gem' – deep purple, flowers late, AGM.
- *L. x intermedia* – a cross between *L. angustifolia* and *L. latifolia*, also called lavandins. This is the lavender grown in the south of France. The plants are taller (about 80cm/32in), with broader and more aromatic leaves than those of *L. angustifolia*. It is used for oil production, but not for cooking. Propagation only via softwood cuttings.
  • *L. x intermedia* 'Alba' – AGM.
  • *L. x intermedia* 'Arabian Night' – AGM.
- *L. stoechas* – also called French or Spanish lavender. The flowers have a couple of fetching 'bunny ears' at the top of the main flower, but are only half-hardy and suffer from damp winters. The plants will reach about 60cm/24in. Hardy only to zone 8.
  • *L. stoechas* 'Kew Red' – striking flowers in deep and light pink, but susceptible to disease.
  • *L. stoechas* 'Regal Splendour' – dark purple/violet, one of the hardiest of this group.
  • *L. stoechas* 'Willow Vale' – deep blue/purple, AGM.

LEMON BALM

Melissa officinalis • Mint family
** • 🌱 • hardy perennial • attracts
bees

Lemon balm originates in the Mediterranean; *meli* means honey in Greek and Melissa was a nymph turned into a honeybee. The Romans introduced lemon balm to Britain, where it became standard in monastic gardens. Reputedly it was Llewelyn, Prince of Glamorgan's regular morning tea, enabling him to live to the ripe old age of 108, and its anti-ageing properties were also recognized in the seventeenth century by the diarist and gardener John Evelyn, who described it as 'Sovereign for the brain, strengthening the memory, and powerfully chasing away melancholy'.

Given all these recommendations, we are sorry to point out that it has a tendency to be invasive, but in a carefully chosen position or sunk into a pot . . .

Soil and position
- Any soil, except very poor or very dry; full sun or half shade.

Propagation, planting and spacing
- Preferably buy as plant.
- Divide established plants in April or September; this is also the only way to propagate golden and variegated forms.
- You can sow seeds in open ground from April. Do not cover, as they need light to germinate.
- Since it spreads so generously, it is a good idea to plant it in a pot and then sink this into the ground.
- 40cm/17in between plants; they will become 40–100cm/17–39in tall.

Aftercare
- Mulch with compost and water well in dry weather.
- Since it self-seeds, cut flowers back immediately after flowering.
- Cut back to soil level after the first frost.

Problems

- Rust. Caused by lack of water and/or nutrients. Cut back hard and feed, and it should grow back fine.

Harvesting and uses

- From late spring, before flowering.
- Use fresh leaves and flowers.
- Tasty when used fresh with green salads, cold herb sauces and fruit salad. Add to apple or lemon juice to enhance the flavour.
- According to herbalist John Gerard, tea 'quickened the senses' of his students. Recent reports claim it boosts memory and eases digestive discomfort.
- If rubbed on the skin it smells pleasant, and some claim it has a mosquito-repellent effect.
- Can be used for potpourris.

Varieties

- *M. officinalis* 'Variegata' – leaves with yellow speckles, fades later in the season, new growth after cutting back is again speckled.
- *M. officinalis* 'Aurea' – parts of the plant have golden yellow leaves, looks best in half shade, also fades, so cut back as for 'Variegata'.

MARJORAM AND OREGANO

Origanum species • Mint family
* • 🪴 • half-hardy and hardy perennials
• attract butterflies and bees

The name 'oregano' is a compound of two Greek words: *oros* meaning mountain and *ganos* meaning joy. The ancient Greeks planted marjoram on graves because they believed it brought happiness to the dead; the Romans used it for wedding crowns.

Marjoram comes in several species: one form is native, others are from the Mediterranean. Amongst these is oregano, indispensable in Italian cooking. The English pot marjoram was grown in medieval times for medicinal and culinary use and as a strewing herb, to make rooms smell better. Marjoram has antiseptic, relaxing and tonic properties. The pretty little flowers come in white and purple shades that attract many insects.

Soil and position

- Dry, well drained, and preferably alkaline soil; sunny site.

Sowing, planting and spacing

- Sow seeds from March on a warm windowsill, several seeds into each little pot.
- Do not exclude light for germination; cover lightly with vermiculite.
- Divide from established plants in spring.
- 25cm/10in between plants.

Aftercare

- Cut off flower heads before they run to seed.

Companion planting

- Do not plant basil next to marjoram.

Problems

- Usually none.

Harvesting and uses

- Main harvesting time for leaves June to August while flowering, but you can always pick a few leaves of hardy marjoram plants throughout winter in mild areas.
- A staple in Italian cooking, together with thyme and basil.
- Leaves can be dried.
- Marjoram tea eases coughs, colds and indigestion, and aids sleep.
- Inhaling steam from marjoram tea helps to ease catarrh.

Varieties

Unfortunately there is still confusion regarding the names, sometimes even amongst suppliers. If in doubt, nibble a leaf (discreetly) before buying!

- *O. marjorana* (sweet or knotted marjoram) – the best taste of all, frost tender, treat as annual, 30cm/12in high.
- *O. onites* (French marjoram) – evergreen, 40cm/16in.
- *O. vulgare* (wild or pot marjoram) – the native form, frost hardy, evergreen, but has less flavour than the others.
- *O. vulgare* subsp. *hirtum* (oregano or Greek marjoram) – fiery aroma, white flowers, 50cm/20in.

MINT

Mentha species • Mint family
** • 🌿 • hardy perennial

Mint grows in damp meadows and along little streams or ponds. Traditionally it is used as tea for digestive problems and, especially in England, the leaves are also very popular for cooking. There is a wide range of different mints available and collecting them can become something of a hobby. Their height varies from 40 to 100cm/15 to 40in.

Unfortunately mint is a very invasive herb, so it is best to plant it in containers. You can sink the container in the soil, but the rim of the container should remain about 5cm/2in above the soil – otherwise the roots simply climb over. The leaves die back in winter.

Soil and position
- Humus-rich, rather damp soil – but still well drained. Sunshine or half shade.

Propagation, planting and spacing
- Buy as plant.
- Divide established plants in early spring (see page 32).
- Distance between plants: 40cm/17in.

Aftercare
- Mulch with compost to retain moisture.
- Divide plants after 3–4 years and plant anew.

Companion planting
- Mint is said to keep caterpillars, aphids and carrot flies away. You could sink mint pots next to plants you hope to protect.
- Do not plant parsley next to mint, as they inhibit each other's growth.

Problems
- Rust – cut plants back and new growth will come up soon.

Harvesting and uses
- Leaves can be picked throughout the gardening season, but the taste is best shortly before flowering. If you cut the plants back, new growth will come up after a short time.
- Fresh and thinly sliced with all kinds of salads, especially potato, bean and lettuce, or with yoghurt.
- Mint tea.
- Can be dried.
- Apparently potatoes in storage sprout later if you put dried mint twigs between them.

Varieties
- *M. suaveolens* (apple mint) – hairy grey leaves, 70cm/28in high.
- *M.* x *piperita* f. *citrata* 'Chocolate' (chocolate mint) – brownish leaves, 'After Eights' in plant form, 40cm/16in.
- *M.* x *piperita* f. *citrata* 'Eau de Cologne' (Eau de Cologne mint) – scented with a hint of lavender, 60cm/24in.
- *M.* x *gracilis* (ginger mint) – golden-green variegated leaves, 50cm/20in.
- *M. spicata* var. *crispa* (Morrocan mint) – fresh green, crinkly leaves, lower menthol content, but rust resistant. 40cm/16in.
- *M.* x *piperita* (peppermint) – 50cm/20in.
- *M. suaveolens* 'Variegata' (pineapple mint) – green and white variegated leaves, wilts slowly so good for garnishes, 50cm/20in.
- *M. spicata* (spearmint) – fruity aroma, 60cm/24in.

and many more . . .

NASTURTIUMS

Tropaeolum majus var. *nanum*
Nasturtium family
* • 🌿 • tender annual • attracts bees and butterflies

This pretty plant is widely used as a bedding plant in bright and cheerful colours, but is extremely useful in organic vegetable gardens. The flowers and leaves have an interesting peppery taste which is somewhere between watercress and rocket. It also is a brilliant companion plant.

Since it is from South America it should be planted out after the last frost. If you want to grow nasturtiums between vegetable rows make sure you sow non-trailing varieties; otherwise they will ramble wildly over all your vegetables. You can also use dwarf nasturtiums as (short lived) edging plants.

Soil and position
- Any garden soil; full sunshine.

Propagation, planting and spacing
- Sow in little pots on a warm windowsill from April.
- Plant out carefully: the plants do not like root disturbance.
- Can also be sown *in situ* after the last frost; the plants grow very quickly.

Aftercare
- Flowers for longer if you deadhead – or eat – them.

Companion planting
- Attracts insects for pollinating fruiting vegetables. Also attracts aphids and cabbage white caterpillars, so many gardeners use them to lure pests away from more valuable crops.
- Deters ants, mice, slugs and white fly.

Problems
- As already mentioned: aphids and caterpillars. If there are just too many, rip the nasturtiums out and plant new ones.

Harvesting and uses
- Check there are no aphids inside the flower as you harvest.
- Flowers and young leaves are good in salads; older leaves are too peppery. Add chopped to herb butter, mayonnaise and cream cheese.

Varieties
Nasturtiums come in a wide range of varieties and colours between pale yellow and dark maroon, and in trailing, semi-trailing and dwarf forms. Look out for these varieties if you want to grow dwarfs:
- 'Alaska' – even more decorative, with variegated leaves, 20–25cm/8–10in high.
- 'Jewel Mixed' – 25cm/10in.
- 'Tom Thumb Mixed' – 30cm/12in.

PARSLEY

Petroselinum species – Parsley family
** • 🐌 • half-hardy biennial •
attracts hoverflies and lacewings

Parsley is probably the most cultivated herb in Europe and the Middle East. It comes with big flat or curly leaves. Sometimes it can be a bit of a primadonna but, as with true primadonnas, it is worth putting up with it.

Soil and position
- Good garden soil, well drained.
- Sunshine or dappled shade. Half-hardy; for parsley in winter, protect it with a cloche.

Propagation, planting and spacing
- Sow in spring, about 10 seeds per module or little pot. Seeds take about 3–6 weeks to germinate; germination can be erratic.
- Soak seeds in warm water before sowing, to speed up the process.
- In areas with mild winters you can sow in August, and plants will be in their prime the following spring.
- Parsley needs a new spot to grow every year; otherwise it will not thrive.
- 20cm/8in between plants.

Aftercare
- Parsley flowers in summer. Cut off flower shoots to ensure a longer harvest. Leave some, however, to attract beneficial insects to your garden.

Companion planting
- Grow with tomatoes (for instance, in the dappled shade behind them): the tomatoes will taste even more aromatic.
- Do not plant with other members of the parsley family because they share diseases.

Problems
- Slugs – especially on small plants.
- Yellowing leaves. Can be several reasons. Plants may have been too dry, or be deficient in magnesium; or they have been attacked by aphids, carrot fly

or nematodes. Remove yellow leaves, check for aphids, feed and improve watering. If problems persist, rip the plants out and plant new ones elsewhere, far away from other plants of the parsley family.

Harvesting and uses
- If grown in mild areas and protected by cloches, can be harvested throughout the whole year.
- Pick the outer leaves, including stems.
- Use for a wide range of dishes, always adding shortly before serving.
- Can be frozen.

Varieties
- *P. crispum* var. *crispum* (curled parsley) – prettier but less aromatic than flat-leaved parsley; more susceptible to fungal diseases.
- *P. crispum* var. *neapolitanum* (flat-leaved, French or Italian parsley) – better for overwintering, as it is hardier and less susceptible to diseases than curled parsley.
- *P. crispum* var. *tuberosum* (Hamburg parsley) – leaves are not very aromatic; it is grown for the root, which is similar that of to parsnip. Cook with soups and stews.

ROSEMARY

Rosmarinus officinalis · Mint family
* · 🪴 · half-hardy shrub · attracts bees

Rosemary is a Mediterranean herb, whose name comes from the Latin *rosmaris*, dew of the sea. The ancient Greeks also valued it, using its scent to improve their memory in examinations. Given that it stood for remembrance, it was carried at funerals, and also at weddings to remind the bride and groom of their vows. In the US, rosemary is hardy only to zone 7; in colder areas, grow it in a container. It can grow into an impressive bush 1m/40in high and wide. Evergreen, it can be easily clipped into hedges or simple shapes. The leaves can be harvested throughout the whole year. It starts to flower early in spring and attracts lots of bees.

Soil and position
- Hardy to –5°C/23°F. If your winters are colder, grow in containers and take it inside.
- Sunny, sheltered site; well-drained soil – can be rocky.

Propagation, planting and spacing
- Buy as plant.
- Softwood cuttings from

established plants between May and August usually root well.
- When planting out bought plants, handle root ball gently, as it hates disturbance.
- Can grow large, so space individual plants 1m/40in apart, or for hedge 45cm/18in apart.

Aftercare
- Occasional clipping is appreciated, but do not cut back too hard into the woody stems.

Companion planting
- Grow close to fruit trees, as it attracts bees in spring.

Problems
- Rosemary beetle – spreading outwards from southern England, these attractive metallic green/blue beetles eat the foliage. Not a problem in the US.
-

Harvesting and uses
- A classic with lamb, but also very good with roast potatoes, soups and casseroles. Use rosemary twigs as skewers for barbecues, for meat or vegetable kebabs.
- Rosemary tea can be used as a mouthwash for fresh breath.
- Evergreen, but dries well if necessary.

Varieties
- 'Albus' – white flowered.
- 'Miss Jessopp's Upright' – pale blue flowers, erect growth, good for hedges, one of the hardiest varieties.
- 'Prostratus' – pale blue flowers, creeping form, can be used as ground cover, but not very hardy.
- 'Rosea' – pink form, compact growth.
- 'Tuscan Blue' – upright growth, porcelain blue flowers, starts to flower very early.

> *'Where rosemary flourishes, the woman rules.'*
> Proverb

SAGE

Salvia officinalis · Mint family
* · 🪴 · hardy perennial · attracts bees and ladybugs

Common sage is one of the few herbs that is reasonably frost hardy. The name comes from the Latin *salvere*, to be well, and it was reputed to aid longevity. Many healing properties are attributed to sage, such as the ability to cure digestive problems, excessive perspiration and throat infections.

Originally from southern Europe, the evergreen, slightly shrubby plant responds well to occasional clipping. The plants can get straggly over the years, so they may need replacing after about five years.

In the Middle Ages sage was chewed to whiten rotting teeth and it is also said to restore the colour of greying hair, and although we cannot guarantee this, there is an old saying, 'Why should anyone die who has sage in their garden?'

Soil and position
- Light, well-drained soil. Sunshine or dappled shade.

Propagation, planting and spacing
- Buy as plant.
- Softwood cuttings from established plants from late

spring root quickly.

- 40cm/15in between plants.

Aftercare

- Cut back into shape once in a while.

Companion planting

- Deters caterpillars, aphids and slugs. Plant with other long-lasting plants like roses.

Problems

- Usually none.

Harvesting and uses

- Can be picked throughout the year, but aroma is best shortly before flowering.
- With pork, potatoes, for stuffings (see recipe on page 113).
- Sage tea works well to cure a sore throat. You can use fresh or dried leaves. Unfortunately the taste of pure sage tea is quite pungent, but it can be mixed with mint or other herbs to improve it.
- Leaves can be dried.

Varieties

- 'Icterina' – leaves are variegated yellow and light green shades. Not for areas with cold winters.
- 'Purpurascens' – pretty purple leaves, needs full sunshine.
- 'Tricolor' – leaves come with white and purple speckles. Not for areas with cold winters.

SAVORY

Satureja species · Mint family
Summer savory: *S. hortensis*, tender annual
Winter savory: *S. montana*, hardy perennial
* · 🌣 · attracts butterflies, bees and hoverflies

Savory is a tasty and useful plant that comes in two forms: the annual summer savory and evergreen winter savory. Both plants are from southern Europe.

Summer savory is a good companion for several vegetables. It grows up to 30–40 cm/12–16in and has a pleasant flavour. In continental Europe it is widely used for cooking, mainly with beans to improve their taste and digestion. Winter savory tastes similar, but is shorter (25–30 cm/10–12in high) and more robust, and since it is evergreen can be used throughout the year for the same purposes.

Both kinds are basically treated the same way, with the difference that the summer form is good in vegetable beds, while the perennial winter savory is better planted into a herb bed. It also makes a good edging plant.

Soil and position

- Not fussy about soil, but it should be free draining.
- Full sunshine.

Propagation, planting and spacing

- Sow seeds from mid-April (May in cooler areas) to the beginning of June *in situ* in rows – or sprinkle into little pots or modules.
- Cover the seeds with a thin layer of vermiculite, as requires light to germinate.
- Take softwood cuttings from winter savory from late spring.
- 25cm/10in between plants.

Aftercare

- Pinch flowers of summer savory off before they open – otherwise taste will be affected.

Companion planting

- Summer savory deters aphids and flea beetles, so is a good companion for beans and cabbages. Sow between beetroot, carrots and onions, where it should deter pests and improve taste.

Problems

- Usually none.

Harvesting and uses

- Flavour of both varieties is best shortly before flowering.
- Helps digestion and is good with pulses and stews. Add while cooking.
- Summer savory can be dried.
- Can be used like lavender to deter moths.

Savory (foreground, left) grows well with beans.

THYME

Thymus species • Mint family
* • 🌣 • hardy perennial • attracts
butterflies, bees and hoverflies

Like so many of our common herbs, most thymes originate around the Mediterranean. Ancient Egyptians used thyme for embalming; Roman soldiers bathed in thyme water to renew their energy. For centuries people believed it had an antiseptic effect and so large bundles of thyme were burnt in an attempt to ward off the plague. Thyme tea was thought to lend courage to the shy.

In the Middle Ages people wore posies of aromatic herbs, including thyme, to ward off germs and bad smells; there could still be a niche for these posies, known as tussie mussies, before a rush-hour trip on public transport.

The plants are evergreen and can be picked all year round. The upright species are good as edging plants; creeping ones make a lovely ground cover.

Soil and position
* Light, well-drained soil; can be poor. Full sun.

Propagation, planting and spacing
* Buy as plant or sow seeds, several per 10cm/4in pot in March on a warm windowsill. Do not cover the seeds, as they need light to germinate; they usually germinate within a week at 16–18°C/60–64°F.
* Can also be sown outside in shallow drills in late spring.
* Plant out when the plants are 10cm/4in high.
* Mature plants can also be divided in April.

* Taking softwood cuttings is frequently recommended, but it is rather fiddly; division is quicker. 30cm/1ft between plants.

Aftercare
* Cut taller varieties back by half after flowering in early summer.
* Some thymes with golden leaves can revert to green. Cut off the reverted twigs.

Problems
* Root rot if grown in too wet conditions.
* Bushes become woody – cut back hard. If a bush does not recover, get rid of it and start afresh.

Harvesting and uses
* Pick small amounts throughout the year as needed.
* Thyme is very versatile for cooking. Fresh or dried, it goes with all meats, stews and many vegetables.
* It is one of the *fines herbes* in French cuisine and also used for bouquet garni.
* As a tea: helps flatulence, painful menstruation, chest infections, sore throat (for preparing herbal teas, see page 81). Good combined with mint, bergamot, lemon balm or rosemary.
* Add thyme to lavender for use as a moth repellent and for potpourri.

Varieties
* *T. vulgaris* (common thyme) – about 30cm/1ft high.
* *T. fragrantissimus* (orange-scented thyme) – spicy orange flavour, for meats, fruit salads, jam, height 20cm/8in.
* *T. x citriodorus* 'Argenteus' (silver-edged thyme) – bushy, rounded shrub, lemon-scented, white-edged leaves, height 20cm/8in.
* *T. x citriodorus* 'Aureus' (variegated lemon thyme) – small, upright, spreading, with gold-splashed leaves, lemon scent, 15cm/6in tall, 60cm/24in spread, good as ornamental and for cooking: especially for fish, lemon-flavoured vinegars, herb butters.

WELSH ONIONS

Allium fistulosum – Onion family
* • hardy perennial

Welsh onions used to be grown in cottage gardens as attractive, edible perennials rather like overgrown chives. They do not develop bulbs and can be used for the same purposes as chives or spring onions. The hollow leaves are evergreen, and the plant makes an unusual edging. It has white flowers in summer.

Welsh onions reach a height of about 30–40cm/12–16in and are very tolerant of extreme temperatures: they survive severe cold in winter as well as tropical temperatures. They are not indigenous to Wales: the name comes from the old English word *welisc*, meaning foreign.

Soil and position
- Not fussy about soil, but it should be well drained. Full sunshine.

Propagation, planting and spacing
- Sow seeds under glass from February, *in situ* in rows April–May. Germination is slow – about 3–5 weeks.
- Plant seedlings out from April.
- Division in spring gives quicker results than growing from seed.
- Distance between plants: 20cm/8in.

Companion planting
- Do not plant legumes (peas, beans) or parsley next to Welsh onions because they will inhibit each other's growth.

Aftercare
- Pinch off the white flowers in July.
- If plants become congested, divide in autumn every few years.

Problems
- Slugs.
- Rust.

Harvesting and uses
- Finely shredded for salads and cooking.

Varieties
- 'Evergreen White Bunching' – most frost-hardy variety.
- 'Red Welsh' – the lower stems have a reddish tinge.

FLOWERS

As well as food and medicine, kitchen gardens of the past provided beauty and perfume for the eye and nose, and an abundance of flowers for decorating the house.

It may sound extravagant to grow your own cutting flowers, but with a bit of planning it should be quite possible to harvest your own blooms throughout summer and it will save you money, as well as giving you the thrill of providing fresh and different flowers for yourself and friends. And if you are at all worried about the cut flower industry — excessive use of pesticides, badly paid labour, greenhouse gases wasted on flights and overheating – then growing them yourself is a good idea. Children will enjoy the bright colours, the lovely scents and the insect life just as much as adults.

Flowers that are specially grown for picking are fascinating for children, but you will have to grow enough to allow for some casualties. Children do not always pick flowers with a long enough stalk, or with as much delicacy as is required, but as long as there are enough blooms for you to relax, they will be really 'helpful'.

Planning your cutting flowers

Most cutting flowers require a sunny position – basically the same conditions as vegetables. If you don't have space for a dedicated cutting bed, it's not the end of the world. Annual flowers can grow somewhere new each year and could be included into your vegetable crop rotation scheme.

This could easily work on the smallest of plots. Sow just three or four varieties of cut-and-come-again annuals, accompanied by one or two dahlias in appropriately complementary colours, and you will be all set for a bit of floristry in the summer.

You could raid your vegetable bed as well: lime-green dill and fennel flowers look brilliant with pink, dark red and blue – and the leaves of certain chard varieties are stunning enough for a vase. So start experimenting!

What makes a plant suitable to be a cutting flower? First it has to be attractive, and it must last for a reasonable length of time in a vase. In general, cutting flowers are picked from plants that will continue to produce flowers; often the more they are picked, the more flowers they will produce. Once you let a flower go to seed, it has fulfilled its mission, and will therefore stop flowering and concentrate on ripening its seed or on bulking up its roots for next year.

Growing cutting flowers

- The site should not be too windy; otherwise you will have a lot of work staking everything.
- Plants are generally happy when you add good compost to your soil. Only dahlias, sunflowers and sweet peas are really greedy and appreciate the addition of well-rotted manure.
- If you do not have time and space to start sowing inside, do not worry – good results can be achieved by sowing hardy annuals *in situ* from April onwards.
- Pinch out young plants by literally pinching off the top two leaves at the junction. This makes them branch out more, which results in more flower stems (see page 32).
- If your flowers need some extra food, use a potassium-rich product such as tomato fertilizer – it encourages the flowers, rather than the leaves.
- Make sure you change the positions of annual flowers each year to keep soil-borne pests at a minimum.

We were very pleased with the flowers featured on the following pages: they provided us with a constant supply of lovely fresh blooms. It does not mean that these are the only flowers out there to grow for cutting – there are many more to explore. But these are pretty uncomplicated, child-friendly, quick and easy to grow.

Blue nigella (love-in-a-mist) flowers and seed heads, lilac *Verbena bonariensis*, poppy seed heads and pinks.

Edible flowers

Flowers can be sprinkled on dishes to add flavour and aesthetic appeal. Use them sparingly, as too many could be a little overpowering.

> *'I hate flowers. I paint them because they're cheaper than models and they do not move.'*
> Georgia O'Keeffe

Plant	Description	Use
Nasturtiums	Peppery taste.	Use whole flowers as garnish; mix chopped flowers into butter.
Pot marigolds, French marigolds	Slightly bitter herbal flavour.	Add to salads or use to tint rice yellow.
Sage, rosemary, thyme, fennel, dill	Flavour similar to that of the leaf.	For cooking or as garnish for dishes where the herb would normally be used.
Basil, coriander (cilantro)	Flavour similar to that of the leaf.	Use as you would the leaves.
Dill	Flavour similar to that of the leaf.	For garnishing jars of pickle.
Lavender: L. angustifolia, L. x intermedia 'Provence' (not French)	Floral with notes of citrus.	Soak in milk to perfume custards and ice creams; dried in sugar, which can be used for baking; in savoury dishes in place of rosemary; in marinades for grilled meats or fish; sprigs to flavour vinegar.
Vegetable flowers		
Radish, mustard, rocket (arugula) , pak choi	Mild to spicy mustard flavour, sometimes with a hint of honey-like sweetness.	Eat whole sprinkled over salads, stir-fries, pasta or soups.
Courgettes (zucchini), marrows, squashes, pumpkins	Delicate, flowery flavour.	Stuffed with ricotta and herbs, grilled, dipped in batter and deep-fried, sautéed or baked.

ANTIRRHINUMS OR SNAPDRAGONS

Antirrhinum majus • Plantain family
** • 🪴 • half-hardy perennial,
usually used as annual • ☺ •
attracts bumblebees

The snapdragon is a wonderfully old-fashioned plant with a long vase life. As it is a half-hardy short-lived perennial, originating from the south of Europe and North Africa, after mild winters you could be lucky enough to enjoy your snapdragons for a second or even a third year. Slugs, snails and rabbits usually avoid them, so if you are having problems growing other cut flowers because of these, try snapdragons.

The flower stems provide a different, vertical shape for bouquets. The flowers are also fun for children, who can squeeze open the dragon's mouth and then let it snap shut on a finger, preferably accompanying the action with a convincing sound effect. The sight of a bumblebee half-swallowed by a snapdragon flower is also memorable.

Soil and position
* Any good soil. Ideally sunny, but dappled shade is acceptable.

Propagation, planting and spacing
* From February on the windowsill in trays. The seeds are tiny, so try to sow very thinly, and do not cover.
* Do not bother sowing them with small children; the seeds are so small that they will either be blown away or stick to gummy fingers, or – at best – you will end up with several thousand per square centimetre.
* Sowing from mid-April outside is possible, but then they will flower later.
* Prick out into small pots when large enough to handle.
* Plant out in April to May.
* If the plants are root bound when you come to plant them out, loosen the roots before planting; otherwise they will not grow on (this applies to many plants, but especially to snapdragons).
* Can also be sown in September in milder areas – will flower earlier the following year.
* Distance between plants: 30 x 30cm/1ft x 1ft.

Aftercare
* Pinch out tips, as they will branch better and produce more flower stems.

Flowering
* July–September.
* Cut when the flower spikes are one-third open.
* Remove wilted flower heads to promote opening of upper buds.

Problems
* Rust – in wet weather. Dig the plant up and bin it; try again next year in a different part of the garden.

Varieties
If you buy young plants, double check that they are tall ones – garden centres usually sell the shorter bedding types. There are varied colour mixes for sale, but if you prefer single colours, hunt them out. The following come in a variety of single colours:
* 'Liberty Classic' F1 series – 60cm/24in high.
* 'Ribbon' F1 series, 50–60cm/ 20–24in.
* 'Rocket' F1 series, 1m/39in.

ASTERS

Callistephus chinensis • Daisy family
** • 🪴 • half-hardy annual

There is some confusion about this plant. When it was introduced to England around 1730, it was named *'Aster chinensis'*, although it is only distantly related to the other asters, which are perennial. The mistake was soon discovered, but the misleading name stuck.

But do not let this worry you. Asters – also known as China or summer asters – are another old-fashioned cut flower. They fell from popularity, although why is not clear, since the flowers come in all shades between white, pink, red and purple, with some newer varieties producing pale yellow and peach blooms, and a whole range of different forms is available: from delicate daisy-like petals to little pompoms of colour and wildly shaggy balls. Recently they have been making a much-deserved comeback.

As long as they are constantly picked, asters will flower for about two months.

Soil and position
• Rich, well-drained soil; sunny position.

Propagation, planting and spacing
• Sow seeds from mid-March on the windowsill, in pots or trays.
• Germinates in 7–10 days.
• Prick out into small pots when large enough to handle.
• Plant out mid/late April.
• Or sow *in situ* in April/May – not later, as they may not flower before being cut down by frost.

• 25 x 25cm/10 x 10in between plants.

Aftercare
• Watering, weeding – picking! That's it.
• Taller varieties will appreciate staking.

Flowering
• From July onwards if sown in March; otherwise a bit later.

Problems
• Aster wilt – plants wilt just before flowering. Unfortunately in organic gardening there is nothing you can do about it. Bin the plants, try a different spot next year and do not plant asters on the same spot for another 7 years.

Varieties
When choosing a variety, double-check the seed packet, as there are usually more bedding types for sale, which are not good for cutting. Unfortunately it is difficult to get single colours, all mentioned varieties are widely available with mixed colours.

Some suppliers claim to sell wilt-resistant varieties, but this information should be taken with a pinch of salt.
• 'Big Boy' – large double flowers, includes shades of apricot and apple blossom, 90cm/36in high.
• 'Duchess' – chrysanthemum-type flowers, pink and purple pompoms, 60cm/24in.
• 'Giant Princess' – large, densely packed flowers, 70cm/28in.
• 'Lazy Daisy' – single daisy flowers, yellow centres, 60cm/24in.
• 'Matador' – densely packed flowers, 80–90cm/32–36in.
• 'Ostrich Plume' – feathery double flowers, in shades of pink, purple and white (illustrated left), 60cm/24in.

CALENDULA OR POT MARIGOLDS

Calendula officinalis • Daisy family
* • 🪴 • hardy annual • ☺ •
attracts bees and hoverflies, deters eelworms

Pot marigolds hail from the Mediterranean, where they were known as calendula because they flowered in nearly every calendar month. They are some of the most versatile plants in our gardens and also at home in the herb bed. Since pot marigolds are beneficial for the treatment of all kinds of skin conditions they are used commercially in a wide range of skincare products.

You can sprinkle the petals on your salads or use them to give rice a nice tint. Apparently the whole plants were used in former times for culinary use – hence the name 'pot' marigold. As well as being valuable in the kitchen, they are good for your soil; they are also valuable companions for your vegetables, because they attract bees for pollination and hoverflies for aphid control, and they deter eelworms.

If you choose taller varieties they also make brilliant cut flowers that are very easy to grow. Pot marigolds are classic children's plants. The bizarre seeds are something to talk about (the little hooks are supposed to cling on to animal fur to aid seed dispersal) and they are large enough to be easy to handle for young fingers.

Soil and position
• Happy with poor soil. Full sunshine.

Propagation, planting and spacing
• Sow *in situ* from April.
• Cover seeds with about 1cm/½in of soil.
• Thin out when plants are large enough to handle, leaving 25–30cm/10–12in between plants.
• For quicker results sow in little pots or trays from March under glass.
• Sow in September for an earlier flower the following year.

Aftercare
- None except picking and deadheading.

Flowering
- June–November.
- Put in water immediately after picking – calendulas wilt fast.

Problems
- Powdery mildew in wet years – do not plant too densely.

Varieties
- 'Art Shades' – double flowers, 60cm/24in high.
- 'Kablouna' – anemone-shaped flowers, 50cm/20in.
- 'Neon' – burgundy buds, orange petals with darker edges, double, 60cm/24in.
- 'Pacific Beauty Mixed' – double flowers, 45–50 cm/18–20in.
- 'Princess Mixed' – flat, 50–60cm/20–24in.
- 'Touch of Red Mixed' – red tips, 60cm/24in.

COSMOS

Cosmos bipinnatus • Daisy family
* • half-hardy annual • ☺ • attracts bees, hoverflies and lacewings

Cosmos are at home in the tropical and subtropical regions of America, especially Mexico. They are wonderful cutting flowers that are easy to grow. Cosmos is therefore a very encouraging beginner plant for children and adults alike.

Although cosmos are quite tall, they appear very fragile with their feathery foliage and flower without pause until the first frost in shades of white, pink and crimson. As an extra bonus they are also drought resistant. If you do not have enough space to start them on the windowsill, you can still sow them directly after all danger of frost has passed – they will come up quickly.

Soil and position
- Light, well-drained soil – cosmos are not too fussy. Full sunshine.

Propagation, planting and spacing
- Sow seeds in trays or modules from March on the windowsill.
- Sow *in situ* from April to May.
- Prick out early-sown seedlings when tall enough to handle; grow on under cooler conditions.
- Plant out after all risk of frost has passed.
- 40cm/17in between plants.

Aftercare
- Thin out directly sown seedlings when they are about 5cm/2in tall.

Flowering
- About 12 weeks from sowing to flowering.
- Make sure you pick them early or late in the day – those picked in full sunshine suffer.

Problems
- Problem-free.

Varieties
- 'Dazzler' – carmine, 90cm/36in.
- 'Daydream' – pale pink with rose central ring, 90cm/36in.
- 'Purity' – white, 90cm/36in.
- 'Sensation Mixed' (illustrated

above) – 1–1.2m/39–48in.
- 'Versailles Mix' – 90cm/36in, especially bred as a cut flower.
Some suppliers also sell single colours of the mixes.

RELATIVES
Cosmos sulphureus
Comes in vibrant yellow and orange shades; 60cm/24in tall, leave 30cm/1ft between plants.

DAHLIAS

Dahlia hybrids • Daisy family
** • 🌱 • tender perennials

Once considered an old-fashioned throwback grown by working-class men on ineffably neat allotments in rigidly straight lines, dahlias have seen a revival in recent years. Great in the garden, in borders and in vases, the national flower of Mexico is a fabulous addition to late summer and early autumn bouquets.

Avoid the short, multi-coloured bedding dahlias, usually grown from seed, and focus on the larger, richly single-coloured specimens.

Soil and position
• Good soil improved with generous amounts of compost or well-rotted manure. Full sunshine.

Propagation, planting and spacing
• Dahlias are bought as tubers – big fat roots. The fatter the tuber, the bigger the plant.

• If you receive your tubers in early spring, cover them with not-very-moist compost with just the tips of the stalks sticking up, in a generously large pot in a dry shed.
• When spring approaches, start watering them gently and put them in the light, by the shed window, or protected with a pane of glass.
• Plant out once you think the last frost has passed.

Aftercare
• If the centre of the plant is rocketing upwards, pinch it out, thereby encouraging the rest of the plant to bush out.
• Make sure each plant has a firm stake to support it, as they get top heavy.

Flowering
• Late summer.

Problems
• The usual worries about aphids and slugs.
• Earwigs enjoy living in the flowers, so when picking blooms give them a little upside-down shake.
• Virus – mottled yellowish leaves. Chuck the plant out immediately – and not in the compost heap.

Varieties
A huge number of varieties are available – the National Dahlia Collection of Britain alone consists of over 1,700 varieties and species. Here are a few we admire:
• 'Arabian Night' – double, dark velvety maroon flowers, 100cm/40in high (illustrated on page 107).
• 'David Howard' – apricot, double flowers, dark leaves, 75cm/30in.
• 'Gerry Hoek' – pink with lighter edge, 110cm/44in.
• 'Jowey Anouschka' – purple pompoms, 80cm/32in.
• 'Ludwig Helfert' – orange flowers, 110cm/44in.
• 'Orfeo' – spectacular cherry red (illustrated left), 110cm/44in.

DAHLIAS IN WINTER
Traditionally dahlias are left in the ground until the first frost has seared their leaves, and then lifted – and we are all for tradition. But given the benefits of global warming, and if you do not live too far north, you could try just heaping some mulch over the plant to protect it, and ignore the rest of this section. But if it got really cold, you might lose the lot, so be warned.

If you go the traditional route, dig up the dahlia, snip off the blackened foliage, brush off the wet soil, admire the big fat tubers and leave them upside down or on their side for a week or two so that the old stalk dries up a bit. Then plant them, as above, in a large pot in not-very-moist compost with just the tips of the stalks sticking up and keep them in a cool, dark shed or garage over winter. Start them up in spring as described above.

FRENCH MARIGOLDS

Tagetes species • Daisy family
* • tender annuals • ☺ • attract butterflies

Like pot marigolds, French marigolds are truly multi-tasking plants. They are good for your garden because they are excellent companion plants and they repel harmful nematodes. The taller ones also make good cutting flowers.

French marigolds are not in fact from France but from Mexico and are not happy with low temperatures. Make sure you plant them out after the last frost in your area. They germinate and grow on quickly, so there is not much need to sow them before mid-April; and they are easy for little hands to handle.

Soil and position
• Not fussy about soil; the only definitive requirement is full sunshine. Drought tolerant.

Propagation, planting and spacing
• Sow 4–6 weeks before the last frost, on the windowsill in trays and pots. Plant out after danger

of frost.
- Or sow *in situ* after the last frost.
- 30cm/1ft between plants for the tall varieties.

Aftercare
- Very tall ones appreciate a bit of staking.

Flowering
- From June for the shorter varieties.
- The tall varieties take a bit longer: expect flowers from July.

Problems
- Slugs love them.

Varieties
Short varieties for companion planting:
- *T. patula* 'Safari Mixed' – mainly yellow and orange shades, 25cm/10in high.
- *T. patula* 'Mars' – single, mahogany flowers with yellow eye, 30cm/12in.
- *T. tenuifolia* var. *pumila* 'Lemon Blend', 'Tangerine Blend' – leaves have a citrus scent, flowers are edible, 25cm/10in.

Tall varieties for cutting (*T. erecta*):
- 'Crackerjack Mixed' – clear shades of yellow and orange, 60cm/24in.
- 'French Vanilla' F1 – creamy white, 60–90cm/24–36in.
- 'Simba' – shaggy orange flowers (illustrated below), 75cm/30in.

NIGELLA OR LOVE-IN-A-MIST

Nigella species • Buttercup family
* • hardy annual • ☺ • attracts bees

Nigella is a delicate cottage garden favourite that can squeeze in wherever there is a little space in your garden. The blue star-like flowers are surrounded by fine, rather lovely, hair-like bracts. There are also white and pink variations. But the flowers are not the only attraction: the plump green seed heads make lovely fillers for bouquets as well. And if you miss picking these, you can also dry the seed pods, which keep for a long time.
   Another really easy starter plant with largish seeds that children can enjoy sowing.

Soil and position
- Any good garden soil. Sunshine.

Propagation, planting and spacing
- Sow all cultivars from seed in March–May.
- *N. damascena* can also be sown in September for early flowering the following year.
- Sow in succession every 4 weeks – if you remember.

Aftercare
- Thin out to 15cm/6in between plants.

Flowering
- From June to September.

Problems
- Does not like to be pricked out or transplanted. If you do not have space to sow directly, you could sow in modules or little pots and transplant very carefully when the seedlings have a healthy root ball.

Varieties
- *N. damascena* 'Double White' – as the name says, with a green centre, 45–60cm/18–24in high.

- *N. damascena* 'Miss Jekyll' – sky blue, 55cm/22in.
- *N. damascena* 'Persian Jewels' – blue, mauve, purple, pink or white, 55cm/22in.
- *N. papillosa* – dark blue, crimson seed pods, 45–60cm/18–24in.
- *N. papillosa* 'African Bride' – white with dark purple stamens, stunning, 75cm/30in.

SUNFLOWERS

Helianthus annuus • Daisy family
* • half-hardy annual • ☺ •
attracts bees

The summer classic, these have to be included. Nothing is more stunning than watching one little seed grow into such a tall plant in just a few months – especially for children. Sunflowers are particularly good for dividing off parts of the garden, or to obscure unsightly views (of the compost bins, perhaps). Any that are left on the stem produce edible and healthy seeds, and for this reason they were cultivated by North American Indians. If you do not eat them, the birds in your garden will be happy.

But this is sunflower as a fun giant, rather than as a cutting flower. There are also branching varieties that can be picked without destroying the whole plant, and that will provide you with big brash bouquets. Ain't much subtle about a vase full of sunflowers.

Soil and position
- Full sunshine; good garden soil, preferably with manure or good compost.

Propagation, planting and spacing
- Sow from seed, from March inside in little pots or modules; cover with about 2cm/1in of soil.
- From mid-April to May sow *in situ*. It should be reasonably warm, as sunflowers do not germinate or grow well below 12°C/54°F.
- Harden off before planting out.
- 40–50cm/16–20in between plants – depending on height of variety.

Aftercare
- Sunflowers are greedy plants. Mulch them with compost or well-rotted manure. Feed with liquid tomato food once in a while.
- Staking may be necessary.

Flowering
- From July to September; will flower about 60 days after sowing.
- Cut flowers before ray petals open.
- Cut sunflowers can shed pollen, which might irritate allergy sufferers. Some new varieties produce less pollen and this also extends the flower's life.
- Sunflowers need a lot of water in the vase, so check daily.

Problems
- Slugs attack seedlings. If you have major slug problems in your garden, grow them in pots before planting out.

Varieties
- 'Earthwalker' – mix in orange and terracotta shades, about 2.5m/8ft tall.
- 'Italian White' – creamy shade, almost white, 1.2m/4ft.
- 'Prado Yellow' – looks like the classic sunflower but with 7–10 flower stems per plant (illustrated left), almost pollen free, 1.5m/5ft.
- 'Valentine' – primrose yellow, pollen does not drop, flowers very early, 1.5m/5ft.
- 'Velvet Queen' – dark velvety crimson, 1.5m/5ft.

SWEET PEAS

Lathyrus odoratus • Legume family
** • half-hardy annual • ☺

This is one of those plants that makes experts very boring, as they start talking incomprehensibly about Spencers, grandifloras and dwarf varieties. And then they start on the great cordons versus wigwams debate. But don't let them put you off. Sweet peas are not difficult to grow: they are pretty tough, and anyone can achieve

WIGWAM OR CORDONS?
Traditionally sweet peas are grown on cordons (in a straight line along a kind of fence) or wigwams (made of a circle of bamboo canes).

- Wigwams make a nice decorative feature. But the plants can get a bit squashed at the top as the canes converge and this can affect plant quality and cause short stunted stems, which are annoying.
- Cordons can be used to make a pretty division in the garden, but probably require a more disciplined approach that may not be feasible for those gardening with children. (Save them for when they have left home.)
- Alternatively you could just let the sweet peas scramble over some boring shrub or bush, or fence, as long as you provide them with enough support. They may need some trellis, or a few twiggy sticks to help them get started.

a long and plentiful season of their delicate and fragrant flowers with a little attention. They are also so prolific that once they are established you can let children loose picking as many as they wish.

Soil and position
- Add well-rotted compost and organic fertilizer to soil. Full sunshine.

Propagation, planting and spacing
- Sow seeds from October/November or January/February on a windowsill.
- In deep pots (at least 15cm/6in) or root trainers.
- Soak seeds the night before sowing in warm water.
- One per root-trainer compartment, or five or six spaced out around the edge of a larger pot in seed compost.
- Once the seeds have germinated they can go outside, but protect with a bit of horticultural fleece or a cloche in cold weather.

• When seedlings are about 8cm/3in tall, pinch off the tip of the main shoot. By stopping the main shoot, you will encourage the sweet pea to push out some side shoots and become short and bushy, rather than tall and lanky.
• Plant out once the seedlings reach about 25cm/10in tall with a support (see box, left).

Aftercare
• Tie in shoots to the support.
• Keep the plant well watered throughout the summer.
• The single most important thing with sweet peas is to keep deadheading. Even if you do not want a bunch of flowers that day, nip off the flowers. Once your sweet peas have run to seed, the plants will no longer bother to make more flowers.
• If you go on holiday, ask a neighbour to pick for you.
• When all that deadheading has got away from you, the stems are beginning to yellow at the edges and you suddenly hate the smell of sweet peas, rip them

SWEET PEA VOCABULARY
Grandifloras: bigger flowers, initially bred by a head gardener, Henry Eckford, in the 1870s.
Spencers: bred by Silas Cole, head gardener to Earl Spencer; even larger than the grandifloras and with wavy leaves.

up and compost them. The roots are particularly valuable to the compost heap.

Problems
• Aphids.
• Powdery mildew. Keep sweet peas well watered.

Varieties
• 'Cupani' – the original wild seed from Sicily, mauve/maroon.
• 'Matucana' – a Peruvian grandiflora, deep maroon-purple.
• 'Glow' – Spencer sweet pea, peachy pink.
• 'Blue Velvet' – very deep blue, ruffled.
• 'White Supreme' – vigorous, long-stemmed.
There is really no point growing a non-fragrant variety, or a dwarf or trailing basket version. Why would you want a sweet pea that does not climb or smell?

SWEET WILLIAMS

Dianthus barbatus
Carnation family
* • 🌱 • short-lived perennial grown as hardy biennial • attracts butterflies

Sweet Williams are one of the classic cottage garden plants. The flowers come in white, red, pink and purple shades, and have a lovely clove scent and a vase life of up to two weeks. Do not rip them out after flowering, as they may last a second or even a third year. The plants are very easy to grow and the only real requirement is a cold phase in winter – otherwise the plants will not flower.

Soil and position
• Any good garden soil, in full sunshine or dappled shade.

Propagation, planting and spacing
• Sow seeds from April to May, either in trays or in rows in a nursery bed.
• Do not exclude light for

germination; cover with vermiculite.
• Plant out when tall enough, usually about 6 weeks after sowing.
• Seeds can be easily collected, but they will not come true. So if you have a particularly pretty plant, propagate it with softwood cuttings.
• 25cm/10in between plants.

Aftercare
• If your plants get a bit straggly, just trim them back.

Flowering
• From June to August, the year after sowing.

Problems
• The leaves can suffer from frosts, but will grow back quickly as soon as it warms up.
• Otherwise problem-free.

Varieties
Look out for varieties tall enough for cutting – most of the ones on the market are rather short.
• 'Auricula-Eyed Mix' – 45cm/18in high, AGM.
• 'Hollandia' F1 – 60–70cm/24–28in. Mixed colours.
• 'Single Mixed' – 45–60cm/18–24in.
Breeders are busy developing varieties that will flower the same year. Sow these from February on a windowsill:
• 'Noverna' – 45cm/18in. Mixed colours.
• 'Summer Sundae Mix' F1 – 45–60cm/18–24in, but only lightly scented.

ZINNIAS

Zinnia elegans • Daisy family
** • tender annual • attracts bees
and butterflies

> *'Il faut cultiver notre jardin.'*
> Voltaire, *Candide*, 1759

A whole bed of tall zinnias can look rather stiff and uptight, but take a closer look at the velvety petals – they are stunning. And the stiffness of the stems can be a virtue when zinnias are used in a vase. They are mainly from Mexico, so choose a warm spot for them and their cheerful colours will give your garden a tropical touch. Zinnias come in all kinds of shades except blue and you can get them with rather flat flowers, round ones that almost resemble dahlias or with little pompom-style flower heads. Once the plants are established, they can tolerate drought.

Soil and position
- Good garden soil. Warm and sunny site.

Propagation, planting and spacing
- Sow from March on the windowsill, in trays or modules.
- Prick out into little pots or trays when tall enough to handle.
- Plant out after danger of frost has passed, 30cm/1ft between plants.

Aftercare
- Zinnias appreciate staking in windy spots.

Flowering
- July–October.

Problems
- Powdery mildew in wet years – rip them out and try again next year.

Varieties
As with other old-fashioned cutting flowers it can be a bit tricky to find tall ones for cutting.
- 'Benary's Giant Lilac' – 1.1m/45in high, vigorous, flowers about 10cm/4in in diameter, semi-double, compact, dark cerise colour, fairly mildew resistant, long flowering season.
- 'Double Envy' – chartreuse green, gorgeous with blue and purple.

Don't bother with single 'Envy'. 60–90cm/24–36in.
- 'Giant Tetra State Fair' – huge mixed flowers, 70cm/28in.
- 'Liliput' – small double mixed pompoms, lovely, 45cm/18in.
- 'Oklahoma' – round flower heads, 4–5cm/1½–2in in diameter, semi-double, less susceptible to powdery mildew, 75–100cm/30–39in.

APPENDICES

Plant families

Plants are divided into different family groupings, based on the biological construction of the petals. This becomes relevant for planning your crop rotation, and for effective companion planting. As a rule of thumb, plants from the same family should not follow one another in a rotation, because they tend to suffer from the same type of pests.

Every now and then there is a surprise – for instance, lettuce belongs to the same family as the sunflower – but in general once you get the hang of it, the family groupings are fairly straightforward.

Beet family – *Chenopodiaceae*
Beetroot (beets)
Chard
Spinach

Cabbage family – *Brassicaceae*
Broccoli
Brussels sprouts
Cabbages
Kale
Kohl rabi
Oriental leaves
Pak choi (bok choy)
Radishes and mooli (daikon)
Rocket (arugula)

Cucumber family – *Cucurbitaceae*
Courgettes (zucchini)
Cucumbers
Marrows
Pumpkins
Squashes

Legumes – *Fabaceae*
Beans
Peas
Sweet peas

Daisy family – Asteraceae
Globe artichoke
Lettuce
Sunflower

Nightshade family – *Solanaceae*
Chilli pepper
Sweet pepper
Potatoes
Tomatoes

Onion family – *Alliaceae*
Asparagus
Chives
Garlic
Leeks
Onions
Shallots

Parsley family – *Apiaceae*
Carrots
Celeriac (celery root)
Dill
Parsley
Parsnips

Winter vegetables for mild areas
Happy in temperatures down to about –5°C/23°F

Beans, broad(fava beans)
Broccoli, sprouting
Brussels sprouts
Cabbage, spring
Cabbage, winter
Cabbage, savoy
Celeriac (celery roots)
Chard
Garlic
Kale
Leeks
Lettuces, winter varieties
Onions
Parsnips
Peas
Radishes, winter
Rocket (arugula)
Shallots
Spinach

Average time between sowing and harvest

Vegetables	Weeks
Oriental leaves	3–6
Radishes, summer	4–6
Lettuces, loose leaf	6–8
Rocket (arugula)	4–8
Onions: spring, salad and Japanese bunching	8–10
Kohl rabi	8–12
Spinach	8–14
Beans, French	10
Pak choi (bok choy)	10
Potatoes, first early	10
Radishes, winter	10–12
Courgettes (zucchini) and marrows	10–14
Pumpkins	10–14
Squashes, summer	10–14
Carrots	10–16
Beetroot (beets), globe	11
Chard	12
Lettuces, heads	12
Beans, runner	12–14
Cucumbers	12–14
Peas	12–16

Vegetables	Weeks
Beans, broad, sown in spring	14
Sweetcorn (corn)	14
Broccoli, calabrese	15
Beetroot (beets), long	16
Squashes, winter	16
Tomatoes	16
Garlic and onions, from sets	18
Peppers	18
Shallots	18
Cabbages	20–35
Onions, bulbing, from seed	22
Potatoes, maincrop	22
Artichoke, globe, from offsets	5–6 months
Beans, broad (fava), autumn-sown	7–8 months
Brussels sprouts	7–10 months
Leeks	7–11 months
Celeriac (celery root)	7–8 months
Kale	8–10 months
Parsnips	8 months
Cabbage, spring	8 months
Broccoli, sprouting	11 months
Asparagus	2 years

Fruit*	
Trees	**Years**
Cherry	3
Fig	3
Plum	3-4
Pear	3-4
Apple	4
Nut	4

* You may get a small crop earlier.

Bushes	Years
Blackberry	2
Currant	2
Gooseberry	2
Raspberry	2
Rhubarb	2
Strawberry	2
Blueberry	3
Vine	3

How much do you need?

Without being swamped by gluts, to use fresh with no preserving or storage

Vegetable	Yield per plant	For a family of four
Artichoke	10–12 heads	1–2 plants
Asparagus	15–20 spears	8–12 plants
Beans, runner (pole)	1kg/2lb	4–6 plants
Broccoli, sprouting	500g/1lb	2–4 plants
Brussels sprouts	1kg/2½lb	2–4 plants
Courgettes (zucchini)	10–15	1–2 plants
Cucumbers	10	4–6 plants
Kale	750g/1½lb	2–4 plants
Marrows	2–3	1–2 plants
Peppers	6–10	4–6 plants
Pumpkins	2–5	1–2 plants
Squashes, winter	8–10	1–2 plants
Sweetcorn (corn)	1–2 cobs	10–12 plants
Tomatoes	1.5–2kg/3½–4½lb	10–14 plants
	Yield per row (3m/9ft)	
Beans, broad (fava)	4kg/9lb	1–2 rows
Beans, French (string)	3kg/6½lb	3–4 rows
Beetroot (beets)	4–5kg/9–11lb	2–4 rows
Carrots	3.5kg/8lb	3–4 rows
Chard	3kg/6½lb	1 row
Leeks	4kg/9lb	2–4 rows
Onions, bulbing	3kg/6½lb	2–4 rows
Parsnips	3kg/6½lb	2–4 rows
Peas	3kg/6½lb	2–4 rows
Potatoes, early	5.5kg/12lb	2–4 rows
Potatoes, others	10kg/22lb	2 rows
Radishes, summer	1.5kg/3½lb	2–4 rows
Radishes, winter	3kg/6½lb	1–2 rows
Spinach	2kg/4½lb	2–6 rows
	What you see is what you get	
Cabbages		
Celeriac (celery root)		
Kohl rabi		
Lettuces, heads		

Sowing and planting calendar

Sow indoors ▨ **Sow outdoors** ▨ **US planting times are generally 1–2 months later**

Plant out ▨ **Harvest** ▨

Legend (shading key):
- Sow indoors = light grey
- Sow outdoors = dark grey
- Plant out = medium-dark grey
- Harvest = pale grey

Each month is divided into 4 weekly columns. Activities are marked as: I = Sow indoors, O = Sow outdoors, P = Plant out, H = Harvest.

VEGETABLES	January				February				March				April				May				June			
Artichoke											I	I	I	I	P	P							P	P
Asparagus													P	P	P	P	2nd year after planting							
Beans, broad (fava) – early																					H	H	H	H
Beans, broad (fava) – maincrop					I	I	O	O			O	O	P	P					H	H	H	H		
Beans, French (string)															I	I	O	O	P	P	H	H	H	H
Beans, runner (pole)															I	I	O	O	P	P			H	H
Beetroot (beets) – early										O	O	O	O				H	H	H	H				
Beetroot (beets) – maincrop													O	O	O	O					H	H	H	H
Beetroot (beets) – late (storage)																	O	O	O	O	H	H	H	H
Broccoli, calabrese											I	I	O	O	P	P					H	H	H	H
Broccoli, sprouting					O	O	O	O	O	O	O	O					P	P					H	H
Brussels sprouts – early									O	O	O	O					P	P	P	P				
Brussels sprouts – late	O	O	O	O	O	O			O	O	O	O					P	P	P	P				
Cabbage – summer							I	I	O	O							P	P	P	P	H	H	H	H
Cabbage – autumn, savoy													O	O	O	O			P	P	H	H	H	H
Cabbage – winter	P	P	P	P	P	P											O	O	O	O	H	H	H	H
Cabbage – spring																								
Carrots – early									O	O	O	O	O	O	O	O		H	H	H	H			
Carrots – maincrop																	O	O	O	O	H	H	H	H
Carrots – late																								
Celeriac (celery roots)										I	I	I							P	P	H	H	H	H
Chard	O	O	O	O	O	O	O	O	O	O	O	O	O	O	O	O				H	H	H	H	H
Courgettes (zucchini) and marrows																	I	I	P	P	H	H	H	H
Cucumbers																	I	I	P	P	H	H	H	H
Garlic									O	O	O	O												
Kale – early													O	O	O	O							H	H
Kale – late	O	O	O	O	O	O	O	O	O	O	O	O												
Kohl rabi											O	O	O	O	O	O	O	O						
Leeks – maincrop	O	O	O	O	O	O			I	I	O	O	O	O	P	P			P	P				
Leeks – late									O	O	O	O	O	O	O	O	P	P	P	P			P	P

July	August	September	October	November	December

Sow indoors ▨   **Sow outdoors** ▨   **US planting times are generally 1–2 months later**

Plant out ▨   **Harvest** ▨

VEGETABLES	January	February	March	April	May	June
Lettuce – spring						
Lettuce – summer and autumn						
Lettuce – winter						
Onions – from seed						
Onions – from sets						
Spring onions (scallions)						
Oriental leaves (salad greens)						
Pak choi (bok choy)						
Parsnips						
Peas – first earlies						
Peas – second earlies						
Peas – mangetout (snow peas)						
Peas – maincrop						
Peas – late						
Peppers, sweet and chillies						
Potatoes – early						
Potatoes – second early						
Potatoes – maincrop						
Pumpkins						
Radishes – spring						
Radishes – summer						
Radishes – autumn and winter						
Rocket (arugula)						
Shallots						
Spinach – spring/summer						
Spinach – autumn/winter						
Squashes – summer						
Squashes – winter						
Sweetcorn (corn)						
Tomato						

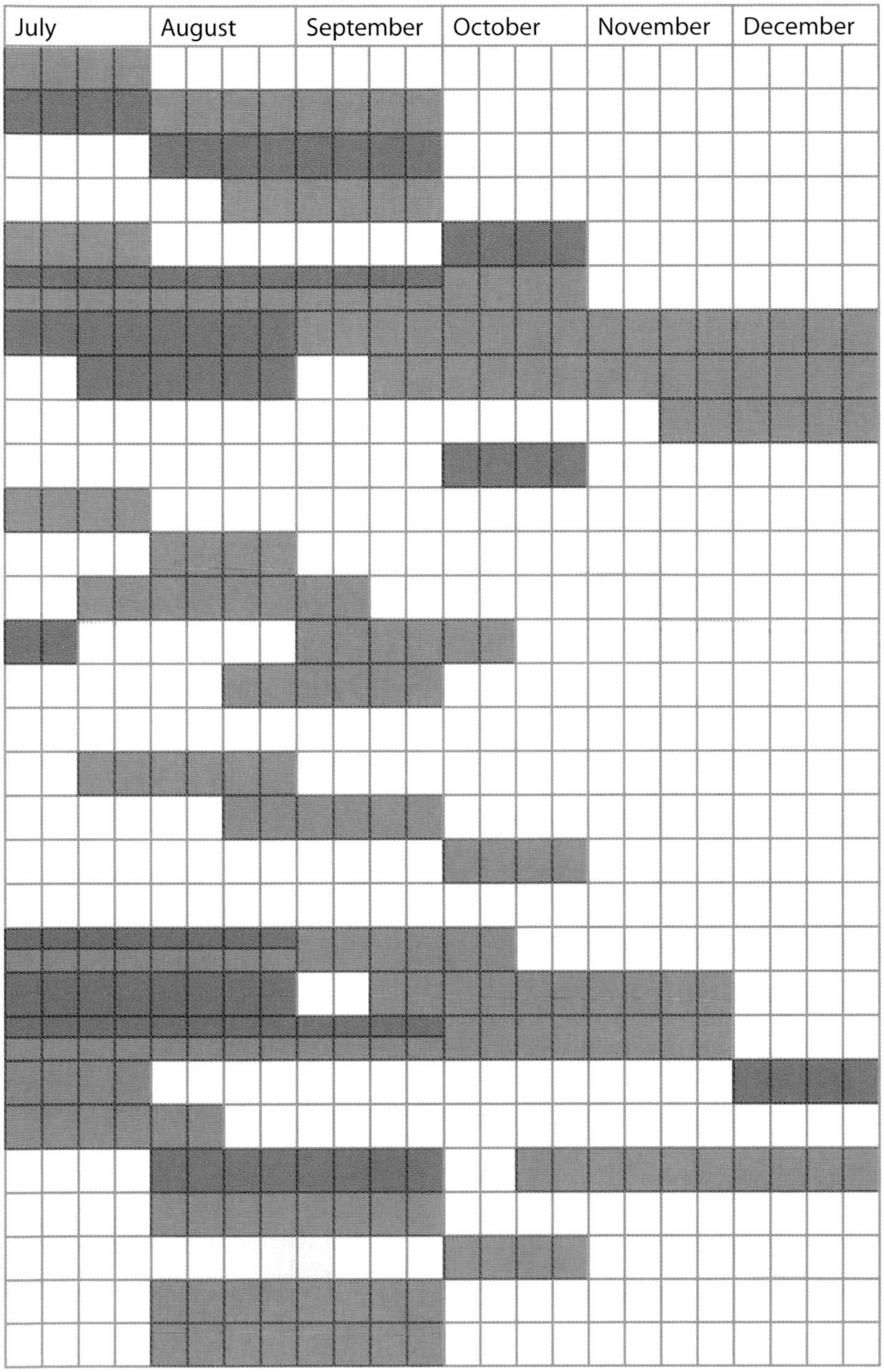
July
August
September
October
November
December

Sow indoors ▢   **Sow outdoors** ▢   **US planting times are generally 1–2 months later**

Plant out ▢   **Harvest** ▢

HERBS	January	February	March	April	May	June
Basil						
Bay laurel (sweet bay)						
Chives						
Coriander (cilantro)						
Dill						
Lavender						
Lemon balm						
Marjoram/oregano						
Mint						
Nasturtium						
Parsley						
Rosemary						
Sage						
Summer savory						
Winter savory						
Thyme						

FLOWERS	January	February	March	April	May	June
Antirrhinum or snapdragon						
Aster, summer – annual						
Calendula (pot marigold)						
Cosmos						
Dahlias						
French marigolds						
Nigella or love-in-a-mist						
Sunflowers						
Sweet peas						
Sweet Williams						
Zinnias						

July	August	September	October	November	December

Ease and effort
Some plants are easier than others to grow, in terms of effort and yield.

	Vegetable	Tricky because
Easy	Artichokes	
	French beans (dwarf)	
	Beetroot (beets)	
	Chard	
	Courgettes (zucchini) and marrows	
	Garlic	
	Kale	
	Kohl rabi	
	Leeks	
	Lettuce, leaves	
	Onions and shallots, sets	
	Oriental leaves (salad greens)	
	Pak choi (bok choy)	
	Parsnips	
	Pumpkins and squashes	
	Radishes	
	Rocket (arugula)	
Less easy	Broad (fava) beans	Need staking
	Runner (flat pole) beans	Need tall and stable poles
	Carrots	Need defending against carrot fly
	Celeriac (celery root)	Demanding regarding nutrients
	Cucumbers	Need a frame
	Lettuce, heads	Has a tendency to bolt
	Peppers and chillies	Need a warm spot
	Potatoes	A lot of digging involved
	Spinach	Has a tendency to bolt
	Sweet corn (corn)	Only good in warm areas
	Tomatoes	Regular pinching out important
Slightly tricky	Asparagus	Very good soil preparation and patience needed
	Calabrese broccoli	Prone to brassica diseases, demanding regarding nutrients, might bolt
	Sprouting broccoli	Prone to brassica diseases; needs staking
	Brussels sprouts	Prone to brassica diseases, need staking, might bolt
	Cabbages	Prone to brassica diseases
	Peas	Need taking and protection from birds

	Fruit	Tricky because
Easy	Currants, black	
	Currants, red and white	
	Gooseberries	
	Hazelnuts	
	Plums, damsons, greengages	
	Raspberries	
	Rhubarb	
Less easy	Blackberries	Can be invasive in a garden
	Blueberries	Require acid soil
	Figs	Need enough sun
	Pears	Late frosts can reduce crop
	Strawberries	Need strawing and defence against slugs
	Sweet cherries	Netting a tree can be tricky
Slightly tricky	Apples	Need regular pruning and thinning of fruit
	Sour cherries	Need netting and pruning after harvest
	Grape vines	Pruning a bit fiddly

	Herb	Tricky because
Easy	Chives	
	Dill	
	Lavender	
	Marjoram	
	Nasturtium	
	Rosemary	
	Sage	
	Savory	
	Thyme	
	Welsh onions	
Less easy	Basil	Has small seeds and requires warmth
	Bay	Might need winter protection
	Coriander (cilantro)	Tends to run to seed
	Mint	Has invasive tendencies
	Lemon balm	Has invasive tendencies
	Parsley	Germination can be tricky

	Flower	Tricky because
Easy	Calendula	
	Cosmos	
	French marigold	
	Nigella	
	Sunflower	
	Sweet William	
Less easy	Antirrhinum	Has tiny seeds
	Aster	Has slight risk of diseases
	Dahlia	Needs staking and winter protection
	Sweet pea	Needs lots of pinching out
	Zinnia	Needs a warm spot

INDEX

Page numbers in *italic* refer to illustrations; page numbers in **bold** refer to the principal text on the subject.

ACKNOWLEDGMENTS

Authors' acknowledgments

We would like to thank Penny Bottari, Fiona Crumley, Roger Morsley Smith, Alan Wadner, Anita Wagner and Helen Whitman for gardening suggestions and helpful criticism; Gareth Gardner, Kate Guest, Suzette Llewellyn, Cathy Maund, Gloria Moore, Jo Rabin and Robert Ward Dyer for their help and support, and all the other kitchen gardeners at Chiswick.

We would also like to thank all the children who helped us out with photography – Diya, Ella, Hannah, Julian, Luisa, Nick, Sienna and Sophia – and all the children who have gardened at the Chiswick House Kitchen Garden. We hope they will continue to enjoy gardening for the rest of their lives.

Photographic acknowledgments

Most of the photographs were taken at Chiswick House Kitchen Garden and in our own gardens and kitchens, with additional shots at the gardens of Anne and Andrew Sawyer and of Delia Fuchs.

We are grateful to Petersham Nurseries and Jonathan Cohen of the Breadshop for the loan of gardening equipment and props.